GROWING UP IN GROUPS

The Russian Day Care Center and

The Israeli Kibbutz

Early Child Development and Care

Early Child Development and Care is a multidisciplinary publication (a periodical and a book series) which serves psychologists, educators, psychiatrists, pediatricians, social workers and other professionals who deal with research, planning, education and care of infants and young children. The periodical provides English translations of work in this field which has been published in other languages, and original English papers on all aspects of early child development and care: descriptive and evaluative articles on social, educational and preventive medical programs for young children, experimental and observational studies, critical reviews and summary articles. In addition to scientific papers, the periodical will contain reviews of books, reports on conferences, and other items of interest.

GROWING UP IN GROUPS

The Russian Day Care Center
and
The Israeli Kibbutz

Two Manuals on Early Child Care
Edited by
JOSEPH MARCUS, Jerusalem
Introduction by
HALBERT B. ROBINSON, Seattle

Gordon and Breach
New York   Paris   London

Copyright © 1972 by

Gordon and Breach, Science Publishers, Inc.
440 Park Avenue South
New York, N.Y. 10016

Editorial office for the United Kingdom

Gordon and Breach, Science Publishers Ltd.
42 William IV Street
London W.C. 2.

Editorial office for France

Gordon & Breach
7-9 rue Emile Dubois
Paris 14e

Play and Activity For Children in the First Three Years of Life by N.B. Kupriyanova and T.N. Fedoseeva, Published in Russian by Izdatelstvo "Meditzina" Leningradskoe Otdelenye.

Methods of Kibbutz Collective Education During Early Childhood by Y. Ben-Yaakov, Published in Hebrew by Ihud Hakvutzot v'Hakibbutzim, Education Department, 1971.

Library of Congress Catalog card number applied for
ISBN 0 677 04800 9
All rights reserved. No part of this book may be reproduced or utilized in any form or by any means, electronic or mechanical, including photocopying, recording, or by any information storage and retrieval system, without permission in writing from the publishers.

Printed in Great Britain by Hazell Watson & Viney Ltd, Aylesbury, Bucks

GENERAL CONTENTS

INTRODUCTION by Halbert B. Robinson   vii

Section One: Early Child Care in the Russian
   Day Care Center and Children's Home

PLAY AND ACTIVITY FOR CHILDREN IN THE FIRST
   THREE YEARS OF LIFE by N.B. Kupriyanova and
   T.N. Fedoseeva xvii

Section Two: Early Child Care in the Israeli
   Kibbutz

METHODS OF KIBBUTZ COLLECTIVE EDUCATION DURING
   EARLY CHILDHOOD by Yona Ben-Yaakov   197

INTRODUCTION

In *Growing Up in Groups*, the reader concerned with the upbringing of very young children will find two extremely interesting and useful manuals, written by professionals for workers who are responsible for day-to-day group care of very young children. For over a half century, both the Soviet Union and the Israeli kibbutzim have provided early group care on a broad-scale basis. The kibbutzim, in fact, have provided practically full-time care for all their children beginning with newborns. The Soviet Union once had extensive residential facilities for the young, but more recently has supported group day care for large numbers of infants and preschoolers, together with a continuing program of residential care for children with special needs. Each has continually sought better ways to enhance the development of its youngest citizens.

Furthermore, though rather different, both systems of early child care have won the profound respect of professional and lay persons throughout the world. It has been my good fortune to visit a number of early child care settings in both countries, and I heartily concur with the high regard in which they are held. I have seen healthy, radiant, alert, and busy children under the fond and adept care of workers who take pride in their young pupils and find fulfillment in the development of each infant, toddler, and preschooler. Caring for and teaching young children is hard work — demanding of physical effort, emotional involvement, ambition for the children, foresight, self-confidence, patience, and tact — and at least in staffs of Israeli kibbutzim and the Soviet preschools I have visited, all these qualities have been abundantly evident. No child care manual can, by itself, create such qualities; indeed, the whole society must be sufficiently oriented toward the needs of the child for excellent care to occur. Yet, good manuals can support and enhance good child care by motivated personnel, and each of the two present manuals has a special contribution to make.

Neither of these important guides has previously been available in the English language, and the literature on early upbringing is surely enhanced by their publication in translation. Yet, these are two very different books which cannot and should not be compared. They differ markedly in intent, in approach, in style, and in breadth and depth of coverage. It would also be a mistake to conclude that either of the two represents "the last word" in its setting. Both systems have published a variety of guidelines, and both systems are still evolving. Let us consider the books independently, primarily seeking from each an enrichment of our own ideas about group care of the very young.

Looking first at "Play and Activity for Children in the First Three Years of Life" by Kupriyanova and Fedoseeva, we find a resource for basic games and explicit teaching situations to be undertaken by the child-care worker in a daily period of planned, directed teaching. These little games and songs, which appear so simple and commonsense, are actually the product of a serious cooperative effort by knowledgeable scientists and pedagogues, spelling out a curriculum for the youngest children in day care, who had not previously been given this kind of detailed educational attention. Although recent Soviet manuals for child-care workers (e.g. Chauncey, 1969) had stressed the need to keep babies active, occupied, and learning, and had even suggested some general types of activities, we have here a much more explicit description of just how to go about such tasks. Such a manual serves also to re-emphasize the role of caretaker as teacher, an especially crucial matter in view of the inescapable pressures of basic caretaking tasks in groups of 15 or perhaps more infants.

Providing playful teaching experiences which help to build basic skills is not "child's play." It deserves — and here has received — the efforts of some of the most expert minds available in the country. In fact, one would have to look long and hard to find in any language, descriptions of suitable teaching games for such young children. In the United States, for example, only within the past year or two have there become available any "how-to" manuals for the mother or worker inspired to extend her repertoire of baby games. Even so, the literature on this topic is sparse and surprisingly little of it emanates from the major publishers whose books commonly find their way to the libraries, bookstores, and newsstands. "Play with your baby," psychologists tell mothers, but they seldom translate such exhortations to practical suggestions. Many mothers, of course, on their own develop rich and varied baby games; many others do not. Some recent studies with disadvantaged mothers and their infants have suggested that, indeed, mothers (and surely, more easily, day care workers) *can* be taught how to teach their babies, and to enjoy doing so. This collection of activities is a welcome resource.

One very real concern about establishing group care for under-threes where it has not been common, is the fear that impersonal "institutionalization" will result from the combined pressures of inadequate finances, undertrained staff, and demand for admission. Even child-care workers who are basically warm, maternal, fun-loving, and ambitious for children's development, under such conditions may find themselves taxed merely to look after the physical needs of the children, to the virtual exclusion of fostering any new learning or *joi de vivre*. Under such pressures, child-care workers often cease to think of themselves as "teachers" at all. It is clear from this and other publications for the operational staffs of day care facilities, however, that the Soviet nurse and her helper *are* teachers in a preschool setting, not baby-sitters, and that it is up to them to foster the development of their small charges in many areas — speech, conceptual ability, music, motor skills, and, perhaps above all, social behavior and moral development.

A number of aspects of this manual draw special attention. For example, the clarity of goals is striking. The Soviet citizen and especially the staff of the preschool, are apt to be rather well aware of an explicit set of values and desirable traits toward which optimal child development leads. In many other countries neither such awareness nor such consensus exists. Furthermore, many educators, particularly in my own country, feel that to a large extent, cognitive development, and to an even greater degree, moral development proceeds automatically from experience, as if by osmosis; the Soviet pedagogue, in contrast, is oriented toward purposeful teaching directed toward well-defined cognitive and moral goals. Certainly, in this manual, it is clear for what purpose the book was prepared, for what general goals of development the worker is to strive, and, for each game and activity, precisely which skills are to be taught. In view of the contemporary psychological research which highlights the necessity for clearly specified behavioral goals in teaching, this clarity of purpose rates a distinct "plus."

Although the background for these early developmental tasks is framed in Pavlovian terms which will be unfamiliar to many readers of this translation, most readers will find the theoretical reasoning generally compatible with their own orientation. The emphasis on the significance of verbal learning, for example, is adaptable to any of the currently popular points of view. This approach to early childhood education is founded upon highly developed theories related to cognitive development, neurophysiology, and personality, and upon empirical norms of development, but of course to conduct the activities it is not necessary to know any of this complex background. It is important to note that this manual does include a brief description of some of the thinking on which it is based, despite the fact that it is addressed to day care workers who have had little education beyond the high school, if that. Again, we see that the *why* as well as the *what* is important.

Early education in this manual is not only play, but playful. The business of learning is expected to be fun for the child and for the adult as well. Consider, for example, "Catching Up," an activity designed to promote motor development in the second year of life. "Our Dana is in the garden, Feels like an apple dipped in honey, Our Dana," sings the group as Dana's head is stroked by the child-care worker. Then Dana dances and everyone claps. Pure entertainment and joy have their place, too, as with soap bubbles and catching sunbeams in a mirror.

The directions for these games and activities are quite detailed. In the hands of an unimaginative worker, such completeness is especially valuable. In the hands of an inventive and clever worker, more likely they are embroidered, interwoven, and modified to suit the children and the circumstances. How the manual is actually used of course depends greatly upon the workers and their directrices; the manual can be a resource or a taskmaster. In terms of my own observations of Soviet preschools, I am inclined to think that most child-care workers there will use it sensibly and judiciously, and not as a daily chore. The care which has been taken to specify details such as the number of children to be involved, their seating arrangements, and the dialogue, does, however, suggest quite a prescriptive flavor.

Many English-speaking readers will be in for some surprises in reading this manual. For example, at times standards for behavior are somewhat higher than might be expected. Color discriminations, for example, are to be taught during the second half of the second year; and throwing balls into a basket during the first half of that year. Groups of up to eight children are expected to sit quietly and attentively at very early ages. Of course, infants and toddlers can and will sit still if the game is interesting enough — I have seen a group of half a dozen 8 to 12 months old American infants enraptured for a half hour at a time by a clever teacher. We may be so caught up with the notion of the self-directed, individualistic child, that our toddlers miss this kind of opportunity for learning and enjoyment.

One matter about which there may be disagreement, is the wisdom of correcting the articulation of the young child. The usual English-speaking teacher, I believe, seeks only to grasp her small pupil's meaning, expecting that his articulation will improve without any special attention if he has decent models. She fears that correcting him will create such self-consciousness that stammering and other forms of speech pathology may result. The Soviet teacher, it seems, pays considerable attention to pronunciation as early as 18 months, though gently. One ought to be able to discover in the Soviet preschools, whether the fears are at all justified.

Finally, the readers will note that although there is some attention to individual differences (e.g. activities with pictures are said not to be appropriate for all infants by the end of the first year), by and large a child's age is given as an accurate predictor of his behavior. And what of the child who doesn't measure up? Or the one whose behavior is more advanced in some respects, less advanced in others? My own observations again lead me to believe that caretakers in the Soviet Union are as sensitive to the individual differences among children as are those of any other country. How fruitful it would be to discover the effect of the lagging child on the caretaker's behavior and vice versa! Can we accelerate the development of the maturationally slow child? The Soviet caretaker will probably try!

Turning now to "Early Childhood Education in the Kibbutz," by Ben-Yaakov, we find a general-purpose manual for the metapelet in an Israeli kibbutz. This book is intended to provide the overall framework by which the metapelet can build healthy relationships with the infant, the young child, and his family, and can establish the everyday routines by which the upbringing process may be made smooth and effective. This manual resembles an abbreviated "Dr. Spock" for the kibbutz, a gentle blend of common sense, psychoanalysis, and a recognition of the realities of living in groups.

The reader will need to understand that each kibbutz in fact determines for itself how its children are to be cared for — although there are many similarities from one to another — and that details in this manual which are appropriate for one settlement may not fit another. The kibbutz settlements, for whom this was written are, in fact, those of only one of three major kibbutz movements in Israel. In some kibbutzim infants are cared for by trained nurses in baby houses and are later transferred to the care of a metapelet in another house when they become toddlers; in the structure outlined here, no such discontinuity exists during the earliest years. This book therefore covers the entire range from the newborn era through the preschool years.

The manual is indeed brief, yet it manages a rather broad coverage of topics having to do with what might better be termed "upbringing" than "education," as the latter is commonly understood. For the typical metapelet, who has probably had no more than a few months' formal training for her job, if any, this little book can, it seems to me, serve a number of purposes. First, it provides a set of guidelines and a rationale which are child-centered and sensitive to the needs of the children; it handles a large number of everyday questions by establishing a rather extensive set of rules to handle routine situations, rules which can be followed flexibly and sensibly. Second, the manual supports the central position of the metapelet, the critical importance of her role as "upbringer," not "caretaker," thereby serving to enhance her status within the kibbutz. As in every country with which I am acquainted, the child-care worker in Israel tends to fall rather low in the status heirarchy, a sad state of affairs considering the crucial nature of the position of those who so deeply affect children's lives and their potential as eventual citizens of the community. Finally, by implication, this manual indicates the kinds of supportive help which the metapelet needs from other kibbutz members if she is to concentrate her efforts with the children themselves, rather than with details such as housekeeping, procuring supplies, laundry, etc.

According to Ben-Yaakov, and in actual fact, the job of the metapelet is extremely demanding. She must give herself quite completely to rearing growing children. During the child's first year of life, especially the first half of that year, the mother shares in his care in the children's house, cooperating closely with the metapelet. Except for this period, however, the metapelet has primary responsibility for four to five children during all their waking hours except for those few which they spend elsewhere with their parents and siblings. She is expected to devote herself unstintingly to the children and to remain their metapelet for at least the first three and a half or four years of their lives.

Dr. Spock's mothers have their own needs and moods; the metapelet's are unnoticed here. For example,

"The presence of the metapelet and her willingness to help the child in every instance prevents tension, anger, and various collisions and in large part assures quiet in the house and relaxation for the children," Yet, Burton White's study of especially effective American mothers with their own toddlers reveals that such mothers do not *always* respond to the children's pleas for help and that in fact, each goes about his own business with only occasional interchanges. Ben-Yaakov is, of course, not alone among authors of manuals for all sorts of persons in helping relationships in this expectation that the person to be helped is the only one of the two who is permitted foibles. The metapelet's intimate and long-range relationship with the children makes this perhaps a heavier burden for her than for the day care worker in other settings, however.

The goals for upbringing in the kibbutz are in this manual rather loosely defined. The routines for caretaking, the "positive, quiet, and balanced physical environment," the toys, and the warm and supportive interaction with the metapelet, are all designed to promote healthy physical and emotional growth. A sense of trust in others, the establishment of autonomy and self confidence, and the control of instinctual impulses, are seen as the paramount tasks for the earliest years. Learning tends to be defined in these terms, rather than in terms of skills or intellect, and little direct teaching is suggested. In an ordered and loving environment, the child is expected to flourish happily, escaping the hazards of either over-inhibition or over-excitation. There is no need to "push" or to "instruct" in any but the basic rudiments of coping with day-to-day situations; the ideal child is a quiet and relaxed child, in both internal and external equilibrium. Consonant with the psychoanalytic framework, healthy living today is seen as a more effective guarantee of fulfillment in adulthood than is any sort of structured, sequential teaching for more specific goals.

Play, for example, is seen as serving the child's current psychological needs. "Fears, disappointments, and insecurity which bother him occasionally, find their expression in the play language of the child. Play helps the child 'repair' the disappointing reality and turn it into a satisfying fantasy." Plentiful toys should be provided, including a broad variety of creative materials, for, "Through touching and using materials, he obtains positive sublimating instinctual satisfaction... He simply enjoys the activity, the use of his muscles and his control over the material..."

We should remind ourselves that not only do kibbutzim differ among themselves, but that they differ from time to time as well. Marcus (1971), for example, in his very engaging and enlightening description of kibbutz group care in early childhood — a "must" for the interested reader — takes note of a recent move toward attention to early cognitive stimulation, as well as a replacement of earlier overpermissiveness with a more balanced approach. the active Israeli programs of compensatory education for disadvantaged preschoolers, quite apart from the kibbutz movement which encompasses only some 4-5 percent of the Israeli population, also reflect this newer philosophy. Yet, there remains a strong emphasis on the fulfillment of the child's emotional needs; the baby has not yet been thrown out with the bath water, and probably never will be.

Although this little manual suggests a number of routines for the celebration of holidays, for weaning, toilet training, feeding, and the like, it is clear that the metapelet is in charge and that it is up to her to adapt these suggestions to her own group of children and, to some extent, to their parents. What the manual does *not* treat are some of the harder questions: the "problem children", "problem parents", and the inevitable imperfections of the metapelet. What *does* one do about the mother who upsets her baby, is late for feedings, or is jealous of the metapelet's skill in handing her child? How *does* one deal with tantrums, biting, hitting, overpossessiveness, or whining when these persist longer than they should (or than the metapelet can tolerate that day)? Despite Ben-Yaakov's positive and helpful suggestions for management of everyday behavior, there are times when these do not work as one expects. What then?

The quality of care, the happiness of children, the loving and sensitive ways in which metaplot care for the young, and the degree to which the children's house is part of the total community with mothers, fathers, and other relatives in and out throughout the day — all these are most impressive to the observer. They are even more impressive when one realizes that child rearing in the kibbutz has taken shape as a community effort, a matter of central concern to all and a frequent focus of questioning and discussion. Metaplot are generally chosen by a vote of the membership, and for the most part, they are remarkable women indeed. In this manual, Ben-Yaakov has provided, perhaps more than anything else, support for their own healthy "instincts."

In summary, then, both these manuals are commended to the reader as substantive, valuable, and fascinating documents. How very different they are, and yet how deeply each reflects the determination that young children shall be accorded the very best opportunity which their society can devise for a healthy childhood! Even though the experts may disagree on many details, it is fortunate for the world's children — and ourselves — that fine minds are today being turned to the creation of optimal environments for the young.

> Halbert B. Robinson
> University of Washington
> Seattle, Washington, U.S.A.

REFERENCES

Chauncey, Henry (Ed.), *Soviet Preschool Education, I*, New York: Holt, Rinehart, and Winston, 1969.

Marcus, Joseph, Early Child Development in Kibbutz Group Care, *Early Child Development and Care*, 1971, 1, 67-98.

PLAY AND ACTIVITY FOR CHILDREN

IN THE FIRST THREE YEARS OF LIFE

Section One: Early Child Care in the Russian
Day Care Center and Children's Home

PLAY AND ACTIVITY FOR CHILDREN

IN THE FIRST THREE YEARS OF LIFE

by

N.B. KUPRIYANOVA

and

T.N. FEDOSEEVA

(Translated from the Russian)

CONTENTS

THE AIM OF SPECIAL PLAY AND ACTIVITIES IN EARLY
CHILD DEVELOPMENT 1
    The Programming of Activities 3

PLAY AND ACTIVITY DURING THE FIRST YEAR OF LIFE . 7
    Play and Activities with Infants from 3-5 Weeks
        Until 2½-3 Months 9
    Play and Activities with Children From
        2½-3 Until 5-6 Months 12
    Play and Activities with Children From
        5-6 Until 9-10 Months 18
    Understanding of Speech and Widening of the
        Child's Impressions 21
    Play and Activities with Children at the Age
        From 9-10 Months Up to 1 Year 25
    Indexes of Neuropsychological Development of
        Children in the First Year of Life 32

PLAY AND ACTIVITY DURING THE SECOND AND THIRD
YEARS OF LIFE 36
    Children's Play and Activity in the Second
        Year 37
    Demonstration with Names (From 1 Year Up to
        1 Year 6 Months) 41
    Demonstration of Objects in Action (From One
        Year Up to One Year Six Months) 43
    Demonstration of Live Animals 48
    Hiding Objects 49
    Walks With A Purpose 49
    Activities for Developing Imitations (From
        1 Year 3 Months) 50
    Carrying Out Instructions 52
    Activities With Pictures for Children Aged
        From 1 Year to 1 Year 2-3 Months 53
    Activities With Children From 1 Year 2-3
        Months Till 1 Year 4-5 Months 56
    Activities With Children From 1 Year 4-5
        Months Up to 1 Year 6-8 Months 57
    Demonstrations With Names (From 1 Year 6
        Months to 2 Years) 59

CONTENTS

Demonstration of Objects in Action (From
    1 Year 6 Months to 2 Years).   60
Demonstration of Live Animals (From 1 Year
    6 Months Up to 2 Years)   65
Purposeful Walks in the Backyard or in the
    Fields (From 1 Year 6 Months Up to
    2 Years)   65
Implementation of Instructions   66
Searching For a Certain Toy Among Similar
    Ones   66
Story Telling With Pictures (From 1 Year
    6 Months Up to 2 Years).   67
Showing Slides   70
Story-Telling-Conversation   70
Purposeful Acts With Objects in the Second
    Year of Life   71
Activity to Develop General Motor Ability
    During the Second Year of Life   82
Organization of Motor Activities   83
Entertainment During the Second Year of Life.   92

PLAY AND ACTIVITY IN THE THIRD YEAR OF LIFE . . .   95

Speech Development and Orientation in Three
    Year Olds   95
Organized Observations   97
Observations While Feeding Fish in an
    Acquarium   98
Walks With a Purpose   98
Demonstration on Simple Topics With the
    Use of Toys 100
Using Pictures to Tell Stories 106
Slide Shows Accompanied by Stories 109
Fairy Tales and Stories 110
Poetry 115
Didactic Games 116
Didactic Games to Encourage Speech Develop-
    ment and Orientation Within the
    Surroundings 116
Didactic Games to Differentiate and Name
    Colors 121
Didactic Games to Differentiate Forms . . . 122

CONTENTS

Didactic Games to Differentiate Contrasting Forms 124
Didactic Games to Develop Numerical Concepts 125
Didactic Games to Develop Auditory Perception 126
Didactic Games for Concentration and Memory. 128
Ability to Develop the Small Motor Muscles of the Hand 131
Organization of Motor Games 133
Modelling 148
Drawing 149
Puppet Shows 161
Holidays in Children's Homes 173
Planning of Play and Activities 174
An Approximate Enumeration of Play and Activities With Two Year Old Children . . 177
An Approximate Plan for Play and Activities With 3 Year Olds During the Spring (March, April, May) 180
Motor Development 181
Painting and Modeling 181

REFERENCES 194

THE AIM OF SPECIAL PLAY AND ACTIVITIES IN EARLY CHILD DEVELOPMENT

In early childhood the infant goes through an intense development of the sensory system. He masters movement and speech, he develops his memory, his thought processes and his imagination.

In order to achieve full development of infants up to the age of three in day centers, it is necessary to have a complex and carefully thought out system of education. The work has to be organized so that while taking care of a group of children the child-care worker at the same time can consider the peculiarities of individual child and find the individual approach to him.

The younger an infant is the more important it is for his physical and neuropsychological development to have an exact regime according to his age, and an appropriate way to satisfy his physical needs (food, sleep, toilet etc.).

Play is an important factor in the process of his development, and the formation of his personality. Play creates a pleasant, joyful atmosphere, and heightens the vitality of his personality. Under the influence of play connected with motor movements, children become more mobile and dexterous.

Play promotes sensory development. Through play he begins to recognize colour, form, and other qualities of objects, and begins to understand the cause and connection between different occurrences. A child playing often reflects his surroundings, and develops perceptiveness, arbitrary consideration, thought, memory and imagination.

Play promotes speech. While playing a child learns connection of different qualities of objects, and through his handling of them, their verbal meaning. During play, talk arises between children and adults.

Through play children learn to live in groups, they learn to obey rules, function cooperatively, give in to one another, and to wait their turn to accept a leading role. Thus, play disciplines a child, and helps to develop his relationships to other children.

Play promotes the development of will and character. He will learn to overcome difficulties which interfere with his play. Thus he achieves his aim, which is to develop persistence.

Art and decoration of children's games, the viewing of pictures, folk songs and fairy tales all promote a sense of beauty, and provide a beginning to aesthetic education. Play promotes love and respect for work, as well as the acquirement of elementary skills, such as the use of a pencil, clay, shovel and other building materials.

The activity of children moves in two directions. On the one hand, the children play under the guidance of their child-care worker, who organizes and conducts special plays and activities. On the other hand the children play by themselves, on their own initiative, and in this way gain knowledge and abilities acquired in interaction with adults. The role of the child-care worker is to create a proper play atmosphere, according to level of the child's development, and accordingly to guide the child's so-called independent activity.*

This book describes the content and organization of special play, and activities with children.

N.M. Aksarina characterizes special activities with children in the following way; "They are organized on the initiative of the child-care worker following an

---

*[Translator's Note: The Russian authors keep stressing the central role of the adult, apparently as part of their overall philosophy.]

exact educational aim. They are carried out according to a previously prepared schedule and every activity has definite methods. During these activities a child has to behave according to definite demands. The action of the child is regulated by adults. The basic significance of special play and activities organized by the child-care worker by her ability to stimulate the development of the neuropsychological activity, which helps the child to gain a new experience".

The definition of "play" and "activity" is relative. Each of them can be either "play" or "occupation" depending on who initiated it. For instance, putting a doll to sleep can be an independent act of a child in the "play" situation. But the preliminary teaching of this act by the child care-worker, carried out as a demonstration during activity time, would be called "activity".

In addition to playing, which is the main form of children's activity, they also observe their surroundings, obey orders, paint, model (clay), listen to stories, see puppet shows, etc. All these activities are occupation, and not play. However, it is commendable to carry them out in a warm emotional atmosphere so as to interest the child, hold his attention and thus obtain desirable results.

THE PROGRAMMING OF ACTIVITIES

Special play and activities can be carried out with a single child, within a small group of children (subgroup), or with a whole group.

Individual activity prevails during the first year, when the developmental needs of the child call for an individual approach. During the second and third years the individual approach is gradually reduced though the individual approach remains essential for retarded children, or children newly accepted into the group.

Ordering of children into small groups can be carried out in the first year of their lives. When the child-care worker sings or plays an instrument or demonstrates something during activities, the children should be grouped according to developmental level. Still, even in this subgroup she should view each child as an entity and associate with it.

Work in small groups (4-6 children) is carried out mainly in the second year of life. The main stress is the development of speech, and the handling of objects. In the third year the main attention is focused on activities which further the development of speech. These didactical games are carried out in subgroups. Each group contains 10-12 children of the same intellectual level. Otherwise the more developed, more verbal children will suppress the activity of the less developed, shy and passive children. The whole group should not participate in didactic play with games such as picture matching, lotto, etc. Because then the play would not fulfill it's aim. New activities such as kneeding of clay, are also carried out in the subgroup. The child care-worker carries out individual and subgroup activities while all the other children are playing independently under the supervision of another adult.

Activities (such as shadow pictures) are carried out in a place where all the children can be spectators, and also where common participation is necessary in games of movement, musical activities, painting, etc. As mentioned before the child-care worker must keep each child within her field of vision.

There are special rules which should guide all play and activities:

1. In order to achieve its aim, each activity has to be carried out according to an exact, previously planned program.

2. A daily schedule with exact hours is essential.

3. Methods should be prepared by the child-care worker beforehand. The same material used in group work should not be given to the child during individual activities.

4. Adults are categorically prohibited from walking in the play area or to talk.

5. The child-care worker should create the proper atmosphere before starting the daily activity. She should suggest to the children to set up the toys and chairs in the wanted order, and explain to them what their play or activity will be about.

6. The children should be comfortably seated in order to use their materials properly and so they can all see well.

7. Care should be taken to watch if the babies are in proper posture.

8. Children should be stimulated to speak during all activities.

9. The children should be given an active part in all activities, use materials, and not to be passive. This is necessary in order to stimulate perceptiveness.

10. The program should be planned according to the child's ability to master the materials.

11. Upon completion of the play, the children should be given individual activities, and not be left to themselves.

12. The children should be given some analogical material for independent use.

The correct evaluation of these activities should be the degree of achievement of the expected goal, the amount of interest shown by the children, the degree of concentration and activity attained, and the speech development (according, of course, to their age).

The methods used in carrying out these activities have to be guided by thorough knowledge of the norms of child development. They must be evolved according to the age group as well as to individual capability.

The goals to be achieved should be:

1. Development of speech, and broadening interest in the immediate environment.
2. Development of the sense of aesthetics.
3. Development of motor ability.
4. Use of increasingly complicated forms of activity (handling of objects, figurative and constructional activities).
5. Creation of positive emotional states.

PLAY AND ACTIVITY DURING THE FIRST YEAR OF LIFE

A newborn infant sleeps during much of the day. Approximately at the age of 4 weeks he responds by smiling to such stimuli as: petting, stroking, a friendly voice, and the gaze of an adult. This indicates that an infant has visual and auditory abilities. From that time on there is need for systematic contact of a grown-up with the child. The contact should be through short, purposeful activities.

The first year of an infant is life characterized by a rapid tempo of physical and neuropsychological growth. According to the development of these and other functions we can differentiate different age periods:

1. *From 3-5 weeks to 2½-3 months*. This is a period when visual and auditory attention begins. The appearance of positive emotions and the ability to raise its head from a horizontal position and to hold it straight in a vertical.

2. *From 2½-3 months until 6-7 months*. Development of grasping, turning over and crawling commences.

3. *From 6-7 months until 9-10 months*. During this time span a period of purposeful activity with objects, comprehension of speech, development of babbling, crawling, standing up with some help, pulling himself up and making scissor movements of the legs takes place.

4. *From 9-10 months until 1 year*. Now pronunciation of the first meaningful words, the first independent steps, and the further development of purposeful activity with objects is observable.

All play and activity in every age group has to be directed, in order to achieve the mastering of these functions, which in turn are necessary for the further development of the child.

At first play and activity is carried out mainly in a play-pen. All the toys which were used by the child beforehand have to be eliminated and there should be nothing to distract him. The child needs to be dressed and dry.

Sometimes we can engage an infant while changing him on a dressing table. For instance, an infant who cannot yet lift up his head can be put for a few seconds on his belly, before he is laid on his back to be dressed.

While comforting a baby in one's arms one can stimulate his understanding of speech, simply by pointing to and naming objects in the room, such as a clock, a doll, or pictures.

With more grown-up infants, the activities are carried out on the floor or on a low sofa. With children who can sit, short activities can be carried out at a children's table.

Preserving the child's good mood is of great importance in attaining proper psychoneurological development. This can be achieved by an exact and planned organization of the daily schedule.

The child is strongly affected by the attitudes of the child-care worker's behaviour. She has to love the children of this age group. She has to be tender and attentive and give a lot of individual care to every infant. She should speak continuously and use an emotional, expressive tone with a melodious voice and varying intonations. Of no less importance is the mimicry of her face, and her movements. These should be soft and slow (Fig. 1).

The following activities with children up to one year of age are systemized by the authors on the basis of the data of Prof. N.M. Shchelovahova and Docent N.M. Aksarina.

PLAY AND ACTIVITY: FIRST YEAR   9

Fig. 1. Emotional contact of the child-care worker with the child.

The play activities "Wonderful Bag", "Who lives in the little house?" and "Show a toy" were suggested by Prof. E.I. Ticheeva and V.A. Petrova. The other material was worked out by the authors on the basis of material collected by the Leningrad Method Municipal Study.

PLAY AND ACTIVITIES WITH INFANTS FROM 3-5 WEEKS UNTIL 2½-3 MONTHS

An infant is born with sensory organs that are more or less ready to react to outside stimuli. Comparatively more mature are his sense of taste, sense of smell and vestibular system, which determines the child's sense of his position in space. Centers which react to distant stimuli (visual, auditory) are less developed. An infant blinks his eyes at a bright light and trembles at a high voice, but he does not notice different objects or react to low voices. Gradually the visual and auditory centers develop under the influence of actual stimuli, such as contact with adults and special games.

From the age of 3-4 weeks an easy way is to attract the infant's attention to mobile objects which are held close to his eyes. Therefore in order to develop his visual attention we put a bright toy near him for short periods of time, and move the toy in different directions. After 4 weeks the child should have the ability to follow visually a bright, colorful mobile toy.

The toys have to be held at a height of 45-50 cm and at an angle of vision of 45°.

The child's attention span is greater if the visual stimulus is accompanied by an auditory one. A preferable toy at this age is a bright rattle with a pleasant noise or a light melodious bell attached to bright red ribbon.

A newborn infant is unable to hold up his head. To help him accomplish this at the beginning of 4-5 weeks, one has to turn him over on his belly a few times a day, and let him try to lift his head. As soon as he puts his head down he should be turned on his back. When he can hold his head more steadily, he should be put on his belly for longer periods. When an infant is 3 months old he usually lies on his belly freely and leans on his forearms.

To hold his head steadily in a vertical position he has to be picked up under his arms and held vertically several times a day.

Positive emotional responses

Goal: to stimulate the development of visual-auditory attention, smiling, pronouncing of sound and general lively movements.

Procedure: before each training period the child is put into a play-pen. Each child gets individual training. The child-care worker bends over the baby, catches his eye, fondles him, smiles and talks to him softly with a melodious voice, or sings lullabys. After achieving her goal she moves on to the next child.

At the end of the first and beginning of the second month the child responds only with a smile. After repeating the same exercise daily the child in his second and third months will listen to the voice of the adult, concentrate his gaze on her face, begin to utter happy sounds and quickly and rhythmically move his arms and legs. That indicates the appearance of the "positive emotional response" or, "the response of animation".*

Lifting of the head

Goal: to develop the ability of lifting the head while lying prone.

Procedure: the child is on a dressing table or in a play-pen. The child-care worker puts him on his belly. To do that, she holds the child, who is on his back under his shoulder blades, turns him over and rests him on her right forearm. With her left hand she picks up the legs of the infant and puts him on the table. When his legs touch the table she uses her left hand to support the child's head, so as to avoid his hitting his forehead. Then she frees her right hand and corrects the position of the infant's arms.

To put him back, the child-care worker puts her hand under his chest, turns him face up, and rests him on her right hand. With her left hand she supports his legs and softly lowers him on the table. The moment the child touches the table with his buttocks, she puts her left hand under the back of his head, and puts him down on the table, freeing her right hand.

---

*Editor's Note: Russian psychology is built on the theory of conditioned reflexes. Thus each bit of behaviour is seen as being a specific reaction to a specific stimulus and such reactions or responses are often given names--like "the positive emotional response".

Holding the head in a vertical position

Goal: to develop the ability of holding the head upright while in a vertical position.

Procedure: The exercise is carried out on a dressing table or in a play-pen with each child. The child-care worker lifts the infant with both hands, raises him under his arms and holds his head with four fingers as she holds his body with her forearms, and carefully lifts him towards her right shoulder. Then she frees her left hand, and supports the child's buttocks with her left. The right hand is on the child's chest. Holding him with both hands, she moves him from her shoulders. The moment he lifts his head the child-care worker returns him back to her shoulder. First her right, then her left hand is moved under his arms. Supporting his head with her fingers, she takes his arm and softly puts him back. When the child learns to hold his head up, one should keep him in the vertical position for a longer time while warmly talking, or joyfully singing to him.

PLAY AND ACTIVITIES WITH CHILDREN FROM 2½-3 UNTIL 5-6 MONTHS

When awake a 3 month healthy child is usually cheerful. He coos and lies on his belly while leaning on his forearms, or lies on his back watching the toys dangling above him. During the next months he learns to recognize familiar faces and nearby objects. He begins to differentiate the tone of a voice and turns his head toward the source of sound.

When in a happy mood the child coos and babbles in varying ways, in accord with his ability to articulate. When he is 3-4 months old he pronounces laryngeal sounds, and when he is 5 months old he pronounces vowel sounds. Therefore it is essential to maintain the child's wholesome emotional state during this period.

PLAY AND ACTIVITY: FIRST YEAR   13

Fig. 2. The children practice grasping toys.

The stimulation of vowel sounds at this age is of great importance for speech development. Also, it is of importance to teach the child to take hold of objects. Consequently, the mobile toys at which he previously looked, passively, should now be lowered towards his chest. This enables him to occasionally touch them while waving his arms and to catch them. The toys should be within easy reach, such as a rattle fastened to a large ring (Fig. 2).

The child at the end of his 5th month not only occasionally stumbles upon a toy, but he sometimes deliberately reaches out, grasps it, and takes the toy from the adult, or even from the bottom of the play-pen (when he is lying prone).

Fig. 3. The leaning on forearms is changed to leaning on the hands with straightened arms.

During this period the posture of his prone position changes. He already leans on the palms of his hands and raises his body. There is no longer need to hang toys above him (Fig. 3). The toys are placed on the floor of the play-pen in order that the child should change the position of his body when trying to grasp the toy.

While the child is on his back the child-care worker should occupy his hands with a toy in order to divert him from thumb sucking.

During this time the baby turns over from his back to his stomach and makes some efforts to crawl towards the toy. This strengthens the muscles of his hands and legs, his chest and stomach, and promotes the development of crawling.

At this stage a child should not be placed on a pillow leaning against the wall or the side of a play-pen, as his vertebra are still underdeveloped. The whole weight of his body is on the vertebra and this can cause deformation. Now, when a child sits, but is unable yet to independently change his position, he might become satisfied in this position, move too little, and get flabby and passive. He may not develop the ability to crawl. This is very important for muscular development, and good posture.

Auditory attention

Goal: the development of the already existing auditory attention, and the ability of the child to search with his eyes for the source of a noise.

For this activity one uses objects which make various sounds (a rattle, bell, triangle, or xylophone).

Procedure: the child is in a play-pen. The child-care worker takes one of his toys in her hand, rings it from right and then to left until the child turns his head towards the sound. At the end of 4 months this activity should become complex. To do this she rings the toy continuously as she walks around the play-pen. Inducing the child to turn his head, she attempts to make him discover the source of the sound with his eyes.

Fig. 4. Bright toys producing various sounds develop visual and auditory concentration.

This activity is carried out with each child. Afterwards it is advisable to return them to a group of 3-4 children of the same age. They are placed in a play-pen, each at a small distance from the other.

Cooing-babbling

Goal: to achieve a joyful mood in the child, to elicit imitation of the child-care worker's voice.

Procedure: the child-care worker bends over the child who lies on his back in the play-pen, she handles him, trying to cheer him and arouses his positive emotional response. She continues the sounds previously made by the child in order to elicit imitation.

Consequently the 5 month old baby starts to repeat sounds, by imitating the adult.

This activity has to be repeated daily during this period.

The moving object

Goal: to develop the following of a moving object.

Procedure: the child-care worker takes 3-4 children and puts them on their backs at a short distance from one another. She talks with every child, pats them, and cheers them. For instance: "Lyusenka lay down here, this way, here, and Irochko this way...".

The child-care worker then takes a small flag, and slowly shakes or waves it, trying to bring the flag to each child's attention. She moves it about and sings a known children's song. The melody is chosen freely. Every movement is repeated. This is necessary in order to enable the child to follow the object. Sometimes the procedure has to be prolonged while the child follows the object.

When the children learn to follow the flag, which is moved in one direction only, the child-care worker walks around the play-pen and taps on its sides from different directions. As she does so, she tries to get the children to turn their heads in the direction of the sound.

The song

>Here is my flag
> yes, yes, yes,
>And the children are having fun
> yes, yes, yes,
>I'll raise the flag
> yes, yes, yes,
>I'll lower the flag
> yes, yes, yes,
>With the flag I'll lightly tap
> yes, yes, yes,
>I'll bring it closer to you
> Take, take my flag.

Similarly, the activities can be carried out with ribbons, by fastening ribbons to the rim of a ring, the ribbons being 25-30 cm long.

During the activity the child-care worker holds the rim in a horizontal position, and moves it back and forth so that the ribbons wave freely.

Grasping and holding of toys

Goal: to teach a child to hold a toy that is put into his hand (from 3-4 1/2 months) and grasp and hold a toy (from 4-4 1/2 months).

For this activity one uses toys easily discernible such as a light, bright rattle with a handle.

Procedure: The child is on his back in the playpen. The child-care worker offers the toy. When the child follows it with his eyes she should move it slowly. After letting the child hold the toy for a short while, she should move his hand and the toy together. During the following activities one should get the child to execute each activity independently.

Turning over

   Goal: to stimulate turning over from a supine to a prone position (from 3-3 1/2 months).

   Procedure: The child-care worker must assist the children to turn over from their back on to their stomach. To turn a baby who is on his back to the right, she takes the baby's left hand in her right hand and with her left hand holds the lower part of his legs, and puts her index finger between the baby's legs. Next, she turns her right hand clockwise, while pulling up the child's left hand.

   After a few times the child begins to turn over without the help of an adult. To do this, his attention has to be stimulated with a bright toy, which should be near his side.

Initiation of crawling

   Goal: to initiate crawling.

   Procedure: The child-care worker puts a toy in front of the child just far enough so that he will not be able to grasp it. The baby will then stretch towards the toy, and at the same time raise the upper part of his body. The adult should then place her palm on the child's sole to enable him to push against it. With the other hand the child-care worker moves the toy and attracts the child's attention. She encourages the child verbally to crawl. Several children of the same developmental stage may be combined in a subgroup.

PLAY AND ACTIVITIES WITH CHILDREN FROM 5-6 UNTIL 9-10 MONTHS

   From 5-6 months the children are more mobile, and should not be with younger ones. When a child begins to crawl he has to be put into a play-pen without a stand for hanging toys, as is the case with younger children. Toys for children this age, as mentioned

PLAY AND ACTIVITY: FIRST YEAR   19

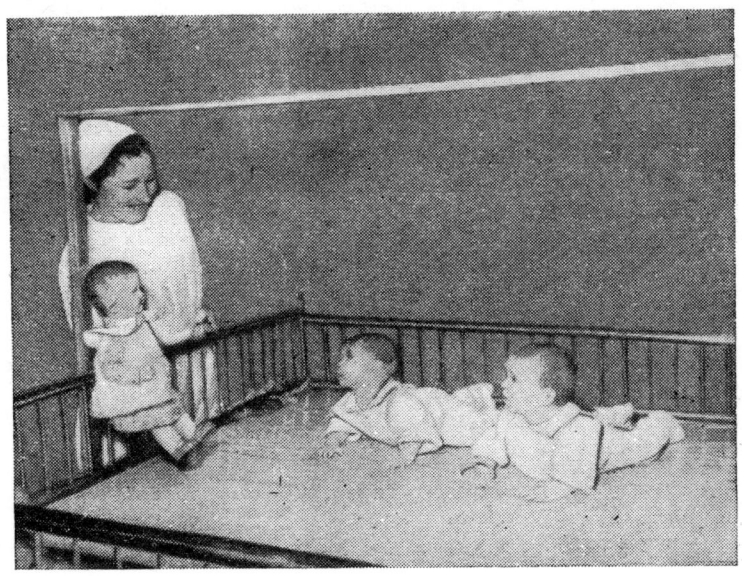

Fig. 5. Acquaintance with a doll.

above, are put on the floor of the play-pen.

The main task for this age group is to develop the comprehension of speech, as well as the ability to repeat syllables.

The decisive role of an adult in the development of speech during the first 6 months is effected by the intonation of his voice. After the 5th-6th months, selection of words becomes of major importance. The child-care worker should name the objects surrounding the child, and the activities carried out by the child or by herself. In this way she combines the objects and activities with their verbal designation.

While changing a baby, feeding him or putting him to bed, the child-care worker should talk to him and name the different objects and actions connected with this process. For instance: "Yurochka will eat now, he will eat cereal", or "I will wash Ninochka's hands, stretch out your hands Ninochka". The child-care worker introduces the children to the names of some of the objects and toys about them. They should be arranged in such a way as to be seen by him. On each shelf there should be a single topical toy.* After showing the child a doll the child-care worker can ask "Where is the doll?" The child may then turn his head in the direction of the toy and find it with his eyes.

At the end of 8-9 months the infants develop the ability of purposeful manipulation. They now can use not only rubber toys, as before, but a special collection of toys which help develop purposeful actions: i.e. balls, balloons, and other round objects, and containers into which they can insert and take out small objects.

Children at 8-9 months walk while they hold on to some sturdy support or railing. They should also be allowed to move around on a partitioned part of the floor, which has enough space to permit free movement. To allow them to practice these movements it is recommended to have a space on the floor which is somewhat raised, with sloping sides. Also, one can have a sofa with springs, or a box one meter square and 10-20 cm high, where children can climb independently. A "didactic table"** is used for toys and objects which involve purposeful movements: (putting objects into a container, rotating a wheel, sorting rings). Special play and activities with children of this age group have the following aims:

---

*Editor's Note: The authors often use the term "topical toy" to designate a toy which represents some topic - i.e. a play house, a toy animal, or a lifelike doll, in contrast to non-representational toys such as rattles and blocks, and which are used for initative games.

**Translator's Note: The author means of course a regular low table, but every piece of equipment has a specific planned aim, and so she calls the table a "didactic table".

PLAY AND ACTIVITY: FIRST YEAR

1. Understanding of speech and widening of the child's impressions.

2. Developing the repetition of sounds, and repetition of simple words.

3. Developing general movements.

4. Developing purposeful manipulation.

UNDERSTANDING OF SPEECH AND WIDENING OF THE CHILD'S IMPRESSIONS

"Where is Liala?" (after 7 months)

Goal: the recognition of objects through the naming of objects.

For this activity topical toys are used (doll, cat, dog, hen, etc.). In this activity the doll "Liala" should be placed within the field of vision of all the children.

Procedure: The children sit in the play-pen or stand near the railing. The child-care worker lifts the doll out of the play-pen. She walks with the doll along the railing of the play-pen, makes the doll bow to the children, and dance, and walk along the rail. Then she brings it to each child and says: "Give a hand to Liala". We shall say to Liala: "Good day Liala". Stroke her head: "Sleep, sleep Liala". Suddenly she should hide the doll behind her back and say, "There is no Liala, Where is Liala? Here is Liala". Liala appears again, bows to the children. These exercises should be repeated several times daily.

After each activity the doll is put in her regular place. The child-care worker asks the children: "Where is Liala?" Gradually the children then begin to follow the doll with their eyes.

Using this same principle, activities are carried out with various topical toys.

Pat-a-cake (from 7 months)

Goal: to develop the understanding and the naming of simple movements, and the repetition of these movements (for instance: "pat-a-cake", "Good-bye", "Give a hand").

Procedure: The child-care worker stands in front of the child, claps her hands and repeats: "Pat-a-cake...". As the child cannot execute these movements with his hands, she takes his hands and clasps them while repeating "Pat-a-cake,". After constant repetition the child will begin to clap independently, as he imitates the adult. Afterwards he will begin to repeat the movement when he hears the word "Pat-a-cake".

When an adult leaves the room (Nanny, doctor, parent) the child-care worker makes use of the opportunity to teach the child by saying "Goodbye".

In addition to this she can teach the child to reach out his hand in response to the words "give me your hand". If the baby shows no reaction to this, she herself takes his hand and prods it lightly. She repeats this several times. The result is that the child begins to extend his arms when asked: "Give your hand".

"Hide and seek"

Goal: to acquaint the child with his name, and the names of other children (from 8-9 months).

Procedure: The children sit in the play-pen. The child-care worker takes a large napkin and puts it over the child's head. "Where is Vova - she then takes the napkin - "Here a-a-a-ah, here is Vova". Again she covers the child's face. He then tries to uncover his face. At first he is helped. Later on the child puts the napkin over his face himself. Also, the adult may cover his face so that the child should uncover it. The child can be in the arms of the child-care worker, the nurse hides behind the child-care worker's back, and suddenly reappears from one or the other side. The child-care worker asks: "Where is aunt Katya?" Whereupon the nurse shows herself. The child is gleeful, and the child-care worker exclaims: "Here is aunt Katya".

Imitation of simple and complex sounds

"Call-over"

Goal: the development of the articulation apparatus and the ability to imitate (from 7-8 months).

Procedure: There are several children in the play-pen. The child-care worker addresses a child, who knows how to repeat several syllables, like "ma": Tanechka, say "ma-ma-ma". The child will listen and after a few minutes will repeat this himself. Then one may elicit the repetition of new syllables not previously pronounced by the child.

"Call-over" can be carried out by eliciting an answer reaction from several children at once. The child-care worker, who may be busy with one child in the play-pen should listen to the sounds made by another and should softly repeat them, and thus encourage other children to repeat these syllables.

The development of general movements - crawling

Goal: continued development of the visual and auditory systems and the inducement of crawling (5-6 months).

Procedure: 3-4 children are put on their abdomen. They should be put in different corners of the play-pen while facing the center. The child-care worker should then take a large colorful top which makes a pleasant tinkle while spinning, and spin it in the center of the play-pen. The brightness of it and the noise attracts the children's attention and they may make an attempt to crawl towards the center of the play-pen in order to grasp the top.

Standing up along the side of the play-pen

Goal: to develop the ability of standing up along the side of the play-pen (from 7 months).

Procedure: When the child tries to stand while clinging to the side of the play-pen, the child-care worker should stand with a bright toy near the play-pen. This will increase the child's aspiration to stand up and reach the toy. It is also recommended to hang toys along the sides of the play-pen, in order to stimulate other children to make similar attempts.

Side stepping

Goal: to teach side stepping along the side of the play-pen (from 8 months).

Procedure: When a child is able to stand freely though holding on to the side of the play-pen, the child-care worker should stand aside at a given distance so that he would not be able to take the toy she is holding. She should gesticulate and call him to her. The child will then reach for the toy and make a step to the side. With every step the toy should be put further away. In this way the child gradually masters the ability to walk along the side of the play-pen, and finally starts walking independently.

Development of purposeful actions with objects

Insertion and extraction of objects from containers

Goal: to teach insertion and extraction of small objects from a bag.

Procedure: The child-care worker places a bag in front of the child who is near the side railing of the play-pen. A small colorful wooden or plastic ball is put into the bag. She inserts the child's hand into the bag. The child will start to repeat these movements independently, putting the ball into the bag and taking it out.

PLAY AND ACTIVITIES WITH CHILDREN AT THE AGE FROM 9-10 MONTHS UP TO 1 YEAR

Towards the end of the first year there is rapid progress in the development of speech. The child now comprehends his surroundings, not only through direct sensations but also through words which he has heard in connection with objects ("signal of signals" of I.P. Pavlov). This becomes possible due to the emergence of new cerebral cortical functions, such as distraction and attention. Thus, the word "Dolly" begins to mean any doll (rubber, plastic, cloth, large or small), the word "how-how" - any dog, and not just a special doll or dog. Taking this into account, the group of children should be given a number of the same kind of toys which, however, differ outwardly and are made up of various materials.

To develop the child's understanding of adult speech, one has to increase the number of words and sentences that the child understands. For instance, he learns from the meaning of words to perform described movements (stand, sit), and carry out a series of different acts with objects (to put one cube on another, to remove and replace a ring on a peg - "put on", "take off").

To encourage the development of active speech (i.e. first words), it is necessary to continue to stimulate the child to imitate an adult, to pronounce various sounds and syllables, and then let him form from them his first words (from the syllables "ma-ma" the word "mama", etc.).

At this age one leads the child to carry out purposeful acts with objects, for instance, to put small objects into big ones, to cover and uncover a toy, etc.

Around 12 months a child may walk independently.

To help the child achieve a proper general development, one has to make use of every moment while attending him, in addition to carrying out different activities.

The child-care worker should have the following aims: to introduce the child to his environment, to develop the understanding of speech; to stimulate the repetition of sounds and the first meaningful words; to stimulate purposeful acts with objects and to teach the child to walk independently.

Continued development of speech and comprehension and acquaintance with the environment, imitation of sounds and formation of the first words

Demonstration of a toy (a cat)

Goal: to stimulate the imitation of sounds "me-ow", and the formation of a meaningful word "meow".

Procedure: 3-4 children are seated on a low sofa. The child-care worker sits on a child's chair at the distance of an outstretched arm. She shows the child a toy - a cat. While holding it in her hands she shows it to the children, repeating "me-ow - me-ow". She speaks expressively to the child, underlining the syllables "me-ow", she strokes the cat, hides the cat; "Where is meow? There is no meow. Call meow-meow, do with your hands like this". (She demonstrates stroking). The children imitate, and the child-care worker shows the cat again. "Here is meow". When repeating this exercise, one has to show various cats. It is desirable to carry out these exercises after the children have seen a live cat.

"Who lives in the little house?"

Goal: to achieve the pronounciation of the words "meow", "how-how", ku-ku-re-ku".

Three topical toys are used for these exercises, a dog, a cat, a hen, and also building material or a small plywood house.

Procedure: 3-4 children lie on a low sofa. In front of the sofa is a low table. The child-care worker should build a small house from blocks, or use a ready made house. She should turn to the children

PLAY AND ACTIVITY: FIRST YEAR   27

Fig. 6. Demonstration of a toy.

and say: "Look, who went into the house - Meow, meow. Meow went away, there is no meow. How-how-how, the dog came running, it also went into the house. The dog went away, there is no dog. Ku-ku-re-ku, the hen came in. The hen also walked into the house, there is no hen. Lets call all the animals, we'll call the meow, we'll call the doggy, and we'll call the hen. Let's call the meow; do with your hand this way". (Waves to the cat to come).

The child-care worker again shows the cat: "Look children, the meow came in, what a nice meow". (She lets the children stroke the cat). Now we'll call the dog: "How-how-how, come to us doggy" - the children make a gesture with their hands. "The doggy did come", says the child-care worker.

In this way the children call all the animals. At the end of the exercises every child gets the same toys for individual play.

When the children learn the names of the animals, they will call them not only with gestures, but with words as well. Then one can exchange the initial toys with other toy animals.

Activity with a bag

Goal: the same as above.

For these activities toys (cat, dog, hen) are put into a bright bag.

Procedure: The child-care worker says: "What a beautiful bag I have. Let's see what's in it!" She takes out a cat - "Who is this, children? Meow me-ow". She strokes the cat. The child-care worker then hides the cat, and takes out the dog and the hen, and talks about them in the same way. At the end of the exercise each child receives a toy, and she suggests that he put it into the bag. (The same toys are given later for individual play).

Hiding and finding of toys

Goal: to understand the names of toys, and to name them.

Three topical toys (horse, dog and bear) are used for this exercise.

Procedure: The child-care worker shows a horse to the children. "Here is a horse - stroke the horse, a dog - bow-wow-wow, and here is a Teddy bear - that's how Teddy bear walks: tap-tap-tap".

While the children watch, she hides one of the toys (and in later exercises all three toys): "There is no horse, where is the horse?" She takes two children by the hand, walks with them to the place where the horse is hidden.

During the next exercise the children move and find the hidden toys by themselves while crawling. If the child brings the wrong toy, the child-care worker says, in an appropriate intonation: "No, this is not a horse, this is a Teddy bear, put Teddy back, and bring the horse..." If the child brings the suggested toy, she compliments him: "Yes Yurochka, this is a horse".

Giving directions

Goal: carrying out a verbal suggestion.

For this activity one uses toys known to the children.

Procedure: The child-care worker talks with a child, near her, and gives him a toy, encouraging him to do certain things with it. "Here is a Dolly. Take Dolly's hand. Stroke Dolly like this, bye-bye Dolly", or: "This is a dog - bow-wow. Feed the doggy, here-here doggy", or: "Meow-me-ow, stroke the cat".

Continued purposeful acts and development with objects

Rolling of a small ball

Goal: to teach the child to place a small ball into the opening of a "didactic box".

For this activity one uses a box with an opening, the bottom of which is sloped, and has holes for the insertion of small colored balls. 1-2 children sit near the box.

Procedure: The child-care worker shows how to place a ball into the opening. She gives the child a ball, and shows him what to do with it. When the ball rolls in, she once again takes hold of his hand and adds another ball. Afterwards the child by himself may take the ball, and slide it into the opening.

Putting rings on a peg

Goal: to teach a child to put a ring on a peg, and take it off and to carry out these activities while

---

*(Translator's Note: Again the author uses the word didactic to stress the purpose of the box).

learning the words: "Take off the ring", "Put on the ring".

A ring (diameter of 10 cm) and a peg (length 10 cm) fastened onto a wooden base are used for this exercise.

Procedure: The child-care worker takes the child's hand and puts rings on the peg, accompanying the movements with words like: "Put on the ring. This way. Put on another ring. This way". - Then, she takes off the rings with the child's hand. "Take off the ring. This way. Take off another one. This way". The result of these exercises is that the child independently carries out these actions when he hears the words: "Put on", "Take off".

Opening and closing toys

Goal: to teach to open and close a toy, and to understand the words "open", "close".

Procedure: The child-care worker sits with 3 children at a table with 4 places. She gives each child a toy, and takes a toy for herself. She opens up a toy, directs the child's attention to herself and helps those who cannot open it. Sometimes she performs it together with the child by laying her hand on his hand. "Here, open it, this way. Yurochka close it, oh very nice, good boy". She strokes the child's head. One can give the children boxes and pans with covers. Thus the children gradually learn the names of the action, "open", and "close".

Shifting of blocks

Goal: to teach the child to take blocks out of a box or a bucket, to pile them on the table, and then them back into the box.

Procedure: 3 children and the child-care worker sit at the table. Each one receives a block which is in a box or a bucket.

PLAY AND ACTIVITY: FIRST YEAR

The child-care worker takes out the blocks, and suggests that the children should do the same: "Lenochka take out the blocks, this way; and you Yurochka take out, that way". Afterwards she shows how to return the blocks into a box. "Put in the blocks here, this way, what a fine fellow Yorchka. Lenochka also did well". The children imitate the child-care worker, and each other.

These toys are given to the child for individual play, as soon as he has mastered this task.

Development of movement

"First steps"

Goal: to teach the child to walk without support (take his first steps).

Procedure: The child-care worker calls for the child who stands near her, and stretches out her arms towards him. When the child tries to make the first steps she catches him. She turns him towards the nurse, who then holds out her arms and calls him to come back to her.

"Catch you, catch you"

Goal: to stimulate walking.

Procedure: The child-care worker makes quick, small steps on one place cheerfully saying: "I'll catch you, catch you". The child often laughs, and tries to crawl or make a few steps away from the child-care worker.

Collecting of scattered rings

Goal: stimulation of walking, and teaching to carry out an action while being verbally instructed by an adult: "Bring", "Put on".

For this activity 10-12 rings are taken with a long rod (1 meter long).

Procedure: The children stand near the child-care worker, who holds the end of the rod with the rings. The child-care worker recites some well known poem. She pulls out the rod and all the rings scatter on the floor.

The children step over, come closer to the rings, gather them, and bring them to the child-care worker, who puts them back on the rod.

The text of the song

> You, little ring, turn around, turn around.
> Show yourself to our kids.
> Turn around this way, this way.
> We cannot catch up with you.

The same method is used for activities - "bring", "give", "put in place" - with other objects: small balls and other round objects.

The text of the song

> Here, high, high, I'll throw the small balls
> Scattered far away, far away are the small balls
> And the children come up, come up to the small balls
> They'll bring to aunt Katya the small balls.

INDEXES OF NEUROPSYCHOLOGICAL DEVELOPMENT OF CHILDREN IN THE FIRST YEAR OF LIFE

(worked out by Prof. Schelovanova, N.M.)

At 2 months

1. Is calm when awake; watches toys hung above him.
2. When an adult talks to him, he smiles continuously.
3. Follows a mobile toy hanging in front of his eyes.

At 3 months

1. Laughs loudly.
2. In response to speech directed toward him by an

PLAY AND ACTIVITY: FIRST YEAR

adult, expresses his joy with a smile, cooing, and animated movements with his arms and legs.
3. Holds his head well, spends much time on his belly while leaning upon his arms.
4. When held under his arms, partially supports himself upon his legs, which bend at the hip joints.

At 4 months

1. Searches for objects which make a sound, finds an adult when hearing his voice (finds the source of a sound).
2. While awake is in a joyous state: smiles, coos loudly, moves with straight arms, bends and straightens his legs.
3. Is occupied with toys which hang in front of him a long time - touches and grasps objects.
4. When fed, supports the bottle with his hands.

At 5 months

1. Recognizes different faces (differentiated response).
2. Differentiates the tone of a voice addressing him.
3. Hums melodiously for periods of time.
4. Accurately directs his hand towards a rattle which an adult holds over his chest. Holds the rattle for relatively long periods of time.
5. Lifts his body, lies on his stomach for long periods of time while leaning upon the palms of his outstretched hands.
6. Turns over from his back to his stomach.
7. Stands steadily when held under his arms by an adult.

At 6 months

1. Pronounces syllables.
2. Freely takes toys from different positions, and is occupied with them for long periods of time.
3. Moves in the play-pen, crawls for short distances.
4. Eats well from a spoon, opens his mouth when seeing food, takes the food off with his lips.
5. Turns over from stomach to back.

At 7 months

1. Babbles for long periods of time.
2. At the request of an adult looks and finds with his eyes objects which are in a fixed place.
3. Plays with a rattle, knocks it and waves it.
4. Crawls well.
5. Stands erect when held by his hands.

At 8 months

1. Loudly repeats different syllables.
2. At the request of an adult performs the learned movement of hand clapping.
3. Displays great insistence, when trying to get a toy that attracted his attention, and performs many different movements to achieve his goal.
4. Toys occupy him for long periods of time, he observes them, and taps them against each other.
5. Sits up and lies down again by himself.
6. Stands up by himself when holding on to something. Stands and lowers himself.
7. Eats a piece of bread while holding it by himself.
8. Drinks from a cup, which is held by an adult.

At 9 months

1. Imitates an adult, repeating syllables pronounced by the adult.
2. Finds objects named by an adult and hidden in different places.
3. Performs different movements: ("Give a hand", "Goodbye") at the request of an adult.
4. Is occupied with objects in different ways according to their characteristics: rolls something, puts it in and takes it out, etc.
5. Steps sideways along the side of a playpen.
6. Walks when supported by an adult.

At 10 months

1. Imitates an adult, repeating different sounds and syllables.

2. Knows some adults and children by name.
3. At the request of an adult, finds and gives a named toy.
4. Responds to the game "I'll catch you, I'll catch you".
5. Play with objects (like opening, closing, patting, etc.) become steady activities.
6. Climbs and comes back down.
7. Walks holding on to a walker.

At 11 months

1. Pronounces the first meaningful words (mommy, give, how, how-how, etc.).
2. Carries out familiar activities when requested.
3. Masters new activities: puts one object on top of another, takes off rings from a rod, etc.
4. Stands alone.
5. Walks with little help.

At 12 months

1. Pronounces 6-10 words.
2. Walks by himself.
3. Drinks from a cup by himself.

PLAY AND ACTIVITY DURING THE SECOND AND THIRD YEARS OF LIFE

At the end of the first year a child walks independently, and pronounces his first words. This enables him to establish a widening contact with his surroundings. The child's now better orientated within his environment, he has better comprehension of adult speech, and his vocabulary becomes enlarged. Speech begins to become a means of contact, a means of communication with the outside world. Thus the adult's speech becomes very important, and it should be correct and clear.

During the second and third years of his life his basic movements are perfected: walking, running, climbing and throwing. The movements begin to be purposeful. In addition there is a further development of handling of objects, and the children get acquainted with their main characteristics - color, form, size, etc. Gradually children's play acquires a reflective character. At first when a child is 12-16 months old he repeats what was shown to him by an adult. F.I. Fradkina indicates that at the beginning when the child was shown how to feed a Teddy bear, or to put a doll to bed, he would feed Teddy bears only, and put dolls only to bed. Gradually the child will begin to transfer the actions shown to other objects. For instance, he will feed not only the Teddy bear, but dolls, cats, dogs, etc. From one year and six months the child begins to reflect in his play not only what was shown to him, but what he himself observes (he measures the temperature of his doll, etc.). At the end of the third year reflective play turns into figurative play when the child starts to play a definite role. The child conceives a clearer idea of his role in the play and he now builds more or less in succession. At this age the children begin to paint, model with clay and work with building materials. In this way the children perfect speech, thought, memory, concentration and imagination.

PLAY AND ACTIVITY: SECOND AND THIRD YEARS

The planning of activities in the second and third years depends upon the character of the activities. For instance, when carrying out dramatization and exercises in speech development the children should be seated in a half circle, so that all of them can see the child-care worker facing them. When playing on a table, the children should be seated near the table together with the child-care worker.

The length of time alloted for such activities is between 6-20 minutes, depending upon their kind. The shortest span should be allowed to activities where children need to concentrate and where they tire quickly. For instance, talking without demonstrations, purposeful actions with objects, didactic games, painting. Musical activities, topical demonstrations and clay modelling can be carried on for greater lengths of time.

The activities have to be carried out in a serene atmosphere. The voice of the child-care worker should be warmly emotional and the speech expressive, clear and slow. The child-care worker should see all the children and address each one individually, taking into account his developmental level. She should encourage maximal participation.

To consolidate the knowledge and ability acquired during these activities it is necessary to reuse the toys and appliances during individual play periods which are similar and analogous to those used during group activities.

CHILDREN'S PLAY AND ACTIVITY IN THE SECOND YEAR

The following aims should be before the child-care worker while carrying out activities with children during their second year of life: 1) development of speech and orientation to the environment; 2) formation of purposeful actions with objects; 3) development of general movements; 4) entertainment; 5) musical education.

Speech development and orientation within the environment

When a child is one year old (or slightly younger) he begins to react to a word as a signal, as a designation of definite objects or people: "Mommy", "Daddy", "Meow", "Dolly", etc. Here there is no demand yet to conceptualize. It is still a specific image. In order that a word acquire its general meaning, it should be what I.P. Pavlov called: "a signal of signals". One has to relate a great many conditioned reflexes connected with it from different senses, and data from recent physiological research also shows a wide inclusion of motor centers. The more conditioned reflex connections that are formed around a word, the easier it is for the word to acquire a generalized meaning.

Taking this into account, the adult should not only show and name objects during activities, but should also place them in the child's hand. The more specific actions carried out with the object by an adult or by the child (for instance, to stroke the cat, to feed or put it to bed, etc.) the quicker the word "cat" or "meow" will acquire a generalized meaning. It will then mean to a child *any* cat (a live, toy or one seen in a picture).

When carrying out these activities, one should use varying toys of the same kind. It is important to stimulate a child to imitate syllables and words. (When a toy is used in play one says "fell", "back", etc. When the child pronounces the first words which have a general meaning, it is permissable to encourage him to imitate simple words, like "beep-beep" - car, "how-how" - dog, etc.).

After one year and six months a child has to be taught the correct pronunciation of words.

At the age of 18 months if the child has had a satisfactory education as well as contact with adults, he will understand the names of many objects and actions. He begins to understand and react to complicated sentences and even to speech not directed at him. (While adults talk about an object, he may bring it to them). He understands when addressed interrogatively: "who?", "what?", "where?". One has to frequently mention objects and actions, with which a child comes into contact. In conversation one should use new unknown words accompanied by actions already familiar to him.

With the understanding of speech the child develops active speech. Imitating the adult, the child, like an echo, pronounces many words. He pronounces easy words clearly, and for difficult ones he uses the first or last syllables. To enrich the child's speech, the adult should speak clearly, expressively and exactly. In order that a child repeat what is said by the child-care worker, she has to have a store of stories, tales, short songs and anecdotes.

Toward the end of the second year, one should continue to stimulate the comprehension of adult speech and development of active speech. In addition one should stimulate and consolidate the child's ability to speak to adults. In order to do this the adult should use every occasion to query a child. For instance, while watching through a window one says: "Who walks? - an Uncle?" "What is this - a bus?" When together with a child she should review well known as well as new toys.

During this time as well as later on pictures viewed by the child are of great importance. The child looks, and points his finger; when he masters speech, he names the object seen in the picture. A colorful interesting picture attracts his attention, and helps him concentrate.

The principal sense used in the child's perception of a picture is the visual one. However the auditory, tactile and kinetic senses also play a role in his perception, providing the adult describes the picture to the child while he touches the picture with his index finger. This interaction of senses makes the perception more complete and encourages the consolidation of new words. When a child reaches the age of two he can name all familiar objects and all actions described in pictures.

At two children can look at pictures on a wall (the pictures have to be hung at the height of the child's vision) or he can look at them while sitting at a table with 3-4 other children.

In order that the child acquire clear and exact speech and pronunciation, it is necessary that adults speak precisely. In addition, all speech has to be corrected. A badly pronounced word has to be repeated again by the adult slowly and clearly, stressing the faulty syllable.

Using valid methods in developing speech activity a two year old child can be taught a vocabulary of approximately three hundred words. His sentences may contain three articles. Imitation of sounds and babbling disappear. The child's speech gradually becomes similar to that of the adult.

After 18 months the child-care worker has to enlarge his vocabulary.

To develop the understanding of speech it is necessary: 1) to help children discover the link between object and actions on the one hand, and to give explanations to the meaning of words on the other; 2) to widen the child's perception of his environment; 3) to teach the child to recognize familiar objects under different conditions; 4) to teach the child to recognize similar objects in nature and in pictures though they differ in color, form and size; 5) to teach the child to carry out different orders at the request of an adult; 6) to teach the understanding of simple sentences; 7) to teach the understanding of simple topics, explained by an adult.

To develop active speech in a child it is necessary: 1) to increase the number of pronounced simple

PLAY AND ACTIVITY: SECOND AND THIRD YEARS

words (from mumbling and sound mimicry); 2) to improve imitation; 3) to develop the ability to listen to an adult and to answer with familiar words; 4) to improve the pronunciation of words familiar to the child; 5) to encourage children to use their own words and to respond to adult questions throughout the day.

Activities to develop speech are carried out in sub-groups from about three to seven children while the others are active on their own. Each sub-group has to receive this attention.

DEMONSTRATION WITH NAMES (FROM 1 YEAR UP TO 1 YEAR 6 MONTHS)

Demonstrations with names have to start with the available toys. These may be: a doll, teddy bear, cat, etc. Puppet shows with a doll and toy animals are attractive to children. The doll in the hands of the child-care worker becomes a little girl riding on a horse, or rolling from a hill. The doll is dressed and undressed, she is put to sleep, and a lullaby is sung to it. A dog runs, eats, hides, etc.

In this pleasant manner the child-care worker elicits the imitation of sounds and then the pronunciation of words.

The child is introduced to a new experience and rounds out his knowledge.

The range of the demonstration is determined by the level of development in this group.

This demonstration of toys is lengthened or shortened, depending upon the age and behavior of the children. The number of toys is gradually increased.

At this age demonstrations with names are executed with "Demonstration of a toy"; "Wonderful bag"; "Who lives in this little house"? (Fig. 7).

Fig. 7. "Who lives in this little house?"

This method is described in a book by V.A. Petrovo.

Unlike the first year of life, at this age the children are taught to name objects by their proper names rather than syllables. Also, they now identify, hide toys in a bag and after immediately after them. Activities carried out in this manner help to develop memory.

"Hiding of objects" is an activity for one year olds mentioned on page 29.

The difference is that now they will play familiar games with toys which are taken out of a bag (for instance, feed the horse, put the doll to sleep, etc.).

PLAY AND ACTIVITY: SECOND AND THIRD YEARS

DEMONSTRATION OF OBJECTS IN ACTION (FROM ONE YEAR UP TO ONE YEAR SIX MONTHS)

To put the doll to sleep

Goal: *to teach doll play: to cover it with a blanket, to rock it. To pronounce words: "Dolly", "sleep", "bye-bye".*

A doll and doll furnishings are used. They are hidden under a table, covered with a napkin.

Procedure: Six children are seated in a semi-circle. The child-care worker sits in front of the children. She then puts the doll's bed with sheets and blanket on a table, and shows each object to the children. "Look children, here is a bed, here is a pillow, a blanket, sheets, and here is a chair". She shows the doll: "Dolly wants to sleep. Dolly, go to sleep in the bed. Now I'll take off Dolly's clothes." She takes the clothes off and puts them on a chair. She places the doll on a bed, covering her. She rocks the bed and says: "Bye-bye, Dolly, sleep". She calls on each child in turn, and suggests to them to rock the doll and stroke her while saying: "Bye-bye, sleep, Dolly, sleep". If the child does not respond and does not react, the adult takes the child's hand and lets it stroke the doll and encourages the child to repeat after her. Dana say: "Bye-bye Dolly, sleep Dolly".

When the action is concluded, the child-care worker puts everything back in place.

Feeding the doll

Goal: *to teach the children simple actions with topical toys (for instance, feeding). To teach the pronounciation of the words: "Dolly", "take", "cereal". To teach the understanding of the words: "Hello", "eat".*

A doll, table and a chair are used and toy plates, spoon and napkin are added.

Fig. 8. The child-care worker shows how to feed a doll.

Procedure: Six children sit in a semi-circle and the child-care worker faces them. She introduces the children to the doll and the eating utensils (Fig. 8).

"Children, look, who came to us? Is this Dolly? Dolly bows to the children. The child-care worker presents the doll to each child to greet him. She places the doll's hand into the child's hand. "Hello, Dana", etc.

She calls each child by name. With the child's hand, she strokes the doll's hand, while saying: "Dolly, good Dolly, Hello Dolly". Emphasizes the word "Dolly".

The doll's furniture is put on the table and she accompanies her action with these words: "Here are a table and a chair. I'll seat dolly on the chair and feed dolly some cereal. Here is a plate, here is a spoon. Take it dolly. Eat some cereal dolly". - Brings the spoon to dolly's mouth several times. - "Have some dolly, eat, eat some cereal. How good it tastes. Dolly has finished her cereal. Dolly is satisfied. Wipe your mouth dolly. Here is a napkin."

PLAY AND ACTIVITY: SECOND AND THIRD YEARS   45

She asks the children: "Who wants to feed Dolly? Come here Lyusa. Here is a spoon. Here is Dolly." She calls each child and suggests that he feed the doll. She makes them repeat the words: "Take your cereal Dolly" (Fig. 9).

Fig. 9. Lyusa feeds the doll by herself.

A hen

Goal: the same as above, introducing new words and phonetic imitation. The children learn to imitate the cackle of a hen, to understand the names: "Plate", "Seed", "eat", pronounce the words: "ku-ka-ri-ku", "go", "take".

A toy hen (of plywood, plastic or paper), a plate and some grain are used.

Procedure: Six children sit in a semi-circle. The child-care worker faces them, about an arm's length from the table. From under the table she lifts up a hen and says "ku-ka-ri-ku". She repeats it. "Who is it? This is a hen. How does he call?" The children imitate the call of a hen or repeat after her. "Eat hen. Here is a plate. Come hen, come take something to eat". The hen pecks. "Who wants to feed the hen? Come, Lyda, give something to the hen". Lyda takes the hen into her hands, and lowers its beak into the plate. "Take, hen, take". Each child is given a turn. At the end the hen is brought to its shelf.

A dog

The goal as above: to teach the pronunciation of simple words: "How-how", "tap-tap", "doggie".

A toy dog is used, as well as a cup or a small bowl.

Procedure: Six children are seated as usual. The child-care worker faces them. She shows them a toy dog. "I have a dog, I like it, its a good dog. Vora, come, stroke the dog, say: Good dog, good". The child repeats and returns to his place. "This is the way the dog walks: tap-tap". "Natasha, come near, show me how the dog walks". Gives the dog to Natasha, or moves the dog with the child's hand while saying: "Tap-tap". She stimulates the child to repeat the words. "Natasha, return to your place".

"This is how the dog walks, the dog runs, runs". The child-care worker moves the dog more quickly and hides it behind her back. "There is no dog. Children where is the dog? There is no dog, it ran away". The child-care worker imitates a barking dog and again shows the toy, saying in a lively manner: "Here is the dog. How does it bark? How-how". The children repeat. "The dog wants food. Let's give it cereal". She puts a bowl in front of it and puts its muzzle into its bowl. "Ira, come here, feed the dog. Who else wants to? Lyusa, come here, Lyusa give some food to the dog. How does a dog bark? The dog is satiated. The dog ran away".

The same activities are repeated with different animals.

PLAY AND ACTIVITY: SECOND AND THIRD YEARS

A bird

Goal: as above. To teach children to observe flying birds.

A paper bird on a rubber band or a piece of thread is used.

Procedure: Six children seated in a semi-circle on chairs or on a sofa. The child-care worker stands in front of them and says: "A bird came in" - shows a flying bird to the children. "Look, children, a bird, the bird flies, flies, flies". - She stretches the rubber band and the bird moves. She hides the bird. - "There is no bird. We shall call the bird. Fly, fly bird, and come to us". "The bird wants to eat. The bird eats. Again the bird flies away. It sat on Vova's head. It pecks. The bird flies away. There is no bird".

Swimming ducks

Goal: as above. To teach the children the words: "Duck", "take", "blub-blub".

This activity calls for a basin, a pitcher with water, six plastic ducks, a plate and towel.

Procedure: Six children sit as usual. The child-care worker sits opposite them. She brings a pitcher with water, a basin and duck which are hidden in a bag or napkin. "Children look, I pour water into the basin. Blub-blub. The water is warm. Come on Lenochka, come closer to the water, put your hands in. See how warm the water is. Dry your hands" - She dries the child's hands with a towel and calls on each child in turn. - "Children, look who came to us? A duck - ducky" - She puts the duck into the water and makes a full circle with her hand, moves the duck. - "Who swims? The ducky duck swims". The children repeat this. "Here is another duck. We shall let it swim". She puts all the ducks into the water - "Here, all the ducks arrived. Watch them swim. And now we shall take them out and dry them". - She dries them and gives each child a duck.

Now the basin and pitcher are removed.

"Do you want to feed the ducks? Watch how I feed them?" - She moves the beak of the duck on the plate. "Here duck. Lyda, come closer, feed your duck". - The duck pecks. Each child feeds the duck - "Say: have some ducky, have some".

DEMONSTRATION OF LIVE ANIMALS*

Live animals arouse much interest in children, their movements and sounds invite imitation--all of them, cats, dogs, chickens, rabbits, sparrows or crows. Of especial interest are animals seen in the yard, village or garden. In winter live animals are brought into the room.

When feasible a goat may be brought to their attention. Say: "Here it is, a goat, beh-beh-beh ... Who came to us? A goat, goat, beh-beh-beh. Kolenka call to the goat, say: Come to us, beh-beh-beh."

If it's a cat, she should say:"Vitenko, call the cat, and say: Meow-meow".

The animals should be in a yard where the children can observe them well. Children usually observe eating animals with pleasure. It puts them in a good mood. They speak freely to the adult, making lively gestures, and point out the eyes, ears, and tails of the animals.

Showing of live animals takes place throughout the year.

---

*A demonstration of live animals described in: "Early child care in children's homes". Edited by: N.M. Shchelovanova and N.M. Aksarina, M., 1960.

PLAY AND ACTIVITY: SECOND AND THIRD YEARS

A bird in a cage or fish in an aquarium, are fine when left with the children for several days, so that the children might get well acquainted with their shape and movements. (The fish swim in the water, the bird jumps from one branch to another, while pecking at grain.)

HIDING OBJECTS

Search for hidden toys

Goal: to develop the ability to recognize and name a toy.

Two or three toys in a basket or in a bag are used.

Procedure: Three children are near the child-care worker. She suggests to them that they hide the toys.

"Children, we shall put the hen in a corner, the cow behind the table and dolly on a bed. Now, let's look for them. Where is the hen? Danny found the hen, what does the hen say? Ku-ka-ri-ku" - The children then imitate this. "And where is the cow - moo-moo? Lyda found the cow. Lyda, who is it? This is moo-moo. Katasha found the doll, here she is. Dolly lies in bed. And where are dolly's eyes? And where is her nose? Right, Natasha, and now show where are your eyes and nose".

"WALKS WITH A PURPOSE"

Walking in a play room (from 1 year and 3 months)

Goal: making acquaintance with names of objects in the environment.

Procedure: Six to eight children walk together with the child-care worker. She says: "Children, let's see what there is in our room. This is a sink, in it are dishes". She takes out a plate, shows it to the children - "This is a plate, we eat soup from a plate and this is a cup, we drink milk, coffee, tea from a cup. In the drawer are spoons, now I'll take out a spoon and show it to you, here is a spoon (puts it back). And what is this? This is a table and chair. Natasha, sit on a chair. Vova, do you want to sit down?" This is repeated and the number of objects are increased gradually.

ACTIVITIES FOR DEVELOPING IMITATIONS (FROM 1 YEAR 3 MONTHS)

"Who barks how?"

Goal: to learn to imitate animal sounds.

Toys representing domestic animals and birds are used.

Procedure: The children sit on chairs. The child-care worker sits at the table covered with a tablecloth hanging over the sides. The child-care worker suggests that the children sit quietly and listen. Then she says: "Children, who came to us? (The children are already acquainted with animal sounds from previous activities.) Who talks this way?" ("Ku-ka-ri-ku, how-how, etc."). When the children guess rightly, she suggests they imitate the sounds of the animal. She takes out a hen and says: "Come to us little hen, dance for us dear friend". The hen dances and the child-care worker suggests to one child to give the hen water, and to put him to sleep. Thus the children gradually learn the animal sounds and learn to imitate them.

"Pass on to somebody else"

Goal: to learn the meaning of the words "say", "repeat".

For these activities one uses topical toys of medium size and with simple names (a ball, a doll

PLAY AND ACTIVITY: SECOND AND THIRD YEARS

a bear, etc).

Procedure: Eight to ten children sit in a line and the child-care worker faces them. To the child nearest her she hands a toy and says: "Petya, give the ball to Lyusya, say: 'Lyusya, take'. Lyusya and you say to Vova: 'give the ball'" (the child-care worker stresses the words "take" and "give"). She turns to Lyusya: "Lyusya, give Petya the ball. Say: 'Take the ball'," etc. Each child has to give the ball to the next one. The last child returns the ball to the child-care worker.

"Short amusing songs"

To develop the ability to listen and concentrate and to partially repeat the text of songs, the child-care worker reads and sings short songs, without accompanying demonstrations or pictures.

Pat-a-cake

Pat-a-cake, pat-a-cake,	What did you drink?
Where have you been?	Milk.
At my grandmothers,	Pff, they are gone,
What did you eat?	On the head they sat.
Cereal.	

The child-care worker claps her hands and invites the children to imitate her. Repeating the words in the text, she raises her hands to her head. If the child does not imitate her she carries out this movement with the child's hands.

See-Saw

Up and down,
up and down
Firmly, Lyusya hold on.

The child-care worker cuddles the child, rocks it, while singing.

A little boy rode

A little boy rode   He trotted
On a brown horse   And trotted
Such a smooth ride   Into a hole - wow!

CARRYING OUT INSTRUCTIONS

"Bring a ball"

Goal: to teach the child names of various toys, and how to carry out instructions given by an adult.

Procedure: Three balls familiar to the child, three identical ducks and three identical hens are placed in the center of the floor. The child-care worker addresses the child by name: "Petya, bring the ball. Thank you. And Vova bring the ball, and Lara bring the ball" - She puts the balls aside - "And now Petya, bring me a duck, and Vova will bring me a duck. And now bring me a hen, etc. There, there are no more toys on the floor. Let's do it again". In this manner she continues with other familiar toys. While giving instructions: "Show", "Throw", "Give".

"What should I give"

Goal: to stimulate active speech.

Procedure: The children sit on chairs (3-5 children). Familiar toys are put on the table. There should be more toys than there are participating children. The child-care worker calls a child by name and asks him "What should I give you?" The child names a toy, or silently points to it. The child-care worker names the toy in a clear voice and says: "Say, 'give me Dolly'" (or another toy). The child repeats, gets the toy and returns to his place. Everyone gets a toy. Afterwards the child-care worker calls each child, asks for the toy and puts it away in a box.

PLAY AND ACTIVITY: SECOND AND THIRD YEARS

ACTIVITIES WITH PICTURES FOR CHILDREN AGED FROM 1 YEAR TO 1 YEAR 2-3 MONTHS

Activities with pictures have to be started at the end of the first year. This does not hold for all the children at this age, as one must consider their individual level of understanding of adult speech as well as the level of the child's own speech.

Activities with one picture

Goal: to draw the child's attention to images, to arouse auditory response and concentration to words of the adult and to connect the image with the word, i.e., to develop the understanding of words.

The activities are carried out daily. The adult works with one child after another.

For this activity only pictures of objects familiar to the child, both by form and by name, are used. It is desirable that this be an object which children enjoy and which elicits lively exclamations. For instance, a dog, a cat, a doll, etc. The size of the picture should be approximately 8 × 20 cm. The image should be bright and clear. The bottom of the picture is in one color, and the back is blank. Pictures from children's games, such as "Lotto for youngsters", "Matching pictures", etc., may be used.

Procedure: The child-care worker seats the child on her knees or sits near him (at his side or opposite) showing the picture to him suddenly and pointing to the image in the picture, for instance: "Meow-meow, here is a cat" ...

Later on when his attention is focused she unexpectedly hides the picture (she withdraws it from the child's field of vision). She may hide it behind her back or turn the picture over, and says: "There is no meow. Where is meow? There is no meow" - trying to make the child react to the disappearance of the picture. When he reacts she again shows the picture, emoting strongly "ah-ah" and with words "Here is the cat, cat ..."

Waiting, while the child looks at the image, she asks: "Where is meow?" and answers by herself after a short interval, pointing with her hand to the image: "Here is meow ... Meow?" Afterwards she inquires calling the child by name: "Lyusenka, show me where is meow?" She guides the child's hand to the picture, saying: "Here is meow ... meow".

This activity is repeated 2-3 times. The activity should be ended with the hiding of the picture: "There is no cat". If the child wishes to see the picture once more, it is recommended to show it to him.

The name of the image has to be pronounced slowly and at short intervals. (This aids the auditory perception of the child). When hiding and showing the picture one should change one's intonation (thus emphasizing the difference between hiding and showing). The voice should be clear and expressive.

If one has carried out this activity three to five times and the goal has still not been achieved, the picture should be changed. It is well to carry on until the child reacts as described above. Only after this can one go on to showing two pictures.

Activities with two pictures

Goal: to consolidate the child's interest in an image, to develop recognition of an image, to teach the child to point correctly to the picture when asked: "What is this?", to respond to the word "give", to encourage auditory attention and concentration to the words of an adult, to elicit emotional exclamations, and imitation of sounds and to achieve the ability to pronounce simple words like: "how-how", "meow", "beep-beep".

Now a second picture sharply differing from the first one is added.

PLAY AND ACTIVITY: SECOND AND THIRD YEARS 55

Procedure: The first activity is repeated, hiding and showing the pictures many times and letting the child react to their disappearance. Use a picture of a cat - "meow", or a car - "beep-beep", etc. Then carry out this same procedure with a second picture. Then show both pictures and suggest to the child: "Show me where is beep-beep? Where is meow?" If he does not point to it the child-care worker should point with her hand.

Gradually new pictures are introduced, depending on the child's ability to differentiate between their shape and their name.

Activities with several pictures

Goal: to teach the child to search for and to find named images in gradually increasing numbers of pictures (up to 10-15 pictures).

Participation in these activities increases from two to three or four children.

A combination of pictures is used: 1. Doll-Dolly. 2. Cat-Meow. 3. Dog-bow-wow. 4. Horse-eee. 5. Hen-ku-ku-ri-ku. 6. Grandmother-granny, etc.

Procedure: The child-care worker demonstrates one picture allowing the child time to react. She gives the correct name of the image followed by the right sound. For instance: "dog-bow-wow, or cat-meow, Where is the cat?, etc." (the phonetic pronunciation of simple words should conform to the names used daily. For instance, doll-dolly, car-beep, etc).

The child-care worker shows the whole collection of pictures which were selected for this exercise. The second time she shows only those less familiar to them. At first she shows 3-4 pictures and later gradually adds more. She may group 8-10 children during a single exercise.

In addition to demonstrating and naming pictures, the child-care worker gradually teaches them to carry out various actions simultaniously: "Kolya, show" or "give". If the child points correctly, she says: "Koo-koo-ree-koo, here is koo-koo-ree-koo, here is a hen, Kolya showed it to us". With her voice she expresses praise. If the child is mistaken, the child-care worker should point to the hen, saying: "Here is koo-koo-ree-koo" and suggest again that the child point to this picture, or another one. Or she may say: "See, there is no meow, this is koo-koo-ree-koo, a hen". If the child is passive, she should lead his hand, repeating everything with appropriate words.

ACTIVITIES WITH CHILDREN FROM 1 YEAR 2-3 MONTHS TILL 1 YEAR 4-5 MONTHS

Goal: to freely recognize known objects differing in external form, i.e. to formulate word generalization; to stimulate phonetic imitation; to consolidate the recognition and naming of known images; to arouse interest in new images; to continue training the child to learn and to listen and hear what is said by an adult.

For these activities one uses images of objects known to the child from previous activities, but in a differing external form. Alterations may be made in the outward representations of the object (for instance: a dog - white or black, a smaller or bigger one, it sleeps, eats, runs or sits etc.) or changes may be made in the outward appearance of the picture itself (re: format, or colors). Some of the pictures are pasted on cubes (the measurement of the cube should be 8-12 cm^3)

Procedure: 3-4 children sit at a table. Demonstrating a known object in a new picture, the child-care worker pauses, to give the children an opportunity to recognize and name the image. If there is no response she should ask: "Who is it?" or "What is it?" If the children name the image, she should exclaim:

PLAY AND ACTIVITY: SECOND AND THIRD YEARS

"Yes, it is a cat or a dog, bow-wow". If they do not respond, she should name it while pointing to it: "Where is beep-beep?"

Suggesting to a child the word "show" or "give", the child-care worker stimulates new reactions - namely, repetition of words. ("Say - meow, meow" or "dog - how-how", etc.) Demonstration and naming of pictures should alternate with various actions, "find, show, give, hide, find, this or this".

ACTIVITIES WITH CHILDREN FROM 1 YEAR 4-5 MONTHS UP TO 1 YEAR 6-8 MONTHS

Goal: to teach the comprehension of words which describe the designation of an object and words which describe the meaning of actions (sleep, eat, etc.) and the quality of things and feelings (big, small, angry, etc.); to practice the imitation of single words as well as two-three word sentences, to change over from easily pronounced words to correct ones.

Pictures with images of single objects and images of familiar persons, birds, and animals performing various acts, are shown. For instance, a girl sleeping, eating, running, falling, crying; a cat lapping milk; a duck swimming; a dog running, etc.

The number of children may be increased gradually, depending on the child's mastery of the following activities - sitting quietly, without disturbing the other, listening to given directions, answering sentences with words and appropriate actions and looking at the pictures.

Procedure: She shows the pictures and not only names the object, but also explains the actions. She uses short sentences of two to three words. For instance: "Dolly sleeps, hush, hush" or "Dolly ate cereal". To teach the general meaning of words, it is best to show different pictures, each representing an object performing the same yet differing acts. For instance: "A girl sleeps and a cat sleeps" or "A dog runs and a dog sleeps", etc.

She encourages the children to speak and not only point, to name objects and describe the actions with words. For instance: when pointing to a familiar picture she should not simply name it, but should ask: "Tell me, what is here?" If the child names the object but not the action, for instance: "Dolly", then the child-care worker should say: "Yes, the dolly sleeps, say: sleep".

During activities with this age group one should teach the children correct speech rather than simplified words. For this reason the adult should not use simplified words. On the contrary, she should correct the child when he does not speak correctly.

One may add additional words to the phrase: "A girl sleeps". One may add other words like "quiet, shhh" or "quiet, the girl sleeps" or "Say: sleep, sleep little girl". Referring to a picture of an eating child: "He's eating, he's eating" or "how good the cereal tastes, etc".

* * *

To further develop speech and orientation in the child's environment *during the second half of the second year*, the child-care worker should set herself the aim of continuous development and comprehension of speech.

To develop speech it is necessary: 1) to develop understanding of the quality and condition of well known objects; 2) to teach how to differentiate between objects with similar phonetic names, or apparent similarity; 3) to develop general ability; 4) to develop understanding in naming dishes, furniture, clothes, toys, birds and flowers; 5) to teach acceptance of given commands which include several familiar

PLAY AND ACTIVITY: SECOND AND THIRD YEARS

actions; 6) to teach to grasp the meaning of adult talk concerning their own experience, no longer aided by visual or verbal demonstrations; to teach to understand the meaning of full sentences pertaining to the child's experiences; 8) to teach to see an uncomplicated subject.

To develop active speech in a child it is necessary: 1) to teach repetition of words pronounced by an adult, and simple sentences; 2) to stimulate children to address adults frequently; 3) to change from "simplified" to correct words; 4) to use two to three sentences at one time.

DEMONSTRATIONS WITH NAMES (FROM 1 YEAR 6 MONTHS TO 2 YEARS)

"Wonderful Bag", see page 29. This activity depends on the assortment and the amount of toys.

"What is in the box?"

Goal: name the toys put in the box.

Procedure: 8-10 children sit around a table. Each child receives a box with a toy. The children take out their toy, examine it, show it and name it. The child-care worker stimulates children to name it and looks at the toy of each child.

"Aunt Anya sends us packages"

Goal: naming and describing various toys.

For this game a basket containing the toys is used, and each toy is neatly wrapped.

Procedure: 8-10 children sit on a low sofa or on small chairs. A bell rings, or a knock is heard at the door. The child-care worker asks: "Who is there?" No answer; the knocking is repeated. The child-care worker suggests to the children to repeat the question. The children ask, the door opens and the nurse brings in the basket. "Here children, let's see what Aunt Anya brought us". She takes out a package and says: "This is a package. And what is in this package? A-ah, what a doll. And what does she wear, what is it?..." They observe the doll with pleasure. The child-care worker: "This was sent by Aunt Anya, so I can show it to you. Look, the doll sits on a chair; well sit, sit". Turning to the nurse: "And what more do you have there? For whom is this package?" Gives the package to one child, then to another and gradually draws the children into a conversation: "What did Aunt Anya send? What shall we do with the toy?" etc. The children play with their toys and afterwards wrap them and return them to the child-care worker.

DEMONSTRATION OF OBJECTS IN ACTION (FROM 1 YEAR 6 MONTHS TO 2 YEARS)

"A cat and paper"

Goal: to teach the children the words: "throw away", "catch".

A toy cat and a piece of paper on a string are used.

Procedure: 6-8 children sit in a semi-circle. The child-care worker shows the children the cat (on her hand) and says, "that cat likes very much to play with a paper ball". She waves a ball in front of the cat. The cat catches it with its paw. Now she says to the cat: "throw away", the cat throws it away; she says to the cat: "catch" - the cat "catches", etc.

Afterwards the child-care worker suggests that the children should say by themselves to the cat: "throw away". If they do say the word "throw away", the cat drops the ball from her paw. The second word, "catch", is employed similarly.

PLAY AND ACTIVITY: SECOND AND THIRD YEARS

"Putting the doll to bed"

Goal: to teach the names of clothes and bedding, to encourage active participation in undressing dolls and putting them to bed.

Procedure: "Putting the doll to bed" is carried out in the same manner as described on page 42, differing only in that the child-care worker tries to identify the doll with a child. She talks with the children about familiar activities ("The doll Sonya walked for a long time, she ate, and now she wants to sleep"), she names every object (pillow, blanket, etc.), and tries to get the children to repeat. While putting the doll to bed, she sings a lullaby. Then the children themselves undress the doll and put it to bed.

"A bird sat on a window"

Goal: to consolidate the children's knowledge of the objects around them and to introduce names of different parts of the body.

Cut outs of a bird with wings slid through its body, with a rubber band attached to the head (like balsa gliders), are used for this activity.

Procedure: The children sit as usual in semi-circle. The child-care worker holds the bird and reads a poem the children know.

> A bird sat on the window
> Sit with us a while!
> Sit, do not fly away!
> Oh, it flew away.

The bird is held by the child-care worker, who pulls the rubber band, releases it, and lets the bird glide across the room. Then she says: "Children, tell the bird: Fly to us, say: Fly to us". What fine fellow, it listened to you and stayed with us, and we shall feed it. (She makes a movement, as if feeding the bird seeds). "And now children, you will feed the bird seeds". The children imitate her. "And now give the bird some water". She gives them a bowl of water, and the children give it to the bird. "Say: Drink bird, drink". The bird eats, drinks and flies away. "Children call the bird: Fly to us, birdy". She puts the bird on the head of a child. "Look children, the bird sat on Nina's head. And where did it sit on Natasha? On her shoulders. Kolya? It sat on his stomach, and Yura? It sat on his ear. Oh, it flew away. The bird flew away". The child-care worker suggests to the children to call the bird, the children call and the game is renewed.

A more complex version: the bird sits in the room on different objects which the children should name.

"Feeding a dog"

Goal: the pronounciation of the words: dog, bowl, rug; the imitation of actions.

A toy, a bowl and a rug.

Procedure: The children sit as usual. The child-care worker shows them a dog. She examines it together with the children and asks: "What is it? How does the dog bark?" She examines and points out different parts of the dog's body; tail, back, ears, paws, etc. and passes it around. The children take the dog's paw. "Don't you want to hear how the dog asks for food? Bow-wow - that's how the dog asks for food". She puts the bowl to the dog's muzzle and pretends to feed it. Then each child is asked to feed the dog.

"The little girl and the hen"

Goal: to acquaint the child with objects used for washing, feeding and sleeping. To teach the child to play with a doll, to wash, feed and put it to bed.

PLAY AND ACTIVITY: SECOND AND THIRD YEARS 63

For this activity one uses a medium sized doll with easy fitting and attractive clothes, a hen (much smaller than the doll), a bed for the doll, a table, a chair, dishes, basins, soap and a towel.

Procedure: The children sit in a half circle and the child-care worker at a table, facing the children. The table is covered with a tablecloth which falls over the side of the table. The toys are put under the table, so that the children cannot see them. The adult takes a doll and without showing it to the children says in a "doll's voice": "Children, I am coming to you". Then, changing her voice she says: "Children, who is it coming to us? Who calls you?" The children answer. The child-care worker says to them, that the doll's name is Katya. "Katya is coming to you; children call Katya, say: Katya, come to us, we are waiting for you". Following the children's invitation, the doll Katya appears and greets them all. The adult asks Katya: "Katya, do you want to eat? Let's wash your hands and sit down to eat". Before washing the doll's hands she asks the children: "With what do we wash hands? And what shall we do next?", trying to get the children to say: "Fill the basin with water, wash hands, dry hands, etc". And what will Katya eat? And where shall we put her to bed?" etc. She feeds Katya, while naming all the objects, and encourages the children to talk. With the doll's hands she puts the napkin in place and makes the doll undress and go to bed. The doll should be conveniently dressed to facilitate dressing and undressing. The doll is fed and put to bed in the same manner as the children are. While putting Katya to bed, the child-care worker recites poems. She puts a finger on her lips: "Quiet, quiet, children, our Katya is asleep". After a pause, makes a noise as it were a hen far away: "ku-ku-ri-ku" then says: "Quiet hen, do not wake Katya. Quiet".

Suddenly, at the doll's bed a loud "ku-ku-ri-ku" is heard. The hen says: "Get up, Katya, get up, let's walk together". The doll says: "Good morning hen, good morning, I'll get up now".

The doll is dressed again. The doll feeds the hen grain, the hen pecks, thanks the doll and suggests a dance. They dance and invite the children to join them. Then all the children dance while the child-care worker sings a dance song.

> Comment: At the beginning of the second year fewer number of actions with the doll are desirable, but the children should be encouraged to express themselves. Play with 2 year old children is carried out according to this plan and the children are encouraged to use preliminary but detailed naming of objects and actions.

"The hare and the carrot"

Goal: to teach the pronounciation of the words: *"Hare","eat", "carrot", and perform with a toy hare.*

A toy hare and a carrot are used.

Procedure: The child-care worker says: "Sit down and see what I shall show you. Look children, who is this?" She slowly removes the hare from her pocket so at the beginning the children can see only the ears, then the head and finally the whole hare.

"Children, it's - a hare, a hare. Well children, say clearly so that I can hear: Who is it? A hare". The children repeat her words.

"Here see, we shall put the hare here. Let him sit here and look at us. Oh, what a nice hare we have. We'll give him a treat. He likes carrots. Hare, do you want a carrot? Here, I have a sweet, tasty carrot. Who will give the carrot to the hare? Do you want to Ira? Come on, give the carrot to the hare, tell him, 'eat hare', 'eat a carrot'".

Ira stands up and feeds the hare a carrot.

PLAY AND ACTIVITY: SECOND AND THIRD YEARS

Several children, in turn, feed the hare. They feed him willingly, saying: "Eat, hare, eat the carrot. Well, we fed the hare and now the hare will jump. Hare jump, show the children how you jump. That's how the hare jumps: ju-mp, ju-mp - And who can jump like a hare? You Natasha? Hey, how does Natasha jump? Jump, exactly like the hare. Now all the children imitate the hare and jump. There, what good hares you all are. And now he shall sit on a bench (puts down the hare). This way".

DEMONSTRATION OF LIVE ANIMALS (FROM 1 YEAR 6 MONTHS UP TO 2 YEARS)

Demonstration of live animals is described on page 46.

PURPOSEFUL WALKS IN THE BACKYARD OR IN THE FIELDS (FROM 1 YEAR 6 MONTHS UP TO 2 YEARS)

Walks in the fields (summer to a village)

Goal: to collect flowers and to examine butterflies, dragon flies, etc.

Children up to 2 years old may walk in the backyard or nearby fields, but for only a very short distance. They should not cross roads where there is traffic. They can walk quietly in a group, but not organized in pairs. It is essential that two adults are in attendance.

When the children reach the fields the child-care worker should suggest collecting flowers. She collects a bouquet of flowers and shows the children how to pick flowers with a long stem.

Seeing a butterfly, the adult catches it with a net and is careful not to damage it. She shows the beautiful wings and then frees it, so the children can see how it flies. She imitates the sound of a bee. Walks like this are pleasant, and enrich the children. They teach the children to observe life about them.

The backyard and schoolground should be similarly used to introduce the children to domestic animals and birds.

IMPLIMENTATION OF INSTRUCTIONS

"What to do with the named toy?"

Goal: to carry out actions according to verbal instructions.

Procedure: The children are seated. The adult shows the toys and plays with them, naming the play or actions with words. She calls on a child and tells him what to do with the toy. The child does so. If he did well she compliments him and calls the next one.

"Show me, how"

Goal: to introduce children to the behavior of animals and to teach them to imitate that behavior.

For this activity one uses toy animals and birds known to the child.

Procedure: The adult shows a teddy bear. Holding it in her hands she approaches the children. She growls and walks like a bear. She asks one child, and then the others, to show how a bear growls and walks. In the same way the child-care worker demonstrates the behavior and movements of other animals and induces the children to imitate.

SEARCHING FOR A CERTAIN TOY AMONG SIMILAR ONES

Goal: to develop a sense of orientation within

the environment and to distinguish between similar objects.

A toy which interests the child, perhaps a doll of a medium size, is used.

Procedure: The adult shows them a doll, names it "Katya", and points out to them how the doll is dressed. Then she hides the doll among other toys and asks the children to search for it: "No, Natasha not this doll, bring Katya". When the child brings the right doll she compliments him.

STORY TELLING WITH PICTURES (FROM 1 YEAR 6 MONTHS UP TO 2 YEARS)

Once the children can recognize and name familiar images and scenes in a picture, then they can understand simple and meaningful contents (a girl cries, falls down, or is ill), and can start using sentences of two, three and then more words. Following this one should pass on to a new subject.

The goal of these activities is as follows: 1) to strengthen the children's observation and deepen their comprehension of familiar acts; to reinforce the comprehension of simple subjects or images through verbal explanation; 2) to enrich the vocabulary of a child; to stimulate the imitation of new words, as well as 3-4 word sentences; 4) to teach the correct pronounciation of words without the substitution of simplified words and to correct faulty termination of words; 5) to continue to enrich the emotional expressions of the child; 6) to teach the children to use picture books by themselves.

To achieve these goals one should make demonstrations with pictures and give verbal explanations of simple topics, i.e., by doing this one trains the child to observe and understand various familiar objects and actions which are connected with one another in simple, meaningful ways.

A book by Z.I. Aleksandrovoi "Kitty In a Day Center" contains examples of simple stories appropriate for this age group. The adult should show the pictures in this book, while telling this sort of story: "Look, here children are getting dressed. They will go for a walk, the girl is putting on her boots and the boy his mittens. Auntie is helping the children dress. When they will be dressed, they will go for a walk. Yes, this is a scarf, it is lying on a table. The girl will put it on. Will she be warm"?

When showing different pictures one should always give a verbal explanation (a tale or story) which expresses the basic meaning and content of the subject, and not merely enumerate the different objects and actions which are represented in the picture. Mere enumeration of details without correctly demonstrating their connection to other familiar objects will but serve to impoverish the vocabulary of the child and inhibit the development of generalization.

The showing of pictures with a topic or story is something relatively new to the child, compared to his previous experience. The new activity is essential in nourishing continued speech development. Together with topical pictures, one should continue to show pictures of single objects and actions. Pictures of simple content are good for eliciting active speech, as well as helping to promote introduction to objects - detailed observation.

When pictures are shown for the first time (especially pictures which tell a story), it is necessary to stop between pictures, so as to permit the children to react to them. The length of the interval should depend upon the children's experience and level of intelligence.

To encourage the children to express themselves in various ways (joyful exclamations, single words and sentences), the child-care worker should tell stories. When doing so, she should observe their

PLAY AND ACTIVITY: SECOND AND THIRD YEARS

reactions, and depending on their behaviour, change the tale, repeat episodes and respond to the children's expressions by agreeing with them or correcting them.

If they speak freely while listening, the adult need not talk, but merely encourage the children to continue talking. If the children have misunderstood the contents of a picture or speak incorrectly it is necessary to correct them, to question them, or to point out to them their mistakes.

When the children are able to concentrate (mainly knowing to sit quietly and listen and look at the pictures), then eight children of the same age may be joined together in a group.

"Matching pictures"

Goal: to teach to match and to differentiate.

For this activity one uses identical pictures of the same subject.

Procedure: For this four children are put in a separate room. They should sit next to a table. The child-care worker removes a single picture from a box (for instance a picture of a horse), shows it to the children and names it. Then she asks each child to name the object seen in the picture.

Holding the picture in one hand so that everyone can see it, with the other hand (unnoticed by the children) she takes out a different picture and puts it on the table. Then she says: "Yuzochka, here I have a horse. There, on the other table is also a horse. Go, bring it". Usually the child willingly runs to the table, looks at the pictures, takes the one with an image of a horse and gladly brings it to her. In this manner each child gets a chance to match pictures. Occasionally, at first the child does not take the right picture, or more often he may take several. Then the adult shows him the picture in her hand and persistently asks him to match the same picture from the table. If the child is still unable to find the right picture, she helps him to find it, hands him the one with a horse and says: "Here, Misha, good boy, he found a horse and put it on the table". The number of pictures are gradually increased.

Little by little, after a few repetitions, the children learn to find the right picture, even among three or four.

SHOWING SLIDES

A slide projector is put on a table and the child-care worker shows a series of pictures. She should stop at each picture, talk with the children, ask them questions and try to get them to answer. In this way she keeps up a conversation with them.

The slide projector should be left with one group until the children absorb one subject. Then the subject is changed.

STORY-TELLING-CONVERSATION

Goal: to teach the meaning of a sentence, which describes events in the child's life.

Procedure: 2-3 children sit with the child-care worker on a sofa. If they have seen a cat drink milk, the adult tells them: "I have a cat. A little kitty. I took a plate and filled it with milk. The kitty drank a whole bowl of milk. And you, Natasha, do you have a kitty at home? What does it do with its tongue"? Other children may also enter into the conversation.

Similar short stories may be composed by the child-care worker.

PLAY AND ACTIVITY: SECOND AND THIRD YEARS   71

PURPOSEFUL ACTS WITH OBJECTS IN THE SECOND YEAR OF LIFE

The improvement of purposeful actions with objects is very important for the development of the two year old child. Manipulation of objects (building blocks, matching toys, etc.) helps develop the small muscles of the fingers and hands. By carrying out different actions with objects - (opening and closing, threading, etc.) children exercise their hands, develop dexterity and learn to concentrate while playing.

Fig. 10. Purposeful acts with objects.

When the child is about two years old he begins to differentiate objects while manipulating them, according to their form, size, color.

To teach the child to carry out purposeful acts with objects, it is necessary to use special activities. Besides playing with cubes, building towers and matching toys children should be taught to use topical toys. For instance, bathing a doll and putting it to bed, feeding a dog or a cat and letting ducks or fish swim, etc. (See chapter on "Development of speech - development of objects in action".

To consolidate the knowledge which the child acquires during special group activities, the child-care worker should give the children appropriate equipment for individual play and help them use it correctly. The children should play unaided.

During the first half of the second year the child-care worker should set herself the following aims: 1) cultivation of the ability to observe and imitate adult action and behavior; 2) development of purposeful actions with several identical objects or with two different interrelated objects; 3) coordination of hand movement; 4) elucidation of the connections between objects and actions and their verbal designation and the development of active speech; 5) achievement of the ability to carry out an act which has been verbally requested.

Activity with cubes

Goal: to teach the child to place one cube (or block) on top of another and to put them in a row.

To teach pronunciation of the words: "This way", "cube".

For this activity one uses cubes or blocks (3-4 cubes for each child).

Procedure: Three children and an adult sit around a table. The adult takes several cubes for herself and shows the children a box containing cubes or blocks.

"Look, children, see what kind of cubes I have, they are smooth and beautiful. Yura, what is this? A cube. Say: cube. Natasha, say: cube. I shall put them in a row. This way" - puts 3-4 cubes in a row -

"And now I'll put one top of the other" - puts one cube on top of another - "And now you will build a tower". She puts the cubes in a row in front of each child (3-4 cubes). "These cubes are for Yura, these for Kolya, these for Natasha. Touch them, see how smooth they are". She puts the child's hand on the surface of a cube - "And now do as I do. I take a cube and put it this way". She puts the second cube on the first. "Yura, put the cube exactly, it should not fall. It is alright now. Pick up another and put it on this one. This way. Oh, Natasha's cubes fell down. Never mind, put them up again, Natasha. Take one more and put it on top, here. Good boy Yura, you did it right. Now everbody has beautiful towers. And now we shall take them off and put them on a table". She takes hers off, and the children imitate her. "Let's put the cubes in a box. Yura, put your cubes, this way. Now, Natasha, now Kolya. I'll put them this way. Now the cubes are all in the box and I'll take the box back and put it where it belongs".*

Activity with a pegboard

Goal: to teach the children to place pegs in holes and understand the words "take out" and "put in".

A small table with short legs and round holes, which are used to "put in" and "take out" pegs (or a low table and a pegboard) are used.

Procedure: Three children and the child-care worker sit at a table. She takes the pegboard and says: "Look, children, what a nice pegboard. I shall take out all the pegs and put them on the table. This way. And now I shall place them in the holes. Yes... yes, etc. Now you do it. Take out the pegs and put them on the table. Do as I do". The children imitate.

---

*Translator's note: The authors stress the importance of always putting things back in their place and verbalizing this in order to teach orderliness.

"We shall put them back in the holes. I take one peg and put it in, this way". She leads Kolya's hand. "This way. Look, children what a nice pegboard we have".

Instead of a pegboard one can use a box with holes (Fig. 11).

Fig. 11. Activity with pegs.

Activity with towers of rings on a peg

Goal: to instruct the children to put rings on a peg and to take them off again. To teach the meaning of the words: "Ring" and "peg", and the names of actions: "Put on", "Take off".

Four sets of rings on a peg are used. It is best if the rings are of the same color. Each ring is slightly smaller than the one below it, and there is a knob or cap which fits on top of the peg over the top ring.

Procedure: Three children and the adult sit at a

table: "Children look, what kind of towers we have. Here Yura, a tower for you. A tower for you, Kolya. A tower for you, Natasha. Let's play with the towers. Look, what a nice knob is on the top. Look, I took the knob off, I shall put it here. And now I shall take off another ring and put it alongside this one. Now I shall take off still another ring and put it here. And now I shall put all the rings back on a peg. Here, I take one ring, and put it on, this way. And now another one on the top. Now I have a tower, and we put the knob on top.

Now let's take off all the rings. Let's take them off! First we shall take off the knob, and we shall put it here. Now we shall take off the rings. Yura, what is this? This is a ring, and this is a peg. Kolya, do not take off all the rings together, take off one after the other, this way". She guides the child's hand and removes the first ring. "Natasha, do not throw away the ring, put it here. Let's take off another ring, put it here. Good boy, Kolya. And Yura took one off, and Natasha took one off. Take off another ring. Yes! Put it here. And now we shall put the rings back on the peg. We shall take a ring and put it on a peg, this way! Yura, pick it up with your fingers, I shall help you. Now we shall put on another ring, this way! Good children. We shall put on another ring. And now we shall put on the knob. What nice towers we have. Do you want to do this again"? Children and adult continue thus two or three times.

Activity with nesting toys

Goal: to teach children to open and take apart toys, to quietly and neatly arrange them on a table, and to put them together again.

Matching or nesting toys (such as a nest of plastic eggs) are used.

Procedure: The same as above. She takes the toy and shows it to the children. "Look, children, I have an egg. I shall open it, inside is another egg, a smaller one". She puts it on the table. "I shall put the big egg here. Yura, what is this? It is an egg. Natalie, show me the small egg. Right, it is the small egg, and this is the big egg. And now I shall give an egg to each one of you. Kolya, an egg. Natasha, an egg and Yura, an egg.

Let's open them. Natasha, I shall help you. Yes, good. Let's take out the small egg, and put it on the table. We shall close the big egg and put it next to the smaller one.

Now, let's match them. We shall put the little one here and close it. This way! Yura, let me help you close it. Right. Good children! Now all of you gather the toys. Now we shall put them away on the shelf".

> Comment: In the same manner one should carry out activities with other round objects, like a nest of cups, etc.

During the second half of the second year the child-care worker should set the following aims: 1) improving hand movements; 2) improving the exactness of visual perception; 3) developing familiarity with the size of the objects; 4) developing the ability to carry out an action to a predetermined end; 5) achieving the ability to reproduce several interactions; 6) increasing the ability to name objects and actions which are connected with them; 7) achieving the ability to independently execute actions which have been taught in the group situation.

Activity with towers

This is done in essentially the same way as described on page 70 (Fig. 12).

The difference is that now the child-care worker compares the size of the rings. She'll say: "We shall

PLAY AND ACTIVITY: SECOND AND THIRD YEARS

Fig. 12. Activity with towers.

take the biggest ring and we shall put it on a peg. From the other rings we shall also pick out the biggest one, and now a smaller one, and a smaller one". When taking rings off the peg she should point out to them the size of the ring.

Activity with blocks

Goal: to teach children to put blocks on top of one another, and to match cubes according to their size.

For this activity one uses sets or nests of cubes of varying sizes and colours.

Procedure: Three children and the child-care worker sit at a table. The adult puts a nest of cubes on the table. "Children, what beautiful cubes. Let's play with them". She takes the cubes and puts them in front of her. "I shall take out one cube and put it here, and now another and put it next to the first one. And now I shall put one on the other. This way". She takes a large cube and turns it over, puts a middle-sized one on top of it and a smaller one on top of the middle-sized one. "Look, what a fine tower we have. Now we'll take the tower apart". She takes the little block off, and then the middle-sized one. Now she turns over the big cube. "In the biggest cube I shall put this one, and in this one the smallest cube. Here, I've put together all the cubes. Now I shall give you the same kind of cubes. This is for Yura, this is for Natasha and that's for you Kolya". She puts a set of cubes with the opening on top in front of each child. "Let's take the cubes out and put them on the table". She puts the cubes with the opening down. "Yura, I'll help you". With the child's hand she takes out a block. "That's good! We'll take out another one. Natasha, put the block here, next to the other. Yes, right. We'll turn the big one over. Now we'll build a tower. Take this block and put it on the big one, and put the smallest on top of it. Natasha and Kolya let me help you. Look, take this block, and put a smaller one on it, and then put the smallest one on top. This way. Everyone build a tower. Fine. And now we'll put the blocks in a line". She puts the blocks in a row with the opening on top. "Now we'll put them together. Yura, you took the wrong one, the bigger one. That's good. All of you put the blocks together. Fine. Now, let's put them where they belong".

Activity with nesting toys

This is carried out, as described on page 72 (Fig. 13). But the goal for this age group is to match the parts of a toy which contains two to three nested parts, and to stress the differences in size. As in the activity with towers, the child-care worker points out the difference in the size. "This is the biggest one, this is smaller, and this one is the smallest. We open the egg and put in a smaller one. Now we open the biggest one and put in this one. Here is an egg". Each child receives an egg, the children open it, take it apart, put the parts next to each other, match the parts and put it together again.

PLAY AND ACTIVITY: SECOND AND THIRD YEARS   79

Fig. 13. Activity with nesting toys.

Activity with spherical objects

   Goal: *to acquaint children with the characteristics of spherical objects and with basic colors.*

   A toy bowling alley (40 cm. long, 10 cm. wide, 15 cm. high, and with sides 2-3 cm. high) is used. Also a medium sized box which contains small wooden balls of 4 colors (red, blue, yellow and green). There should be two balls of each color.

   Procedure: Six children are seated in a semicircle, the adult facing them. The "bowling alley" is put in such a position that the balls roll toward the children. She shows how one rolls the balls. She says: "Children, I have some balls in my box. Look, how beautiful they are". She shows them red balls and places them into their hands. "I'll roll the red ball. It rolls this way. It rolled to Natasha. Natasha, please bring me the red balls. It rolled to Yura. Yura, bring the red ball and put it in the box. Natasha sit on your chair". In this way she shows blue, yellow and green balls. Then she says: "Roll the yellow ball. Natasha, please bring me the yellow ball. Take the same ball and roll it in the 'bowling alley'". The children bring the balls, take them out of the box and roll them.

Activity with small toys and objects of various shapes

Goal: to perceive objects of various shapes.

For this activity one uses small boxes (one for each participant, and one for the adult). Each box contains 5-6 small objects: two small balls, a cube, a block, a rod and a button.

Procedure: Three children and the adult are seated at a table. The child-care worker opens her box, and takes out the objects. She names each object and displays them on the table. "Children, now I'll give you each a box. (Distributes them.) Open it, and see what's in it. This is a ball, Kolya, take it and put it on the table. And you, Natasha, what did you take? A rod? Put it next to your box. Kolya, take out something! You took a cube! Put it on the table etc. Nothing is left in the boxes". While naming the objects she sees that the children take them out in order. If the child is mistaken, she shows and names her object, and suggests that he take the same object from his box. She suggests that he name the object. "Kolya, what is this"? If the child does not react, she names the object, pronounces clearly "ball", and asks the child to repeat. In this way the children learn to identify and name objects.

Activity with building material

Goal: to teach the children to build simple constructions under adult supervision, (a fence, an arch, a train, etc.) And to collect the material and replace it in the box after they are done.

A set of building material - cubes or blocks - 8-10 blocks for each child, and a small toy car are used.

PLAY AND ACTIVITY: SECOND AND THIRD YEARS   81

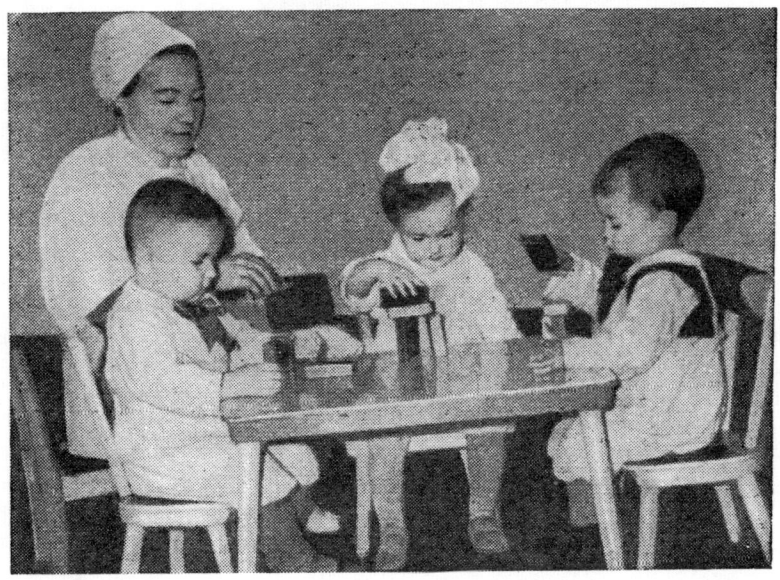

Fig. 14. The children build an arch.

Procedure: Three children and the child-care worker sit at a table. She puts a box of building material on it and says, "Here are blocks, I'll take them out from the box and build an arch. See how I build: I put two blocks here, and then this one on top. Look at the arch! (Fig. 14).

Now I'll give you some blocks. Yura, please take some from the box. Let's build an arch. Put the blocks this way. Right! We'll put a block on top now. Natasha, put the blocks the same way as Yora. Here we have an arch". She takes a toy car out of her pocket and suggests to each child to move the car through the arch.* Now we'll put the blocks

---

*Note: Small toys kept in the adult's pocket may differ. For instance, when building an arch one can take out a hen, or a cat, or a train. One may put a doll on the train so the doll can ride through the arch, etc.

back". She holds out the box to each child to enable him to put his blocks back. Everything is put on the shelf.

*Activity with sand**

Goal: to teach the children to pour sand from one container into another.

Dry sand, a sandbox and two containers of sand on a tray are put in front of each child. The child-care worker uses one of the containers. The children sit at the table.

Procedure: The child-care worker says: "Look, children, what lovely sand. See how I pour it. I'll give you containers. These two are for Natasha, these for Yura and these for Kolya. Natasha, please take your container and fill it with sand from the sandbox. Now Yura....Kolya....and I'll fill my own. Now we'll all pour it into an empty container. This way! Pour this way, carefully, don't let it spill. Good children! Now we'll pour it back into the other container. How interesting it is to pour sand. Now we'll pour the sand back from the container. How interesting it is to pour sand. Now we'll pour the sand back from the container into the sand box and then put everything in place.**

ACTIVITY TO DEVELOP GENERAL MOTOR ABILITY DURING THE SECOND YEAR OF LIFE

Most children begin to walk freely at 11-12 months,

---

*The sand should be carefully prepared. It should be fairly coarse and clean. It's preferable to wash the sand and dry it in an open tray.

**Note: The ability to learn to pour sand from one container into another is practised during the summer time and under supervision of an adult.

but their gait is still uncertain and they cannot yet step over small barriers without support. During the second year of life their movements attain greater perfection and after one year and six months the children's movements are more sure. They begin to move without restriction, and they can climb up and down a few steps on a ladder while holding on to the sides. Some begin to run.

Also some coordinated, fine movements of the hands are developing. The child can already feed himself, and take off some of his clothes.

To insure proper development of motor ability appropriate conditions must be created, i.e. a properly equipped playroom with the necessary appliances: such as low sofas, boxes for children to climb on, boards and logs to walk on and various mobile objects like wheelbarrows, cars, carriages, etc.

In addition to creating the right atmosphere in which the children can play and move, it is necessary to carry out special activities aimed at developing motor skills. These take the form of gymnastic exercises and various motor games with defined rules.

ORGANIZATION OF MOTOR ACTIVITIES

Organized motor activities not only help to develop specific motor skills, but also help to organize the child's behaviour.

Well selected motor activities designed in accordance with the child's abilities and level of development (see appendix) activate different muscle groups. They develop the skills of walking, running, crawling and throwing and teach the coordination of movement. This improves mobility and dexterity. Group activities which demand that the child wait his turn, help train the reflex pattern and develop patience and firmness of will.

Verbal explanation describing the activities should be given in a warm voice. Such explanations, when connected with motor activities, enrich the vocabulary.

Active participation in simple play develops still further the ability to imitate motor activities, contributes to speech development, encourages positive interaction between children, and develops such character traits as patience, bravery, the ability to overcome difficulties and the ability to act in harmony.

In the first half of the second year many activities are carried out with a ball, such as pushing a ball, rolling it in a toy bowling alley, rolling it from one child to another, throwing small balls into a basket (at a distance of 20-40 cm and the basket being 60 cm wide). These activities with a ball do not require special description. In addition, the following activities should be carried out.

"I shall catch up - catch up"

Goal: *to teach a child to walk backwards.*

The child-care worker while playing with a child, begins to run, saying: "I'll catch up with you". The child smiles and moves backwards. The activity is repeated 2-3 times.

"Catch up with a ball"

Goal: *to encourage running in a group.*

The children stand in one side of the room or yard. The adult shows the ball and suggests that the children watch how the ball bounces. She begins to bounce the ball in front of her and calls to the children: "Come, catch up with the ball".

PLAY AND ACTIVITY: SECOND AND THIRD YEARS

"Catch up with a bear"

Goal: to encourage running after an adult.

The children sit in half a circle. The child-care worker holds a Teddy-bear. She approaches one of the children and says: "Catch up with the bear". The child-care worker then runs away with the bear and the child runs after them.

During the second half of the second year it is recommended to use motor play as described by T.S. Babadgan "Organization of Motor Activities in Early Childhood". The following activities were investigated in the program of early child education in children's homes.

"Pat-a-cake"

This activity is carried out with one child, several children or the whole group. The child-care worker sings a song and accompanies it with movements, described in a song. The children imitate the movements of the child-care worker. Repeating words like: Yes, tik-tik, la-la, by-by.

Pat-a-cake

Pat-a-cake, pat-a-cake,
Bing-bang pop-guns,
Clap your hands,
Clap your hands: Yes!

The porridge was cooked,
With a spoon it was
    stirred,
The doll was fed,
The cat got her milk:
    Yes!

Our fists we clenched,
With our fists we banged,
Tik-tak-tak, tik-tak-tak-
    tak,
Tik-tak-tak, tak-tak-tak-
    tik: Yes!

Pat-a-cake, dance,
The children are amused,
La-la-la, la-la-la-la,
La-la-la, la-la-la-la:
    Yes!

The pat-a-cake is tired,
The pat-a-cake is sleepy,
Bey-bey, bey-bey,
Bey-bey, bey-bey: Yes!

"One-two"

The child-care worker takes the child by two hands, moves from one foot to another, then makes some quick steps and sits down. The child imitates her movements.

"Bubble"

Two to three children participate, but gradually the number of children may be increased.

With the help of the child-care worker the children form a tight circle, holding hands. The game is carried out according to verbal instructions and demonstration by the adult. She stands with the children, holding their hands, and regulates their movements.

Words of the play	*Description of the movements*
The child-care worker: "Blow up bubble, Blow up to be big, Stay this way, Do not burst!"	The child-care worker and the children move, holding hands and gradually widen the circle.
The child-care worker: Sh, sh, ...	Small steps forward to the center of the circle.
The child-care worker: Look how small, the bubble is, Lets blow it up.	The child-care worker repeats the words "Blow up" (the widening and narrowing of the circle is repeated 2-3 times), then she says: "clap" and quickly sits down on her heels, clapping her hands. The children imitate her

PLAY AND ACTIVITY: SECOND AND THIRD YEARS   87

	movements and the circle breaks.
The child-care worker: The bubble burst! Blow it up again.	The child-care worker and the children stand up, take each other's hands.
The child-care worker: (To finish the play): Here, what a big bubble and all blown up. (To continue the play): Sh, sh...Oh, again he's small, Blow up the bubble, etc. (The play continues).	

"Catching up"

A melody of a familiar song is sung. The play is carried out first with several children and then with the whole group.

The children sit on chairs, the child-care worker sings about one of the children.

Words of the song	*Description of movements*
Our Tanechka is in the garden, She feels like an apple dipped in honey, Our Tanya.	The named child comes near the child-care worker who strokes her head.
Our Tanya dances, Show us your feet, Our little Tanya.	The child dances, everybody claps hands.
You, my children come and run, Catch up with our Tanya, Our little Tanya.	The child-care worker takes Tanya's hand and runs away from the children.

No, no, no, You can't get our Tanya, I won't give her to you.	The child-care worker hides Tanya behind her back, hiding her from the other children who ran towards her.

Triangle

The children sit on chairs, each child has a small metal rod. The adult stands at some distance from the children and sings.

Words of the song	*Description of movements*
Dim-dim-din-dun, All of you run.	All of the children run towards her, while they run she taps a triangle with a small metal rod.
She who runs to me, Will play the triangle for me, Din-din-din-dun.	The children run towards the triangle and tap it with their metal rods. (It is permissible that two children tap at the same time).

Then the child-care worker runs with the triangle to another place, plays, sings a song. The children again run towards her.

When repeating the game the child-care worker hides with the triangle and the children follow the sound.

Before this game she should let them tap and play with the triangle.

"Where are you Vova"

The children sit in a semi-circle. The adult covers the head of one or two children with a transparent handkerchief, then looks all over the room for the child whose head is covered. While looking for him she sings.

Where is Vova?
I cannot find him,
Children, call Vova,
Come out, wherever you are Vova?

Everybody calls the child.

Vova come here!

The child removes the handkerchief, returns to the child-care worker and hands her the handkerchief.

The adult takes him by his hands and dances with him slowly or quickly.

When dancing with the children she sings a song without words ("la-la-la") and the other children clap their hands.

"A bear walked in a forest"

The children sit on chairs. The nurse pretends to be a bear. The child-care worker says:

A bear walked in a forest,
The bear gathered cones
He walked for a long time,
Until he fell asleep.

While telling the tale the nurse pretends to be a bear, and walks around the room "gathering cones". She too, sits down and falls asleep.

Quietly they all come to the nurse. While doing this the child-care worker says.

The children are moving,
The bear is beginning to wake:
Wake up bear, wake up,
Catch up with us.

The nurse imitates the growl of a bear. This is a signal for the children. All of them run away to their places and the nurse runs and catches up with them.

When repeating the game an older child may take the part of the bear.

"Let's play hide and seek"

One corner of the room is partitioned off with a brightly colored cheesecloth curtain, leaving enough space so that the whole group can get behind it (the curtain is made from 2-3 pieces to enable the children to run out from behind it all at once, both through the sides and the middle).

The child-care worker suggests to play hide and seek. She hides behind a closet, behind a curtain, etc. She cries out, "Hi", and the children find her. Then she suggests that the children hide and that she will look for them. She turns around and waits until the nurse and the children hide. Afterwards she walks about the room, "without hurrying" slowly looking for the children and singing.

> I walk about the room,
> I cannot find my children.
> Well, where shall I turn,
> Where will I find my children?
>
> I'll take out a flute,
> I'll play on my flute,
> Surely they will hear me,
> And they will come to me.

While singing the second part of the song, she goes to a shelf, takes out the flute (recorder) and plays a dance tune. The nurse and the children run out from behind the curtain. Then she dances with them while playing the flute.

PLAY AND ACTIVITY: SECOND AND THIRD YEARS

After the dance she suggests that the children turn around and she will hide. The nurse collects the children in order that they won't see where the child-care worker hides. The child-care worker hides behind a cupboard (or some other piece of furniture), rings a bell or plays on a triangle. The children come and find her. (This part of the play is carried out according to the children's wish).

She suggests again that they hide. This time she "does not find them" in the room and after singing the first part of the song (see above) goes out through the door.

If the children are not tired one may prolong the game this way: when the child-care worker leaves the room, the nurse and the children run from the corner, come near the door and cry out together "Ohh!". The child-care worker answers through the door, but enters the room after a short delay, so that the children may run and hide in the corner. Entering the room she wonders: "It seemed to me the children called me and I do not see a soul", again she leaves through the door. The second time the child-care worker enters the room, while holding rattles in a bag, she shakes the bag and sings (the same melody):

Rattle, rattle, ring,
All the children sing.
When they'll hear it they will run,
With the rattle - the dance will have begun.

The children together with the nurse run towards the child-care worker. She takes the rattles out of the bag and distributes them to the children. They then dance with the rattles.

Comment: The game can be shortened by taking out one episode.

A large and a small ball

Rolling of a ball is carried out individually with each child, and then gradually with several children.

When the children have learned to roll a large ball, the child-care worker teaches them to roll small balls. This is done in the following manner.

The child-care worker takes a number of little balls, according to the number of children. The children sit on the floor in a semi-circle, and she rolls the balls to each child (not in turn, but almost at the same time). When a child rolls the ball back, she returns it to the child, not waiting until the other children return their balls. This way the child-care worker plays at the same time with several children, getting the ball from each child and returning it to him the moment he rolls it to her.

She accompanies the game with a gay rhythmical chatter: "Catch-roll, catch-give back", etc. After playing for a while, she collects the small balls and scatters them around the room. The children get up and run after the balls and bring them back to her.

The scattering and collecting of the balls is repeated several times. Rolling of the large ball is done by the whole group only when all the others have learned to roll it. After rolling the large ball, the game may be finished by scattering and collecting small balls, as described above.

ENTERTAINMENT DURING THE SECOND YEAR OF LIFE

It is important for the healthy development of the child that he be in a cheerful and in a happy mood. The child's first words and play habits usually appear during moments of excitement and curiosity. The child is attracted to everything new and mobile,

PLAY AND ACTIVITY: SECOND AND THIRD YEARS

and to the sudden appearance and disappearance of objects. Games take this principle into consideration and should be carried out with the aim of arousing the emotional response of the child. The games may be carried out individually, or with the group, which gathers around the child-care worker. These games are especially needed for flabby, non-mobile children or children who were newly accepted into children's homes and who have not yet become used to their new environment.

"Toss up toys"

The child-care worker takes a cloth and gives a corner to a child saying: "Hold tight". While doing this she holds two corners of the cloth, puts a teddy bear in the middle and shakes the corners saying: "Teddy bear, teddy bear, dance, Oh, he fell". As she says this the toy bounces and the children may laugh.

The game is repeated many times, while the children willingly repeat two words: "Fell", "Dance", etc.

Instead of the bear one can use a cat, a hare, etc.

"Catching sunbeams in the mirror"

The child-care worker gathers eight children about her and plays "sunbeams with a mirror", accompanying her movements with a poem by V.M Fedieevskoi "To children for joy":

Golden sunbeams,
Dance on the wall,
Touch them with your fingers,
They'll come to you.

If the child makes the right movement with the finger, the adult directs the sunbeam to him.

"Soap bubbles"

The child-care worker takes a paper tube or a straw, inserts it in soap water (in a cup or a bowl) and makes bubbles. When the bubble separates from the straw, she blows the bubble up in the air.

This demonstration can be carried out on a playground where the wind can catch the bubble. The children are happy and run after the bubbles.

Mechanical toys

The child-care worker sits with the children on a carpet and announces that she will show them something. She winds up a mechanical toy and lets it move. This may make the children happy.

Puppet show - Olya and Kolya

Two dolls (one boy and one girl), and a ball on a stick are used. A sheet or a simple curtain is spread between two chairs. The children are seated so that they will see everything. One adult is behind the curtain and a second adult is with the children.

The child-care worker: Children, look who came to us, A little girl came!

The little girl: Good day children, my name is Olya, look at my beautiful dress.

PLAY AND ACTIVITY IN THE THIRD YEAR OF LIFE

Working with Three Year Olds: Activities and Aims:

1) speech development and orientation in the environment, 2) enlarged experience with color, form, size and the connections between time, space and numbers, 3) deepening of concentration, perception, and memory, 4) development of initiative and constructive activities, 5) development of general movements, 6) entertainment, 7) musical education.

SPEECH DEVELOPMENT AND ORIENTATION IN THREE YEAR OLDS

The mastery of speech is of great importance in the third year of life as speech is closely connected with thought, and influences the general development of behavior in the child. Speech in the third year begins to become both a means of communication, and a means of recognition and orientation to the surrounding world.

While a two year old child only approaches his direct surroundings, the three year old child can perceive objects and understand actions related in a story, which do not exist in his field of vision at the moment, but which he has seen before.

The child begins to be interested in recurrent actions and he can come to primitive comparisons, reach conclusions and make generalizations.

The child easily remembers short songs and poems. He masters speech and his vocabulary increases to 1200-1300 words. The child imitates adult speech, remembers what he has heard, and includes new words in his recent speech. However, there still exists a degree of mispronunciation, some have difficulty in pronouncing gutturals and sibilants although others find no difficulty.

The child begins to use most forms of speech in his conversation except the participle and adverb. He begins to use extended sentences, and sometimes even uses a subordinate clause. He asks questions; where? why? what for?

Speech becomes by now an instrument, which enables a three year old child to be explicit, not only to adults but also to other children. Speech is no longer limited to descriptions of the immediate reality. In the "Program for Education in the Kindergarten" it is demonstrated how the teacher can contribute to the child's knowledge and elementary understanding of: the phenomena in nature (the sun is shining, snow is falling, today is cold etc.); animals (cat, dog, horse, etc.); general events (today is a holiday, there are many people on the street, flags, the children receive presents etc.); the work of adults (the maid washes dishes, the driver drives a car, the doctor treats sick children etc.); the recognition and purpose of domestic objects (one sleeps on a bed, one eats on a table, one drinks milk from a cup and soup from a bowl etc.). In addition one should develop primary concepts: space (far, close, here, there); and time (morning, evening, later, now, tomorrow, today). The children should understand the basic connection between occurences (it is raining so there are puddles on the street, we dropped a cup so it broke).*

The child-care worker should converse with the children while they are eating, during any routine work and while they are playing independently. In addition, she should institute special activities to further the development of speech.

The adult's speech should be varied, expressive, correct and clear.

PLAY AND ACTIVITY: SECOND AND THIRD YEARS

The child-care worker should have the following aims: 1) to broaden the child's orientation within his environment; 2) to develop the comprehension of speech which is not related to visible objects and actions; 3) to widen the vocabulary; 4) to teach the child to use sentences, to communicate his impressions and to answer questions; 5) to teach the correct pronunciation of words and sounds; 6) to teach the child to emote and express himself well; 7) to teach him to look at pictures and books independently and to treat them with care.

Activities in this age range which are based on speech development are of great importance. Aim of an action is the development of active speech; it should not be carried out with the whole group, but with a subgroup of 10-12 children who are more or less on the same intellectual level.

There are the following activities: organized observations, outdoor activities, group games, dramatic play, activity with pictures, demonstration of films, conversation and story telling, reading of short poems and games to enrich vocabulary.

ORGANIZED OBSERVATIONS

The ability to observe the surroundings plays an important role in the child's development. Observation widens the child's horizons, and lengthens his attention, as well as memory and imagination.

A young child is quite interested in his environment but he has not quite the ability to specify important factors. His observations are superficial. The child-care worker should direct his attention to things unnoticed by him, and to explain any misconceptions. Observation activities are extremely important.

A sample of an observation: while looking at furniture, explain to the child the purpose of each object; while watching the maid at work point out that the water becomes dirty, after washing the floor, and the floor clean; while feeding fish in the aquarium, emphasize that the fish come to the surface, open their mouths and snatch at the food; looking through a window watching vehicles in the street explain that trucks carry many different loads and cars carry people.

Much may be observed during the summer in a village. This can take on the form of a game: "Let's see what we have?" or "We shall name what we see".

To observe, widens the child's universe, broadens his ideas and conceptions.

OBSERVATIONS WHILE FEEDING FISH IN AN ACQUARIUM

Watching fish feeding should be carried out in a subgroup with 6-8 children and all the children should have a clear view of the aquarium. The children already saw the aquarium and they know how fish swim. The child-care worker lays the stress on feeding fish (Fig. 15). She points out that the fish come to the surface, open their mouths and snatch the food; she scatters on the surface. Subsequently she permits one of the older children to feed the fish.

WALKS WITH A PURPOSE

Purposeful walks enrich the children and provide them with new impressions. The walk should last no more than 15-20 minutes. The children should be accompanied by two adults. In case the children have to cross a street, they should walk in pairs, holding on to a rope with a loop. One adult walks in the lead, and the other guards the rear.

During the summer in the country, one can organize walks to a forest, to the fields, to a water

Fig. 15. The children observe the feeding of fish.

reservoir, a poultry farm, etc. In town they can be taken to a shop window, to a school, to a skating-rink, etc.

When the children come to skating-rink and they watch the skaters: "Children, look at the little boy with the red hat, his legs are bending, he will fall. Here he fell. You know, how hard it is to skate? The ice is slippery. The boy does not yet know how to skate, but he will learn. Oh, but that girl with the white hat skates well, so evenly and she does not fall. Look how the ice glitters! It is smooth, like a mirror. When you'll go to kindergarten, you too will learn how to skate".

DEMONSTRATION ON SIMPLE TOPICS WITH THE USE OF TOYS

Dramatizations also enrich the children's impressions, widen their universe of ideas and concepts and develop their thoughts, imagination and memory.

The telling of stories and fairy tales, aided by topical toys, causes gaiety, activates their speech, develops their ability to listen.

The method of carrying out such dramatization is as follows.

Before beginning the dramatization, the child-care worker familiarizes the children with the heroes. She shows them a doll or another toy, names it, and stresses those characteristics which will be mentioned in the story.

She lets each child touch the toy before the demonstration, so that they will not disturb by wanting to do so during the dramatization of the story.

As soon as they know the main characters she arranges the toys, and tells them about the story she is about to dramatize. While doing this she obtains the children's concentrated attention.

Upon repetition the introduction should be shortened. The adult should be the performer. During the first dramatization, when repeating the story a few roles should be given to the children.

When playing with topical toys, it should take a more advanced form. For instance, if until now they dressed the hare, put it to bed etc, they begin to imitate the specifics of a hare as an animal. The topical toys, illustrate themes of folk-lore stories (Fig. 16).

Fig. 16. A story illustrated by plywood toys.

How a doll builds a room

Small or large building blocks, a doll or a teddy bear matches the size of the building blocks, a tablecloth, a napkin for the bear, a jar, a cup, a plate, a roll made of paper, plastaline or clay, and sweets. The demonstration is performed on a table.

The doll appears and greets the children. "Good day, children, I'll build a room for myself. Look, I'll take some cubes and bricks and I'll put them this way" (erects three walls in a straight triangle and leaves openings in the walls for windows). She looks through the window. "Children, I see you". When the room is ready the doll builds furniture. "Now I build a table". The doll builds the legs from cubes or bricks, and puts a piece of plywood on them. "Here the table is ready. Look, children what a nice table I made".

"But on what shall I sit?" The children prompt her - "on a chair". - "Now I'll build a chair" - puts a block in place, - "here is a seat", - puts another block in place, - "here is the back. Look, what a fine chair I made. I'll build another chair. Here is the seat, and here is the back. The chair is ready. I'll put a tablecloth on the table. And on the table I'll put a cup and a jar. There is milk in the jar. A roll on the plate. What a nice room I have. Do you like my room children? Now, I'll build a road". - She builds a road of blocks at the side of the room.

"I'll walk on the road. I'll invite the bear for a visit". Calls: "Teddy bear, teddy bear, where are you? Well, come to me". She finds the bear and brings him into the room. The bear stands near the road. "Look, how I'll walk on the road".

The bear walks, stumbles, breaks the road and falls. The doll comes towards him: "Teddy bear, how clumsy you are? Look, you broke the road. Let's fix it". - Both of them repair the road. - "Alright bear, let's go; teddy bear, give me your paw. I'll lead you along the road". - The doll brings teddy bear into the room. - "Well, here we are. Look, what a nice room I have. Wash your hands teddy bear. I'll give you something to eat. Are you hungry? Sit at the table. Take a napkin. Here is a cup, I'll give you some milk. Here is a roll!" - Teddy bear drinks. The doll sits on another chair. - "It is tasty isn't it? Do you want a candy? Here is a candy for you, and one for me". - Together they eat the sweets. - "Have you finished? Wipe your mouth with the napkin". Teddy bear cleans his mouth and takes off the napkin. "Now we'll walk. We'll run along on the road. Good-bye, children".

Before going to sleep

A doll, a doll's bed and bedding, a toy horse, a cow, a pig and a dog, bricks and strips of paper are used.

The children sit in a semi-circle. The table is long. She puts the objects on the table. Then she lays the bricks or strips of paper on the table making a road and tells them to watch for someone who will come. She attracts their attention to the animals; she puts on the road, and leads each animal in turn, while telling a story. When the story is ended, she puts a pillow and on it a dog under the doll's bed and sings a lullaby.
The text: (*Often the children answer for the doll*)

	Answer of the doll:
A cow walks on the road and says: "I am tired of walking in the fields and eat and eat to make my milk. Dear child, let me lie on your bed just to pass the night".	No cow I can't let you sleep in my bed. You dear cow are so heavy and my bed is so slight.
A horse walks on the road and says: "I am so tired, either I work in the fields or pull people in carts, I pull and pull. Dear child let me lie on your bed just to pass the night".	No, dear horse. I can't let you sleep on my bed. You, my horse are so big, and my bed is so small.
A pig walks on the road and says: "My feet are tired, my snout is raw. All day long my snout is in the mud. Dear child, let me sleep in your bed, just to pass the night!"	No, pig. You're the dirtiest of them all. I'll never let you sleep on my bed. You muddle in a puddle all day.

A dog walks on the road and says: "My feet are tired. Let me stay overnight. Let me sleep under your bed. Your dreams I'll protect, and your house I'll guard".

Come, lovely dog. Come sleep on a soft pillow under my warm bed.

The teddy bear's holiday

For this activity one uses a furry teddy bear, a horse, a dog, a duck, a pig and ribbons.

A gift is tied on to each toy. Included are chocolate, pencils, sweets and grass. The child-care worker says: "Children, today teddy bear has a birthday, it's a holiday for him, look how dressed up he is! He is waiting for guests. We'll wait and see who his guests are". No one comes (a pause). Then a horse appears: "Look, the horse brought teddy some chocolate"; a dog appears. "The dog brought a pencil"; a pig appears. "And the pig picks up some grass in the yard. 'Oink, oink, I give the grass to teddy bear'". A duck appears: "Ducky came running with some sweets and gave them to teddy bear".

All the animals are put aside, and teddy bear sits surrounded by all his presents. "We gave him all the presents, because teddy bear is so nice".

Teddy bear

A furry teddy bear, pans, a chair, a basin with water, a towel, a comb and a ribbon are used.

The adult brings into the room a toy bear and says: "A bear came for a visit from the forest". The teddy bear climbs clumsily up onto a chair, bows to the children and almost falls off the chair. He gets off the chair and bows in all directions to the children. The child-care worker puts pants on him, places

a basin of water on the floor and brings teddy bear to
the basin. Teddy is stubborn, and does not want to go.
Teddy bear carefully puts a paw into the water and
immediately jumps away, puts in his other paw and also
jumps, and finally runs away and hides under the table.
The child-care worker pulls him from under the table
and forces him to go to the water basin, where she
washes him by force. While he is being washed teddy
bear splashes water all over himself. The child-care
worker dries his paws with a towel, and gives him a
comb. Teddy bear combs his hair, and returns the comb.
Teddy bear shows off, swaying from side to side.

"Now everything is well. Do your exercises".
The child-care worker raises his paws up and down and
the children follow, doing the same exercise. Adult
calls Teddy, and ties a ribbon around his neck.
Dressed up, teddy bear dances, and points with his paw
to some child. The child joins teddy bear in the
dance while all the other children clap their hands.

Masha eats

For this activity one uses a doll, a dog, a cat,
a chicken, a plate, a bowl, a saucer, a pot, a table,
a chair and a tablecloth.

The child-care worker says to the children: "Masha
came in from a walk (shows the doll to the children),
she is very hungry; it is time for dinner".

Dinnertime, Masha sat at the table,
- Bow, wow, wow!
- Who came to us?
- It is me,
- Your reliable dog,
Your Arapta -
With the black nose.
Day and night
I guard your house,
I am tired and chilled,
Isn't it time for dinner?

- Arapta,
Wash your paws.
Meow, meow!
- Who is it now?
Who scratches at the door?
It is your cat Murka,
Murka -
With the silvery gray fur,
I've cleared the cellar,
All the mice have run away,

I've rid you of all the rats.
Oh, how hard I worked, how tired I am.
Isn't it time yet for dinner?
- Well-well, well-well!
Who else hurries to us?
- It's me your chicken,
I have not eaten, nor have I drunk.
But an egg I laid for you.
Isn't it time yet for dinner?
The door is open for all of you,
Masha invites the lot of you.
Arapta with his black nose,
The cat who scratches at the door,
The chicken who laid an egg,
Each one of you will get dinner.
The dog gets his in a bowl,
The cat gets hers in a saucer,
The chicken's is in a pot,
And Masha gets hers in a plate,
But not a deep one, no not in a small one.

USING PICTURES TO TELL STORIES

The telling of stories through the use of pictures has the following aims: 1) comprehension of topics as portrayed in pictures, which reflect the children's experiences and actions, 2) comprehension of adult experiences as illustrated in pictures (Fig. 17), and 3) eliciting verbalization by stimulating the answering of questions, to tell a story independently from memory, 4) enlarging the child's vocabulary, and introducing new details of speech, 5) teaching the child to speak longer more complicated sentences, and to connect the words in the sentences correctly, 6) teaching the child to correctly pronounce syllables and words, 7) continuing to develop the right modulation and to deepen the ability to listen, 8) teaching the independent use of a picture book, i.e., examine the pictures carefully and accurately, relate stories seen in the books, and finally to return the books to their proper place when no longer needed (Figs. 18 and 19).

PLAY AND ACTIVITY: SECOND AND THIRD YEARS   107

Fig. 17. A story illustrated by pictures.

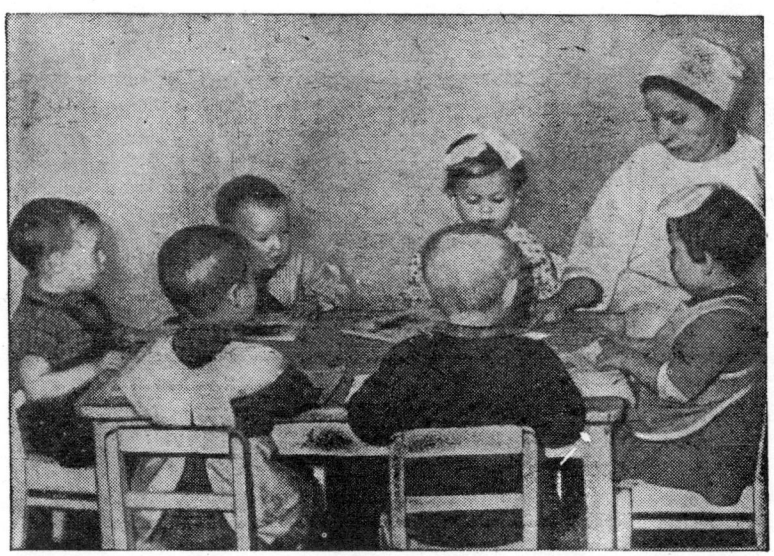

Fig. 18. The children learn to use books.

Fig. 19. The children view books on their own.

In order to accomplish these aims, the children should now be given more complex topics and stories than before.

Complex topics are those in which the images are presented not separately, but together as one whole.

Another elaboration used in these activities is the telling of stories that relate to objects and activities outside of the picture itself, but connected in some way to what is seen in the picture. For instance, when looking at a picture which portrays the feeding of children, one can talk about food the children eat, what they have eaten today, what they like to eat, how carefully they know how to eat, etc. This sort of "story conversation" widens the child's orientation in the surroundings and enriches the meaning of words.

PLAY AND ACTIVITY: SECOND AND THIRD YEARS

Thus elaboration is achieved through demonstrating and talking to the children about subjects with which they have not had any direct contact, but which they can understand on the basis of their previous experience. For instance, by using pictures and appropriate verbal explanations they should be able to understand stories like "The Three Bears" by L.N. Tolstoy.

It is important to determine carefully the meaning and the content of the picture and to compose an appropriate verbal explanation before beginning to tell a story. There is no need to always relate the content of a story in conventional sentences. This does not add to the child's impressions, nor does it enrich his vocabulary. On the contrary, the meaning of words is enriched when various combinations of words are used. It is thus necessary to prepare the text of the stories beforehand.

SLIDE SHOWS ACCOMPANIED BY STORIES

A different way to develop speech is through the showing of slides simultaneously telling stories. In children's homes this activity takes place with the whole group present. The children are ushered into the room when everything has been arranged to show the slides. The children are seated so that the smaller ones are sitting in the first rows, the taller ones farther back.

The showing needs two adults. One operates the projector, the second adult sits on the side by the screen, so as not to interfere with the picture and not to disturb the children. She points at different parts of the pictures while telling the story. It is very important to properly follow these rules if one is to have a successful slide show.

One should differentiate between initial and repeat performances. When slides are shown for the first time, the children should have a chance to leisurely observe the pictures, without being told the content of the topic shown. When repeated this show can be followed with a story. One should use slides made for preschool age children.

It happens that the text written under the picture, particularly if it is in poetry form, is not always comprehensible for young children. A suitable text should be prepared beforehand by the child-care worker. Some words may be omitted, others added. While showing the slides, it is well not to stop to observe separate pictures for too long a time as this may lead to difficulty in perceiving the whole topic, and tires the children as well. It is not advisable to make a too quick summary of the pictures, as this prevents the children from concentrating and understanding the text.

It is well to watch the children's behavior, and not to allow noise that would cause general excitement.

Should the children become noisy, it is worthwhile to pause by switching off the projector, and to continue only when the noise has abated. Children should not become overtired by seeing too many picture stories at one sitting. It is best to show a new story and a familiar one.

FAIRY TALES AND STORIES

Young children like to be told fairy tales and stories.

Listening to the rhythm of a folklore tale and its imaginative expression refines artistic taste. New words and expressions enrich speech and open horizons. Interesting stories help children to concentrate and develop their thoughts as well as their memory. Some stories make children happy and merry, others arouse sympathy etc.

In their third year fairy tales and stories should be told rather than read, as telling a story creates a more intimate contact between the adult and the child. When telling a story she should look at each child, and follow his facial expression. The story assumes a simple and more emotional presentation.

The child-care worker's voice should not be loud, her speech correct, and the tone of her voice serene. She should use her voice with different intonations for the story. For instance, when speaking of a bear, her voice should be low; of a hare, it should be thin, etc.

When telling a story she changes the tempo of her speech. She speeds up or slows down, and sometimes pauses in the middle of a sentence. If the children react strongly to the story, she should pause, and let the children express their reaction to what they have heard. In an expressive way as possible, she should use gestures and words to demonstrate contrasts in size. Questions like: "How big is the dog?" should not be asked. Instead, the children should tell this themselves after they have heard the story often. If they are mistaken about size, they should be corrected in an unobtrusive manner demonstrated with a toy. She may enliven a story by imitating the animals in the story.

The content of a story is perceived better, if the children participate in it. It may be suggested that they clap hands at the right moment or stamp their feet, call out to some one, or answer questions.

The telling of a fairy tale or story should be repeated several times.

The form of a folklore story, its language, and its reiterations must invariably be preserved. However, death of a character may depress the children, therefore it is permissable to change the end of a tale so long as it does not lose its significance.

Repetition of fairy tales and stories is essential. It helps the child remember, and occasionally recollect them. To verify and reinforce the children's comprehension of the content relevant questions concerning the sequence of happenings should be asked after the story is ended. The questions should be simple and concrete.

Here is a sample:

1. A story about a chicken. "'Chip-chip, chip', Aunty calls to the chickens. She wants to feed them grain. The chickens run to Aunty. The young chickens and the old hen all run. They are hungry".

Questions: "Who called the chickens? What did Aunty give them? Who else ran together with the chicks?"

2. A story about a cow. "Moo-moo-moo, who moos in the yard? It is the cow calling her calf. But the calf has opened the gate, and has run into the street. The cow does not see her calf".

Questions: "Moo-moo-moo, who is mooing in the yard? Who did the cow call? Where did the calf go?"

Questions should not be addressed to the whole group, but rather to a single child. If the child does not answer, another is asked. To enrich the child's speech the stories, new words and phrases should be introduced and gradually elaborated.

An example of a gradually elaborated story.

A story about a hare. *Version I*. Once upon a time there was a hare. He wanted to eat, and could not find any carrots. So he ran to the children, and they gave him some carrots.

Version II. Once upon a time there lived a hare. He was white, with a lot of long, fluffy hair. One day the hare woke up and wanted to eat something, but there was nothing to eat. He looked everywhere but couldn't find either carrots or cabbage. Then the hare saw some children. He ran towards them and they gave him carrots.

Version III. Once upon a time there was a hare. He was white with lots of long fluffy hair, and he had small red eyes. One morning he woke up, and saw that it was snowing outside. Everything was covered with snow: the fields, the trees. The hare became hungry, and he ran to the garden. He looked for some carrots, and looked for some cabbage. There were no carrots, and no cabbage. The hare sat under a bush and began to cry. Some children passed by, and they asked: "Why do you cry, hare?" And the hare said: "Why shouldn't I cry? I am hungry and nowhere can I find carrots or cabbage." Then the children gave him some carrots and he ate them, and was happy."

It is well to encourage the children to recall the fairy tales or stories. The child-care worker, while telling a well known story, should stop and allow the children to finish the sentence. For instance:

The child-care worker: Once upon a time...
The children: A grandmother and a grandfather lived...
The child-care worker: They had...
The children: A chicken etc....

This suggestion to the children should be made when they can easily fill in the missing parts.

It is useful to use the following method: the child-care worker does not finish the sentence, but instead asks a question which the children answer. The child-care worker chooses one of their answers, (one which fits the content), and then continues the story.

This method makes story telling more lively, because all the children can participate. They try to guess or remember details. For instance, the name of the character, places where the characters went, clothes they wore, etc.

An example:

"Marusja wanted to go... Where did she want to go? (The children name the place). Vova guessed, Marusja wanted to go for a walk. Marusja put on... What did she put on? (The children mention the kind of clothing.) She took with her... What did she take? etc."

"Marusja went to the street and there she saw... What did she see? Hear her run... Who ran? etc..." The story should end with Marusja returning home.

When telling stories about animals, the children should be encouraged to imitate them; the cackling of a hen, or the barking of a dog. They should also imitate the howling of the wind, or the patter of rain.

When teaching children to listen to and understand stories, one should begin by telling short, simply built stories. Good examples can be found in short stories by L.N. Tolstoy and K.D. Ushinski:

Nastja's doll: (L.N. Tolstoy). Nastja had a doll. Nastja called her daughter. Nastja's mother gave everything to the doll. She had skirts, blouses, scarves. She even had combs, brushes, beads.

A boat (L.N. Tolstoy): Spring came, and the water began to flow. The children took some planks, made a boat, and put the boat into the water. The boat floated down the stream, the children followed it joyously and shouted gleefully. They did not look ahead and all of them fell into a puddle.

There was a squirrel in the forest: (L.N. Tolstoy). There was a squirrel. She had children, and they lived in a hollow. Misha and Kolja came to the hollow. They took the squirrels to their home and then the squirrels lived in a cage.

The geese: (K.D. Ushinskii). The housewife went into the yard and beckoned the geese to come home: "Come, come white geese, gray geese come on home". The geese streched their long necks, they showed their red, red web feet. They flapped their wings and they wrinkled their foreheads. "Ga-ga-ga! We don't want to go home. We like it here". The housewife saw that she would not get anywhere by being kind. So she took a piece of long brushwood and shooed them home.

A dog: (L.S. Slavina). Once upon a time there was a little boy called Petja. He had a little dog called Sharik. Once Petja called to Sharik: "Sharik, Sharik, come to me, I shall give you meat". But there was no Sharik, Petja began to search for him, but Sharik couldn't be found anywhere. He was not in the garden, and he was not in the room. Sharik was hidden under the bed, and nobody saw him.*

POETRY

It is possible for a three-year old child to memorize poetry. However, mechanical memorizing overloads the child's brain with unnecessary detail he does not understand. The memorizing of long poems does not develop or aid memory.

This kind of poetry clutters a child's speech, and he often distorts words. The memorization of poems, which the child repeats without understanding or intonation only causes damage.

The training of memory is useful only when the content of the poem is connected with concrete reality and when the material memorized by the child is understood by him. The child memorizes these kind of poems and enjoys it. This helps develop his speech.

---

*Editor's note: The original contains numerous additional classical Russian folk stories.

Therefore easily understood short poems should be told to the child. When the child-care worker takes the child for a walk she can recite poems. In the winter, they can be about the snow. In the summer when there is a dragon-fly in the fields, she can recite a poem about a dragon-fly, or when picking flowers, about flowers, etc.

When looking at pictures and discussing them with the children, it is useful to finish with a short poem. Short, expressive and understandable poems are easily and quickly memorized. Repetition of poems followed by correction from the adult improves and corrects their pronounciation.

It is not recommended to teach poems through lessons. It is preferable to use poems during activities as didactic material. It is recommended to match poems with pictures, or a toy mentioned in the poem.

DIDACTIC GAMES

Games with toys, table games (lotto), and games with pictures (so-called didactic games, or educational games) serve to develop receptivity, thought, attention, memory, speech and orientation to the surroundings.

The adult should point to and name the objects which have some definitive outward qualities and peculiarities (a red, or blue cube, big size of a toy etc). The child should then be given an opportunity to play with the objects. Thus the child begins to be aware of the outward qualities and peculiarities of objects.

DIDACTIC GAMES TO ENCOURAGE SPEECH DEVELOPMENT AND ORIENTATION WITHIN THE SURROUNDINGS

Who eats what?

Goal: to acquaint children with animals and animal food.

PLAY AND ACTIVITY: SECOND AND THIRD YEARS

Here one uses building materials to build animal houses, toys which portray animals are used (a cat, a hen, a goat, etc.) and appropriate food.

Procedure: "Now, children, we shall build houses. Who will live in them? (builds). This one for the cat and this one for the goat, and another house for the hen. Now we'll feed them all. Who wants to feed the cat? Natasha, do you? Come, along then feed her. Do you know what a cat eats?"

Natasha answers: "Milk, I'll give her milk". "Good, Natasha take a bowl with milk and feed the cat". Alesha: "I'd like to feed the goat". The adult answers: "Well, Alesha, go ahead feed the goat. Do you know what the goat eats? She eats grass or hay. Here, take some hay I prepared for it". Alesha feeds the goat, and gives her some water too.

"The hen too wants to eat - it likes to peck at seeds. Who will give it seeds? Come, Tanja, throw the hen some. Well, now we fed all the animals, and now they'll go to sleep, and we'll go for a walk".

Guess and name

Goal: to acquaint children with the use of various objects.

Various toys and objects, for instance: a ball, a basket, a pencil, a pencil sharper, a rattle etc. are used.

Procedure: Ten to twelve children, seated in a semi-circle are involved. In the center is a table. The objects which she has picked for the game, are shown to them. She asks: "What is it?" The children name the objects one by one.

The child-care worker: "What do you use it for?" (a basket)

The children: to gather berries.

The child-care worker: (explains) Yes, the baskets are used for gathering berries or mushrooms or other things which grow.

If the children do not name the object, the adult names it and explains it's use. For instance: "That's a thimble, mother or grandmother puts it on her finger, when she sews, so as not to prick her finger with the needle. Look, this way". Each object is visible to all on the table. When all the objects or toys are named she suggests to each child in turn that he take a certain toy, but without specifically naming it. She says thus: "Bring me the thing we need together mushrooms or berries, or the one mother cooks soup". etc.

Before executing the exercise, the child must listen intently to the child-care worker. When finished he returns the object into a box held by the adult.

> Comment: There must be 1-2 toys more than the number of participating children, so that the last child too has a selection from which to choose.

Games with matching pictures

In the third year games with matching pictures should be more complex than during the second year.

*Playing lotto**

Before playing lotto, it is recommended to use matching pictures described on page 66. Six to eight children take part in this activity.

Goal: to teach naming of pictures in lotto games. It is an exercise in learning to compare and differentiate between various objects.

This game starts with 3-5 children. Once they master the game, the number of participants is

---

*This chapter is written by Ladiginos.

increased to 8 or 10.

A kind of lotto should be used (toys, animals, clothing, furniture, etc.) which is familiar to the children. The number of cards should equal the number of children. A card is also used for the child-care worker. Two-three children may have identical cards. Two sets of lotto with the same name may be used. There should be no more than 3-4 pictures on the large lotto card.

Procedure: The child-care worker says: "Look, I'll show you cards", - does so and asks "What is it". If there is no response she repeats the question insisting upon an answer. If the children make an error she corrects them.. A big card is placed by her on the table and they all together look at the pictures and name them. Then she displays a small card, and asks what they see on it. Following that she suggests that the children find the identical picture on the big card and point to it. "Here is a hen, where is another hen? There is another hen. On the small card is a hen and on the big card is a hen. Let's cover the hen". She covers the hen on the big card with the small. Thus she shows all the cards, and induces the children to not only find and name the cards correctly, but to cover the pictures as she did, big card with small cards. The game is continued but a different card is added. If they are not tired, a third card may be used. One can also put out 2 big cards on the table. When this game is used again it is recommended that the whole group participate in it. One should distribute a card to each child. She examines the cards together with them. "Children, look, what do you have on your cards? Put them straight in front of you; look, how I do it." While the children examine their cards, she talks to them, answers questions, asks what they see on theirs, names the pictures on hers and confirms their answers: "Yes, yes, you have a deer, and Katja a cow, and who has a horse? Misha and Yura have a horse". Once the cards are examined by them and put on the table, she says: "You have put your cards on the table! Now - see what I have on my card!" - She shows them her card so all can see.

The children name the picture on the card, for instance "a goat"; the child-care worker asks: "Who has got a goat? Look at your cards, which of you gets a goat?" A child holding a big card with the same picture has to verbalize (not only with a gesture!) for the small card. Only when the child asks correctly, the adult hands him the card and shows him how to cover it. In case the child is silent the child-care worker prompts him to give the right answer. Gradually she distributes all the small cards and sees to it that each child is interested and concentrated throughout the game.

The cards shown by her are selected, no child needs wait too long. The child's level of intellectual development is considered and pictures are shown in accordance with increasingly complicated subjects, following the child's growth of vocabulary.

Should children still err in naming pictures correctly, (for instance, a donkey with a horse, or cherries with raspberries) then she not only corrects the error. She points out the difference between the two animals.. "But it's not a horse, it's a donkey. A donkey has long ears, and a horse has short ears, a donkey has a brush at the end of his tail, and the horse's tail has long hair. Now, kids tell me, where is the donkey and where is the horse?"

Gradually the children play the card game independently. The child will show a picture and name it, and no longer waits for another child. "A goose, who has a goose?" The goal of this activity is to promote active speech.

When they master the rules of the game then one may give 2 or 3 children a familiar lotto to use independently, though organized lotto games should be continued.

Lotto of objects

Goal: to teach children to differentiate between real objects, and to compare them with their pictures.

Small wooden objects and plywood cards with pictures of the same objects are employed in this game.

Six children and an adult are seated at a table.

Procedure: A number of objects removed from a box are shown. The adult asks the children to identify them, then she names names and returns them to the box. She then distributes a card with 4 images. Each child examines the pictures. Then she asks: "What are they called?" She holds up one object and asks: "What is this?" When they name the object, she turns to the children: "Which of you has a pitcher?" The child whose picture shows a pitcher, says: "I have one", she gives him the pitcher, names it and puts it next to the picture of the pitcher.

After they have mastered the game the children may play independently.

DIDACTIC GAMES TO DIFFERENTIATE AND NAME COLORS

Sorting of colored balls

Goal: to teach children to differentiate between basic colors (in this game - red and blue).

Red and blue balls and red and blue baskets are used.

Procedure: 8-10 children participate seated as usual, the adult faces them. The child-care worker shows them red and blue baskets and balls of the same color. She gives each child a ball and asks them to say the right color. The baskets are on the table. She says: "Natasha and Vova, look. Vova, what color is your ball?" - Vova answers. The child-care worker says: "Put your red ball into the red basket. And you Natasha, what color is your ball? Your ball is blue. Put your ball into the blue basket. You put the ball into the wrong basket, you put your blue ball into the red basket. Now take the blue ball out and put it into the blue basket. Now it's right".

The child-care worker calls two more children and asks them to name the colors of their balls and put them back in the identically colored baskets.

Rolling of colored balls

Goal: to teach children to differentiate and name the basic colors, and to stimulate the development of coordinated hand movements.

Four gates (red, blue, green, yellow) and balls of the same colors, two balls of each color in a box are used.

Procedure: Seating arrangement as above. She shows 4 colored gates, asks which color they are and arranges them in a row on the table. She calls on each child and asks them to take a ball of their choice out of the box. Then she asks: "Natasha, tell me please, what color is your ball?" - "Red". - "Right, roll it through the red gate. Take a green ball. No, this is not green, it is blue, take a green one. Roll it through the green gate. Now take a blue ball, right, roll it through the blue gate. Sit down. Now Vova, it's your turn". Each child gets a turn.

To acquaint the children with basic colors, colored scraps of cloth, brightly colored preferably with pictures of small objects in corresponding colors may be used.

DIDACTIC GAMES TO DIFFERENTIATE FORMS

Tactile recognition of toys

Goal: to teach children to recognize different forms through touch, to identify and to name objects.

For this game a muff and bag of toys (according to the number of children) are used. For instance, a ball, a doll, a car, a plate, a cube, a brick, etc.) Toys the children are familiar with are used.

Procedure: 5-6 children sit on chairs. The child-care worker shows them the muff and bag with the toys. She tells the children to turn around and not to look, while she puts one toy in the muff. She gives the muff to a child and explains how to put his hands into it. She asks the child to name the toy which he can feel inside the muff. While feeling the toy, he is asked to identify it. He then may take the toy and show it to the others.

During the game the child-care worker suggests to each child to put his hands into the bag, feel one of the toys, name it and take it out of the bag.

"Touch, and guess what I gave to you"

Goal: to teach children to identify objects by touch and to name them.

Small objects familiar to the children are used. The number of objects corresponds to the number of children (a ball, a cube, a brick, a pencil, etc.)

Procedure: 5-6 children participate. The adult instructs them to put their hands behind their backs, shows the bag containing the toys and says: "Now I'll put something which is in the bag into your hands. Don't look, only feel it and guess what it is. Afterwards I shall ask you what you have". She turns to each child: "Natasha, what do you have in your hands? Do not look, only say". - Natasha replies. - "Now show it to us. Right. You have a ball, put it back into the bag". When repeating this game, the number of toys is increased when the number of children is increased as well.

DIDACTIC GAMES TO DIFFERENTIATE CONTRASTING FORMS

A big and small doll

Goal: to teach to differentiate and name objects according to their size.

Dolls, tables, chairs, and dishes of large and small size are used now.

Procedure: The children are seated. The adult fronting them. On the right side of the table she places a big doll, table and chair. On the left of it she puts small furniture and a small doll. She faces the children: "This is a big doll, and this - a small one. The big doll sits on a big chair near a big table. The big doll's name is Katja, and the small one's Katjusha. Why do they sit at the table, Natasha?"

"It is probably time for breakfast. Ask Katja and Katjusha, if they washed their hands?" She bends over, looks at the dolls and says to the children: "Katja and Katjusha both say that they washed their hands. We'll tie napkins around their necks and feed them. Nina, come to me (shows two plates - a big and a small one). From which plate shall we feed Katja? And Katjusha? Right, in front of Katja you put a big plate, and in front of Katjusha a small one. Vova, come closer. I have two spoons, give one spoon to Katja and one to Katjusha. Correct. Big Katja has a big spoon, and Katjusha is little and we have to give her a small one. Marina, come here, what kind of doll is this? (shows Katja). A big doll, correct. Feed the big doll Katja from a big plate with a big spoon. And you, Olja come now, "tell me, what kind of a doll is this one. A big or a small one? (Shows Katjusha.) Right, it's a small doll, it's Katjusha. Feed Katjusha from a small plate, with a small spoon".

Other toys than dolls may be used (Fig. 20).

PLAY AND ACTIVITY: SECOND AND THIRD YEARS   125

Fig. 20. A big and small dog.

DIDACTIC GAMES TO DEVELOP NUMERICAL CONCEPTS

"Many", a "few"

Goal: *to develop the concepts of "many" "few" "one".*

For this activity one uses a bear, a doll, a bag of toys (balls, nuts, cones) and two bowls.

Procedure: 10-12 children take part in this game. The adult puts a bear and a doll on the table and a bowl in front of them. She shows her bag and says to the children: "In my bag I have many cubes, but Katja and Teddy the bear haven't even one. Watch now, I'll put some cubes into the bowl". She shakes many cubes into the doll's bowl, but only 2-3 cubes into the bear's bowl. Look, children, Katja has many cubes, but Teddy bear only a few. Katja and Teddy should divide their cubes". She shakes the bag. "Now Teddy has many cubes, and Katja has only a few".

"Teddy bear share your cubes with the children". The child-care worker bends down to Teddy bear and asks:

"Teddy bear, whom do you want to give your cubes to?" After a pause: "He wants to give his cubes to Serezha. Come to me Serezha, take the cubes from Teddy bear. Now you have many cubes and Teddy bear has none, do give him one. And with whom do you want to share the cubes? With Natasha. Give Natasha all the cubes but one". In this manner the children divide the cubes, always leaving one cube for themselves. At the end of the game they return the cubes to the doll and the bear.

Exercises to differentiate color, forms and sizes are also carried out with didactic toys (towers, nesting toys, etc.) which the children are already acquainted with since their second year of life.

To make the game more complex, big towers of various colors or nesting toys are used.

This enables the children to observe size and numbers while assembling and diassembling them. Such activities heighten the comprehension of "few" and "many", for instance: "Before there was one nesting egg, now there are many eggs; there were many eggs, now there is one".

DIDACTIC GAMES TO DEVELOP AUDITORY PERCEPTION

"Tell me, what you hear"

Goal: to differentiate between the sounds of various musical instruments: (a bell, a drum and a flute).

Procedure: Seating procedure as usual. The childcare worker is seated opposite them. "Children, look what I brought - this is a drum. Listen, how I beat the drum with the drumsticks: tum-tum-tum-tum. And now, Vova, come close and beat the drum with the drumsticks. Anybody else wants to beat the drum? This is a bell-ding-ding-ding. Hear how it rings. Come here, Ljusja, ring the bell, right this way. And that's a flute, listen how I play on it: too-too-too (she does not let them hold the flute).

Listen now! What is this sound? Stand up, turn your backs to me, and listen carefully. Stand, but do not turn, can you hear? Now turn around, and point out the instrument on which I played. Correct, Natasha guessed it. I played the flute. Again turn around and listen! What's this sound? Right, Vova guessed it. It's a drum".

To make the activity more complex, new instruments may be introduced. For instance, a triangle, a xylophone, a tambourine, rattles, etc.

"*What do I do?*"

Goal: to teach children to differentiate between different manipulation of various objects according to their sound.

For this activity one uses: a ball, 2 cubes, a speaking doll, etc.

Procedure: The children sit on chairs and the child-care worker is partly hidden behind a curtain (the curtain covers her up to the waist). Toys are hidden behind the curtain. The child-care worker tells the children to sit quietly, to listen, and to guess with what toy she is playing. She goes behind the curtain, takes a ball and bounces it on the floor. She asks one of the children: "Lena, what am I playing with?" If the child does not guess, she repeats the game and asks another child.

Then she bangs one cube against another etc. She should allow enough time to pass for the children to listen before asking what she is doing. If a child answers correctly the child-care worker and the children clap their hands.

Passive children should be called behind the curtain, where they can play with the toy, reproducing the same sounds.

Where does it ring? Where is Vova hidden?

The child-care worker gives one child a rattle or a bell, and suggests to the rest to turn their backs and not to look where their friend is hiding. The nurse may call the children to her so as to distract them.

In the meantime the child-care worker hides with the child and tells him to ring the bell. The children search for their hidden friend following the sound. The game is repeated if the children wish. Later the children may hide independently.

DIDACTIC GAMES FOR CONCENTRATION AND MEMORY

"Fix it the way it was"

Goal: to teach children awareness of changes in the arrangement of toys.

Four to five toys that are familiar to the children (a car, a doll, a doll's bed, etc.) are used.

Procedure: 10-12 children sit as usual. The adult faces them. She takes some toys from a bag, examines them together with the children, names them, and puts them on the table. "Children, look at the toys. See how are they arranged on the table? Come here, Natasha, look attentively, and remember where each toy is. Then you will turn around, and I'll move one of the toys. Then you look and tell me which toy I moved, and then you'll put it back where it was. Turn around". She moves the doll, puts it on the bed, and turns to Natasha: "Now you look and fix it as it was before, tell where the doll was. Right. The doll was not on the bed, but was here on a chair". Natasha returns to her place. The child-care worker calls another child and again repeats what she said to Natasha. When the child turns around, she puts the cubes on the can. In this manner by moving toys, she asks each child in turn to say what has been changed, and to put it back into place.

This game can be made more complex by increasing the number of objects. When the children have mastered the game, all the children can be asked to turn their backs while one of them moves the toys in the manner described above.

"What is missing?"

Goal: to determine which specific object has been hidden, when one out of a number of objects is hidden.

For this game one uses middle sized toys, or household articles (4-8 pieces).

Procedure: 10-12 children are seated, the child-care worker facing them.

"Children, look what I brought you! I'll put it on the table, and you name it". The children name the objects, the child-care worker puts them on the table and again names each toy. She covers the objects with a napkin, and unobserved by the children hides one in her cap. To arouse the children's attention, she counts to three and pulls off the napkin. "Children, who can tell what I hide? What's missing here? Who wants to tell? You, Natasha? Correct, Natasha, it was a doll. There it is, take it. Lets see again what we have". She names the objects, tells the children to identify them, and hides a new object in the same manner as described above. The game is repeated several times.

To elaborate the game more toys may be introduced. In the same way, one can carry out the game: "What is added?" To do this one begins with 3 objects, and gradually adds up to 5-6. By varying the objects on the table it is possible to include children with different levels of concentration and memory.

Surprises

Goal: to remember and to name objects that are wrapped up.

For this game one uses small objects and toys. Each toy is wrapped in a paper napkin (use one toy per child).

Procedure: A subgroup of 8-10 children are seated around two tables which have been joined. The child-care worker brings a box with wrapped objects and puts it on the table. "I brought you a box, in it are a number of small packages. I wonder, what's in them? Would you like to see?" She takes out a package, displays great interest in it and unwraps it. "What is it?" The children name the object. If the children do not name the toy, she does and puts it on the table. Then she puts a package in front of a child, suggests, that he unwrap it, tell what is inside and show it to the other children. In this way all the packages are unwrapped. The napkin is neatly put away. All the toys are put on the table, and the children examine them. She explains which object is used for what purpose, and describes it's color, form etc. Then the child-care worker suggests to each child to wrap the toys and put them back into the box. "What did you wrap up Natasha? And you, Vova? And you Kolja?" etc. In this way the child-care worker helps the children recall the name of the wrapped toy.

Guess what

Goal: to guess the action of the children.

Procedure: The children are seated as always, the adult is opposite them. She suggests to one of the children, to hide some place and not to look what the other children are doing. She poses a movement which the children imitate. For instance, all of them wash their face, comb their hair, drink from a cup, or lace their shoes, etc. The child-care worker suggests that the children call the absent child. She recites a poem familiar to the children. They repeat the poem after her.

Come back dear friend,
Do look at us,

PLAY AND ACTIVITY: SECOND AND THIRD YEARS

Guess, our friend,
What we're doing now,
We won't tell you,
What we're doing,
But we'll show you,
What we are doing.

The child approaches the group and the child-care worker and the children start to carry out the pre-agreed motion. After the child has guessed, he joins the circle and another child leaves the room. The game is then repeated.

Who went out?

Goal: to guess who leaves the room.

Procedure: Half of the group are sitting on chairs. There are chairs for participants. The child-care worker explains that they guess which child leaves the room. She calls 4 children. Three children sit in one row, and the 4th child sits opposite them. The child-care worker tells him to carefully examine the other three children, to name them, and to leave the room. One of the three children hides. The child who has to guess returns to his place: "Misha, look carefully and tell us who went out?" If he guesses correctly the hidden child runs out, and the children clap their hands. These four children then return to their places, and the child-care worker calls on 4 other children.

The game can be made more complex by increasing the number of children hidden (4 or 5) and having the others guess who they are.

ACTIVITY TO DEVELOP THE SMALL MOTOR MUSCLES OF THE HAND

Embroidery

Goal: to put a thread through an opening.

For this activity perforated cardboard strips are used. A thick colorful thread is tied to a hole. The activity is carried out individually.

Procedure: The child-care worker gives to a child a perforated strip of cardboard and shows him how to "embroider". At first the child is most likely to handle the thread clumsy but learns through practice how to pull the thread through the holes, in a manner that is pleasant and esthetic.

After the children have learned the method of embroidering, one should let them do it freely.

But the adult should watch, and see to it first that the children do their work with care and neither bend nor tear the cardboard. After they are done everything is put back into a box, and the box put into the cupboard.

Threading rings

Goal: to pull a thread through rings.

Rings with a small opening (1-0.5 cm), or colored beads painted in basic colors are used. The activity is carried out individually.

Procedure: The child-care worker hands the child a handful of "rings" and some thread or string. The string is knotted at the end; so that the ring should not slip off. The adult shows them how to hold the ring with the left and the string with the right hand, and to thread it through the ring.

Talk should be omitted to enable the child to concentrate. The adult however, may suggest to the child, to choose red rings only and to thread those only. The adult then asks the child to name the color of its ring. Should the child be mistaken, the adult should name the color. As soon as the child is finished threading all the rings, the child-care worker ties both ends of the string, compliments the child and suggests that he put the rings into a box. If the child is not tired, he may be given another string and rings.

After a child has acquired this skill he should be given an opportunity to work independently during quiet play activities.

Development of movements

The child perfects his movements during the third year of life. The task of muscle development during this period are: 1) to promote increasing perfection of crawling, walking, running and throwing; 2) to develop abilities to stop a movement in response to a specific signal; to develop the ability to change from one movement to another and to change the speed of movements; 3) to help to remove unnecessary associated movements, to form more economical rhytmic movements, and to develop proper posture.

The movements of children throughout the third year (as in children during the second year) develop in the course of everyday life. It is therefore of great importance to properly equip rooms and playgrounds for all seasons of the year.

Exercises in movement development are carried out in the form of gymnastics which follow definite rules (K.D. Cubert and M.C. Riss, 1963).

ORGANIZATION OF MOTOR GAMES

In addition to special exercises for the development of movement, special games are organized for this purpose. They are more complicated than before for children now in their third year.

Children in the third year can carry out a variety of movements, and thus achieve a number of definite activities. Running with the whole group in a definite direction, performing complicated gaits, jumping and

Fig. 21. The game "Bubbe" teaches children to move in coordination with one another.

hand movements, changing movements in the midst of a game are now possible.

In motor games the whole group participates. Each child has to coordinate his own movements to these of the whole group and he should not be isolated from the others (Fig. 21).

The rules of the game define the character of the movements, their direction, speed and changes in tempo. A text acquaints the child with these rules. (The text is often in form of a poem; which helps the children remember the rules.)

The adult when leading a new game takes a direct part at the beginning, later on she gives the children an opportunity to fulfill their role in the game by themselves.

The execution of motor games has a positive influence on the development of the child's character.

It directs their movements according to a definite plan, and teaches them to fill clearly defined roles (i.e. to imitate the movements of animals and children). These games stimulate lively movements and cause laughter.

To ensure a positive emotional state in a three-year old child, further training of the nerve mechanism (especially of the internal inhibition reflexes) takes place aided by motor games. The children have to learn to wait and then to shift from a state of inhibition of reflexes to a state of motor activity. They learn to execute the movements at a given signal, such as the calling out of numbers 1,2,3, or verbal instructions appropriate to the text of the game.

The change of movements during a game (in the third year the child can make as many as 5-6 changes) follows when a definite signal is given. The inhibition of reflexes is trained when a child has to catch-up in a game called "catch-up" or when a child has to pretend that he's asleep, inspite of the liveliness of the whole group, and "wake-up" at a definitive time.

The child-care worker has to differentiate between different games and to understand which of the games is easier, and which more complicated (depending on the quality and quantity of the movements and the training of the nervous system). She should give the children games in definite succession, taking into account the degree of complexity of each game.

When games are selected they should be chosen in accordance with the state of excitation of the nervous system of the children in a given group: if children in a particular group are more excitable, they should be given games which train inhibition. In contrast, if the children are passive or inactive, only games which demand much activity should be introduced.

One should consider not only the state of the group, but also the state of the individual child: If a child is passive or disinterested he should be given an active part. If the child is stimulated and active he may be chosen to act out the role of "catch-up" with another child.

Therefore the selection should be made purposefully, not merely by rote as is usually done. The training of the inhibition reflexes is most effective in motor games.

Firmly hold hands

After the child-care worker demonstrates and issues verbal instructions, the children hold their hands firmly and form a circle. One child stands in the center of it. The child-care worker sings a song and participates in the movements of the circle.

Words of the song	*Description of the movement*
1. We hold our hands firmly, And walk around Vova, Around Vova, around Vova, Around Vova we walk.	1. The children circle around Vova.
2. We run towards Vova, And we say "Hello Vova", "Hello Vova" (twice) "Hello Vova" we say.	2. The children walk with small steps to the center holding hands. On the words "Hello Vova" etc. they bow, holding hands and say Hello Vova etc. Vova also bows while standing in the center of the circle.
3. We'll walk from Vova, Far, far away, We walk away, Far, far away.	3. While holding hands the children walk backwards widening the circle. When the circle is widened, they stand on

PLAY AND ACTIVITY: SECOND AND THIRD YEARS   137

4. Vova, Vova dance for us, Your feet are strong, Dance, Vova dance, Your feet are so strong.	one spot and put out one foot, then the other. 4. All the children clap their hands. (The circle is broken.) Vova dances freely.
5. Vova danced so hard, so hard, And now our Vova ran, Ran away, far, far, Where oh where is Vova, Lost! He is gone.	5. Vova hides behind the child-care worker's back. All the children stop clapping hands and watch where Vova hides.

The child-care worker suggests to the children to call Vova. They all call: "Vova". Behind the child-care worker's back one hears a quiet "oh". The child-care worker suggests that they call out louder. The second time Vova replies "oh" louder. The third time the children call out very loud.and Vova replies as loud as they and comes out from behind the child-care worker's back.

Afterwards the game is repeated with a different child in the center.

> Comment: If there is more than one child, willing to be in the center, one can allow 2-3 children to stand together. The words can be changed accordingly.

An even circle

The children stand in a circle while holding hands. The child-care worker says:

> In an even circle
> You and I we walk,
> and now we stop,
> Wake up don't dream,
> Vova will tell us,
> And do as he says.

The child standing in the circle improvises some movements and the rest imitate him.

The child-care worker or the child standing in the center chooses another and the game is repeated.

A bell

The children sit on chairs in half a circle. The child-care worker faces them. One child holds a bell in his hand. The child-care worker says:

"I run, run, run,
I ring a bell,
Auntie got the bell,
I sit down".

Obeying the adults' instructions a child circles while ringing the bell. Then he returns the bell to the child-care worker, and sits down.

Another child gets the bell and the game is repeated. If he is too slow and does not end in time the adult may repeat the lines of the song.

Subsequently the bell is returned to the child-care worker who names the child whose turn it is.

A sparrow

"The children-sparrows" sit on chairs ("in nests") and pretend to "sleep", according to the words of the child-care worker.

Sparrows living in their nests woke up one early morning. The children open their eyes and holding hands sing:

"Squeeck-squeeck-squeeck,
Merrily they sing".

PLAY AND ACTIVITY: SECOND AND THIRD YEARS

Singing the children run around in the room. On hearing: "To the nest now fly", the children return to their seats.

The children and the bear

The children walk in the room. Suddenly the nurse or someone else appears with a bear. The children scatter and the child-care worker covers them with a large tablecloth (1.5 m × 1.5). The nurse (speaking for the bear): Where are the children?
The child-care worker: There are no children here.
The nurse: And who is this?
The child-care worker: This is a kitten.
The nurse: And why doesn't she say meow?

The children imitate the meow of a cat.

The nurse: Well, I don't need kittens. Goes away.

The children jump and dance. Again the "bear" appears. There is a conversation between the "bear" and the child-care worker. This time the children imitate dogs. While repeating the game, the children imitate different animals.

The game is repeated as often as the children wish.

The birds and bus

The children run in a crowd flapping their hands like wings. The child-care worker stands aside and sings.

> The birds are flying,
> Flying away,
> They fly, and fly and fly,
> They flapped their wings,
> They flew this way and that,
> They flapped their wings,
> Till they came to a road,
> Where they ate picked grains.

With the words to a road they come etc., the children stoop and tap their fingers on the floor (the birds pick grains).

The birds pick grain for some time. Then the child-care worker stops her singing. She takes a wheel in her hands, pretending to be a bus and she runs in the direction of the birds.

The children run to a place in the room - to the "nest" (which was agreed beforehand).

Then the game is repeated from the beginning.

Subsequently the role of the bus can be given to one of the children.

The hen and the chicks

One takes a hat for the hen, and a wheel.

One of the children is a "hen". It stands in the middle. Another child is a "driver" (it holds the wheel in its hands) and stands at one end of the room. At the end of the room the children are imitating chickens. They sit or stand around freely.

The child-care worker says:

"Hen-hen-little hen,
With your bright red comb,
She walks through the yard,
Loudly her song she sings:
Ku-ka-re-ku!"

"The child-hen" walks in the middle of the room, and at the word "ku-ka-re-ku" the child-care worker continues:

"The chicks run to the hen,
Run and flap your wings,
Go chicks pick some grains,

Tap tap the ground with your beaks.
Tuk-tuk-tuk".

On hearing the words, "the chicks run to the hen, run and flap your wings", the children raise their hands to their shoulders. To the words, "pick grain, tap the ground, etc.," all the children sit on the floor and tap their fingers on the floor.

The child-care worker continues:

"Suddenly a car drives by,
Toot-toot-toot,
Our chicks run away,
Toot-toot-toot".

To the words "suddenly a car drives by, toot-toot-toot" the child with the wheel runs to the center of the room and all the other children to their seats.

Good and bad weather

The child-care worker and the children sit in a "little house". The child-care worker says:

"The sun shines into the window,
It brightens our room.
We clap our hands,
'Cause the sun shines so bright".

The children clap their hands. The child-care worker invites them for a walk. They go out of the "house", and gather flowers and berries. Then the child-care worker says:

"It's raining, raining, drip, drop, drip,
All the roads are wet,
Let's run, hurry run!
Or we'll all be wet!
We'll all be wet".

All run towards the "house" and hide. The game is then repeated.

The bear in the pine forest

The nurse imitates a bear. The bear sits on a chair in a "den". The child-care worker and the children go to the bear, they bend over as if they are gathering mushrooms and berries:

"At the den where the big bear lives
I gather berries and mushrooms,
But the bear does not sleep,
And he growls at us.
Oh the bear hears us...
Oh, he runs after us!"

The children run away, and the bear catches up with them. After this, the game is repeated.

The chicken

The child-care worker, or a child, imitates a chicken, and the children imitate little chicks. The nurse, or one of the children, imitates a cat. The child-care worker says:

"A chicken went out,
With her yellow chicks.
'Ko-ko', do not go far away".
The chicken warns:
"On a bench near the road,
A cat lies fast asleep,
The cat open his eyes...
And runs after the chicks".

The mice and the cat

In one part of the room there is a "hole" for the mice, and on the opposite, a pantry, in it cubes, pine cones, and other small objects. At the side of the room there is a house for the cat. The nurse or one of the children plays the role of the cat, the child-care worker and the children play mice.

The cat falls asleep in her house, and the mice run from their "hole" to the pantry, where they eat food. The child-care worker recites a poem, the last line of which is a signal to catch the mice:

"The cat watches the mice,
But pretends to be asleep,
The mice are coming!
And the cat does hear,
They come closer, closer,
They all run from their holes...
Catch the mice!"

Upon learning the last word, the wide-awake "cat" catches "the mice".

The game is repeated 2-3 times.

Running and jumping over obstacles

A big circle is painted on a large floor or in a yard where children are about to run. A few obstacles are put up at a distance of 1.5-2 m from each other: a plank is placed for the children to jump over or step over it. A row of bricks are put up for the same purpose. The children should not ruin it. A plank is laid over two boards over which the children should walk. A rod is held across the plank. The children should either jump over, or crawl under it.

The children form a line and start jumping over the obstacles. The game can be carried out smoothly if the children who participate in it, do not differ sharply from each other in their motor ability and habits.

The obstacles are chosen according to the age and development of the children.

The merry geese

The children imitate geese. The child-care worker plays a grandmother and "sends" them to the yard.

The grandmother (calls the geese): Geese, geese!
The geese: Ga-ga-ga!
The grandmother: Do you want to eat?
The geese: Ga-ga-ga (or yes-yes-yes!)
The grandmother: Come along home!

The geese run to the grandmother bringing an imaginary bowl to each child. Following this she sings a song.

	Description of movement
Grandmother had some geese Ga-ga-ga (twice) The geese lived in a pond. They washed their feet right in the pond. Ga-ga-ga (twice) They are hiding in the rushes. Granny calls: "Where are you?, my geese. Are you lost, lost, my geese, my geese? Look here come the geese, And curtsy to grandma, Ga-ga-ga (twice) Bow to grandmother.	The geese "pinch grass" (while sitting or squatting on the floor, tap the floor with their fingers) They sing: "Ga-ga-ga" the children wash their feet with their hands while singing ga-ga-ga. They hide behind chairs. The Granny looks for her geese. The geese come and bow. They sing, ga-ga-ga, Granny sweetly strokes their heads.

A white hare sits

The children squat.
The child-care worker recites:
    A white hare sat,
    And wiggled his ears,
    This way, and that way he wiggled his ears.

The children move their hands above their heads, imitating the ears of a hare.

The child-care worker recites:
   The hare got cold while he sat,
   He ought to warm his paws,
   This way, that way,
   He ought to warm his paws.

The children rub, and clap their hands.

The child-care worker:
   Standing there, the hare felt cold,
   So he decided to jump,
   This way, that way, jumped the hare.

The children stand up, and jump with both feet.

The child-care worker:
   The hare sees a bear,
   And jumps away and whoop he jumps.

The child-care worker imitates the growl of a bear, and the children run into their "house".

Take care of the flag

   The children stand in a circle, their hands free, their faces turned to the center. The adult distributes flags to each child, and one for herself demonstrating various movements. For instance: the children march in one place, putting their flags on their shoulders or moving them (the child-care worker sings a marching song or counts off "one-two" etc.), they wave the flag calling "Hurrah". They knock the pole of the flag on the floor, holding it in a vertical position.

   After each such activity the child-care worker suggests putting the flag on the floor in front of each child. She sings a dance tune, and claps her hands. The children dance freely. Suddenly she stops singing, and says: "I shall take away the flag", and runs to the children, "trying" to grab up the flags, which are on the floor. The game is repeated if the children request it.

*Butterfly**

The children run about imitating butterflies.
The child-care worker says:
>In a green field,
>Butterflies are flying,
>They fly from flower to flower,
>Fluttering wings in the wind.

The child-care worker takes a butterfly net:
>Auntie went out to the fields,
>With a net in her hands,
>Take care butterfly,
>Or you'll find yourself in it!

The child-care worker catches one of the children, touching his head with the net. This child is "caught" and has to squat on the floor.

Airplanes

Flying airplanes have to be shown to the children before playing this game.

The children imitate airplanes. A place for the airplanes is marked off. Upon the adult's signal the children, with outstretched hands "fly, from the airport". The children have to maneuver so as not to collide. At the next signal "the airplanes" return to the airport. The game is repeated.

We raise our hands

The child-care worker has the children arranged in a half circle, and induces them to imitation, by saying "we raise our hands" (does it), "we put our hands down" (repeats a few times), "we put our hands down this way".

---
*A.I. Annfieeva and O.I. Mitiukova, "Play and Activity for Youngsters", M., 1962.

PLAY AND ACTIVITY: SECOND AND THIRD YEARS   147

The children repeat the movements after her and gradually they begin to carry these imitations on their own merely upon hearing the verbal instructions and no longer need to see the movement demonstrated.

Picking apples*

The child-care worker pretends to be an apple tree. She holds an apple or a ball in each hand. Her arms are "branches" moving in the wind. The children are to pick an apple. The children try to reach her hands so as to "pick an apple".

Games with balls

When playing with a ball, it is well to teach the children to use it independently when they play in a room, or when walking or while walking down a village street during summertime.

In ball games one can carry out the following movements: 1) rolling the ball downhill; 2) rolling the ball on a floor, and driving it through a wicket, rolling it on the ground and driving it into a hole; 3) catching a ball thrown by an adult, or catching several balls; 4) throwing a ball to each other standing in a circle; 5) throwing a ball to each other; 6) throwing a ball into some goal; into a basket or into a jar with water (at a distance of 1 meter); 7) hitting a target such as a hoop with a bell; 8) throwing a ball over a horizontal net; throwing a ball over a vertical net at the height of a child's outstreched arm.

Drawing and modelling

Drawing and modelling have a positive meaning in children's development. These processes heighten the child's perceptiveness and make it more specific. The

---

*A.I. Annfieeva and O.M. Mitiukova, "Play and Activity for Youngsters", M., 1962. The content is shortened.

child develops the ability to compare, fit objects according to size and form, and to differentiate a part from the whole, as well as developing speech, memory, and thought.

The child-care worker should teach children the specific use of materials and should arouse interest in drawing. She should teach them to recognize and name familiar objects in adults' drawings. During the first stage of teaching the child is gaining skill in holding a pencil. While making involuntary movements with a pencil on a sheet of paper he produces different shapes and lines.

At the beginning of the third year the child begins to name shapes ("a house", "a bird") but this is in fact imitation, a result of the children observing the adult specifying things he draws. There is not yet any recognition of objects through drawing itself. Only at the end of the first half of the third year the child may incidentally observe in his own drawings, something akin to an object he knows, and may mention the name of it; "Here I have a bird". Often after naming of an object the child announces: "I shall paint a bird!" and tries conciously to paint a figure, which reminds him of a bird and resembles a bird. Only at the end of the third year does the child begin to draw with premeditation, announcing beforehand what he will paint. For instance: "I'll paint a bird".

In the same manner the child develops his skill at modelling.

MODELLING

Activity I

Goal: to acquaint the child with clay and its characteristics. To stimulate interest in modelling and to learn to recognize objects modelled by an adult.

For modelling, specially prepared clay in the form of bars ought to be used.

PLAY AND ACTIVITY: SECOND AND THIRD YEARS

Procedure: 4-5 children sit at a table. The child-care worker distributes pieces of clay and says: "Children, here I have clay. Soft clay". In front of the children she kneads it, she asks the children to touch it. After all the children have tried to work with the clay, the child-care worker says: "From this big piece of clay, we can break off small pieces of clay, and from them we can roll some sticks. She demonstrates this on the table.

Activity II

Goal: to teach the first technical methods - rolling.

Clay in the form of balls (one for each child and one for the child-care worker) is taken.

Procedure: Same as above. She asks the children: "Kids, what do I have?" If a child names it, she agrees: "Correct, Vova, this is clay" and names it again: "Children, I have clay. I'll roll sticks. She breaks off small chunks and rolls sticks. She accompanies all her activities with explanations. After this, she distributes clay among the children and tells them to model. She follows and checks if they use it correctly, sees that they don't throw it around, and shows each child separately how to break it off and roll sticks. She must direct the child's hands. These activities are repeated until the children learn to carry out the elementary, specific actions with the clay. Afterwards the child can model with the whole group.

DRAWING

Activity I

Goal: to acquaint the child with pencil and paper. To stimulate interest in drawing. To teach the child to recognize images in the drawings of adults.

The children are given a sheet of paper, notebook sized.

Procedure: As usual she says: "Kids, look what do I have?" - and shows a pencil. If the children name it correctly, she agrees: "Yes, it's a pencil". In the same manner she asks about the sheet of paper. She says: "Look, I'll now draw something for you!" She draws a few horizontal and vertical lines. "See now I have a ladder. Do you want to draw too?" Responding to their positive answer she distributes paper and pencils, and shows them how to hold a pencil. They hold it with the fingers of the right hand, not too close to the end of the pencil. Then she demonstrates how to hold the paper. "Hold the pencil this way, and hold the paper with your other hand like this. Do not draw here, as here I have already drawn something". The child-care worker sees to it that the children use the paper and pencil as instructed and that they do not crumple the paper. They should not tap the pencil, and she must teach them how to press it gently on the paper, so that it makes lines, as the first movements of the child are very timid. If the child-care worker feels that interest in drawing is waning, she suggests that the materials be put where they belong and the drawings be given to her.

In the next exercises the child-care worker teaches the children how to draw straight, curved, and zig-zag lines. She teaches them how to close a circle or angular line, and gives some simple demonstrations of what can be drawn (a road, a ladder, a window, a ball, a sun, etc.). As with modelling, she should help the child see the similarities between the drawing and the object itself. "Look, you drew a line, and got a road". This encourages the child to self-examination of his own drawings.

If the child incidently finds a resemblance between his drawing and some object and names it, (for instance, he drew a round line and it reminded him of an apple, and he exclaims, "Oh, I got an apple!") -

PLAY AND ACTIVITY: SECOND AND THIRD YEARS

the child-care worker must emphasize this incidental resemblance, and ask the child to draw it again.

The adult herself draws in order to teach the children to draw something identifiable. First she tells the children what she intends to draw, and while drawing the different parts she explains: "Here is a round head, and here is a long tail" and thus stimulates the child to recognize what is being drawn. If, as happens the children have guessed the identity of the object from its individual parts, she stops drawing and asks the children what is still lacking. For instance, after having drawn a head, and a body, she stops, and asks: "What else should I draw? Correct, its got no feet" and while going on she says: "Here I drew legs below for the little girl". It is desirable, that she gives the children a sample of the objects that they will draw before the lesson. For instance, they can be given a ball, stressing that it is round, and suggesting that they touch it. It is proper to examine successful drawings with the rest of the children.

It is desirable to keep the children's work, as it reflects the developing drawing process during these activities.

Besides group drawing the children should be given the opportunity to draw singly. For that purpose there should be available a blackboard and chalk, pencils and sheets of paper. In different ways, the children should be encouraged to draw independently, using the methods described in group work (Fig. 22).

When they draw and model correctly and systematically 3 year-olds achieve the following: 1) they now know how to correctly use a pencil and clay; 2) they draw and model willingly, name their drawings and clay work, if an incidental likeness occurs, and recognize the object drawn or modelled by the child-care worker; 3) sometimes they predetermine what to draw, although usually they change to some new object in the middle of the activity; they may achieve a resemblance in their drawing even if only a vague one in relation to the real object.

Fig. 22. Natasha drew a fir tree independently.

in their drawing even if only a vague one in relation to the real object.

A construction activity

The two year old block building is simple manipulation. In the third year constructive manipulation begins.

From simple manipulation the child gradually arrives at constructional activity through observing the resemblance between his building and that of an object. Demonstrations and teaching how to use blocks so as to build a clearly defined object permits the children to begin to plan building by themselves.

Construction sets and building materials help develop creative initiative and imagination.

In addition to building material, nesting toys also develop constructional skills, they further concentration and encourage determination and exactness.

After mastering methods and use of different building materials, these should be given to the child for independent work.

For this activity a variation of building materials of varying geometric shapes, and construction materials such as rods and wheels should be used.

The aim is to stimulate interest in building, to teach the proper use of building and construction materials and to teach the child to carry out simple constructions which are first demonstrated by the adult.

Activity with building material

In addition to constructional materials of varied shapes (blocks, bricks, prisms, cones, boards, sticks, etc.) dolls and small animals may be used. Each child is given 8-10 items.

Procedure: Usual seating arrangement. The adult takes a set of building materials and builds something, accompanying her actions with words: "I'll build a house, I'll take some bricks, put them in a row, here are some more bricks and I'll put them on top", etc. Then she distributes building material to the children and suggests to each to build something they like. She helps and demonstrates how to use the materials correctly.

"For whom are you building a house? For dolly, Marusja? But how will Marusja go into the house? You should build a door". If the child is unsuccesful the adult does this building herself. While working she takes care to explain all she does paying careful attention to each child.

They may build various structures; a house, a garage, a ladder, a railroad etc.

Besides building with small material on a table, there should be more use of the floor with larger materials. This is done in the same manner but fewer children are involved.

Concentration and exactness of execution are developed with the following materials: toys accompanied with subjects of matching shapes, flat colorful mosaics, collapsible houses.

The set aim for the educator is to teach children to concentrate while building which demands exact, clearly defined execution and thus stimulates the child to achieve good final results.

Topical form boards

A form board with colorful cutouts, made up of simple objects such as a tower, a train, a mushroom, etc.

Procedure: 4 children and the child-care worker sit at a table. She holds a form board, examines the pictures together with the children and shows them how to fit the pieces into the spaces. Then she distributes the form boards, examines them with the children and helps them to fill them (Fig. 23).

A more complex way is to use a jig saw puzzle into which several pieces are inserted so as to make a picture. Form boards with geometric figures may be used as well.

Constructing houses

Four parts of a house and a colored roof are used for this.

Procedure: The child-care worker illustrates to the children how one builds a house from parts. She gives two parts of the house to the children, and shows them how to fasten them together, she helps them and finally adds the other parts (Fig. 24). Once the children have learned to work with this toy, they

PLAY AND ACTIVITY: SECOND AND THIRD YEARS   155

Fig. 23. Topical form boards require concentration and attention.

may work with it independently. It is necessary to see to it that they conclude the activity so as to obtain a successful result. They should put the toys back in place.

Entertainment

Entertainment for children in the third year includes: 1) games: "Hide and Seek" and "Catch-up" (see p. 128); 2) mechanical toys (they have to be more complex than in the second year); 3) plays: shadow plays, puppet shows; 4) children's holidays.

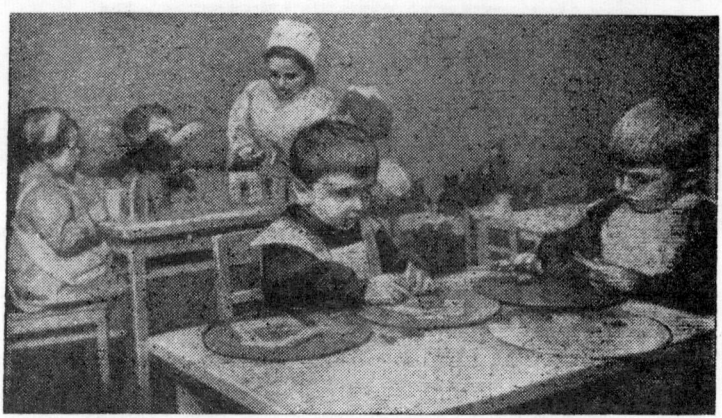

Fig. 24. Constructing houses demands exactness of movement.

Shadow plays

Shadow plays are performed with a screen, on which flat cardboard cutouts or plywood figures, are held against the back of it, leaving shadows. When the figures are moved their shadows move as well. One may show the children not only single figures, but full-scale plays (Fig. 25).

A piece of plain tracing-paper is stretched over a 110 × 120 cm frame. The screen with a curtain in front is put so that it is between the source of light and the children. Thus, during the day the light should be from the window, in the evening from a lamp placed behind the screen.

The figures (which should be in profile), should be drawn first on paper, and then transferred onto cardboard or plywood. To make the cardboard figures firm, a double thickness of cardboard is used.

If part of the figure is to be movable (a hand, a leg, or the head) it should be cut out separately and fastened to the figure with a string. Another string

PLAY AND ACTIVITY: SECOND AND THIRD YEARS   157

Fig. 25. Demonstration of a shadow theatre play "The Tower Room".

is attached to the movable part and is used to pull the parts. Finally, a round piece of wood (a pencil may be used) is glued to the center figure and is used as the handle.

The size of the figure should be 13 to 30 cm. and exact proportions between figures are not necessary. For instance, a chick can be a quarter of the size of the little girl and a chicken twice as large as the chick! The figures can be colored in order to give a brighter impression. To achieve this an opening is cut in the figure, and covered with colored cellophane.

The crows

Figures: Two crows and a pine tree, the text is read by the leader.

The leader: The forest is quite still. Two crows are flying. They start to jump under the pine tree.

Under a green pine tree
Jump and caw two crows:
Caw-caw, caw-caw!
How they fight over a crust,
Loudly they fight and shout:
Caw-caw, caw-caw!

The crows (they fight in the air, and afterward sit on the ground under the pine tree).

The leader: Came night and they fell silent and quietly went to sleep.

The chick

Figures: A chick, a rooster, worms, a black cat, a hen, a frog.

The leader: Once upon a time there lived a chick. He was little, this way (shows it). But he thought himself very big and he proudly lifted his head, like this (shows it). He had a mother. His mother loved him very much. His mother was like this (shows it). Mother fed him worms and flies. And the worms were like this (shows it). Once a black cat jumped at the mother hen and chased her out of the yard (the hen and cat disappear). And the black cat was like this (shows it). The chick was left all alone in the yard. Suddenly he saw a rooster at the gate. The rooster stretched his neck and loudly called "Ku-ka-re-ku" - then he proudly looked around to all sides.

"Am I not a fine fellow?
Am I not a bold fellow?"

The chick liked it very much. He also stretched his neck - like this (shows it). And with all his strength began to squeak:

"Peep-peep-peep!
I too am a fine fellow!
I too am a bold fellow".

PLAY AND ACTIVITY: SECOND AND THIRD YEARS   159

But he stumbled and fell into the puddle - this way. In the puddle there sat a frog. It saw him and laughed.

"Ha-ha!!! Ha-ha!!!
You have a long way to go
To match the rooster!"

And the frog was like this (shows it). Now his own mother ran to him, she felt sorry for him, stroked him, and kissed him - like this.

The squirrel

Figures: A squirrel, two children, a sled, two pine trees.

Two children arrive at the forest. They have a sled and they watch a squirrel jump from branch to branch on a pine tree. The leader says:

The squirrel on a pine tree
Jumps up and down.
Hold on you little, squirrel
With your paws hold on, hold on to the pine tree.

The children address the squirrel:

Furry, curly, little squirrel,
Wait, don't move,
We shall catch up with you,
We shall snatch you,
And bring you home with us.

The children take the squirrel and put it on the sled. The squirrel jumps off and runs to the pine tree. The show ends with the children catching the squirrel and taking it home.

A ladder

Figures: A ladder with five rungs, a little girl, a boy, a mother, a hen, a cat, a dog.

A ladder stands in the yard. It has five rungs. A hen jumped onto the first rung. She flapped her wings, and sang loudly. "How did she sing, children?" (The children imitate).

A cat jumped on the second rung. She sat there and licked herself with her tongue and purred. "How does she purr?" (The children imitate the purring of the cat.)

And the dog jumped onto the third rung. He wagged his tail on the rung and he growled at the cat. "How does he growl, children?" (The children imitate the growling of a dog).

The boy climbed onto the fourth rung. He sat there, looking down to the ground and dangled his legs. "How does he dangle his legs, children?" (The children dangle their legs).

And the little girl sat on the last rung and sang a song: "We sit on the ladder and sing songs". "How does she sing, children?" (The children sing). Suddenly the wind blows. "How does it blow?"

Quickly, softly the raindrops patter. "How do the raindrops patter?" (The children tap their fingers on the floor.)

The hen flapped her wings, jumped under the porch and hid herself. The dog also crawled there.

The cat jumped ever so cleverly through the open window. "How did she jump, children?"

But both the children sat on the ladder, they could not climb down, and they sat and cried. "How did they cry, children?"

Then mother came to the porch, and took the children off the ladder. They stamped with their feet on the porch. "How did they stamp, children?" (The children stamp with their feet.)

The children went inside the house, and ladder was left all by itself.

Any story can be adopted for such shadow plays.

PUPPET SHOWS

Puppet shows make good entertainment for children. Their educational significance is quite great. A puppet show enriches the children with new impressions.

Fig. 26. An interesting show arouses many emotions in children.

It is easier for children to grasp the meaning of stories when they are acted out with puppets than when they are simply related verbally or shown in pictures.

Puppet shows bring happiness to children, cause merry laughter, stimulate concentration, and sustain attention, and generate feelings such as sympathy, etc. (Fig. 26).

Puppet shows have great influence on the child's speech. Reacting directly to the plot, the child responds, gives a clue, and answers when queried by the puppet.

The puppet show should not be cumbersome. The height of the stage should be constructed so as to hide an adult with outstretched hands. The stage can be improvised - for instance a curtain falling to the floor, which is held up by a string stretched between open doors.

During a puppet show, one adult - the leader - should be among the children, while one or two adults play the roles of puppets.

The adult - the leader - sits among the children, sometimes stands up and walks to the screen, talks with the children and with the dolls, and explains the action or the plot to them. (The head and the hand of the adults behind the stage should not be visible.) The players should enunciate clearly and slowly, so that the children can follow the plot.

The imitation of sounds (the barking of a dog, the growling of a bear etc.) should be neither sharp, nor frightening. The adults manipulating puppets should be well acquainted with their roles. If the children become overstimulated the show should be slowed down or stopped and continued when the children are calm again. At the end of the show, the puppets should be removed so as not to be seen by them in ugly poses, like with hanging heads, wide-spread legs, etc.

The seating arrangement should be planned well so the children can see the show. It's preferable not to seat them at the sides, but rather in two rows directly in front of the stage.

The stage which is used for puppet shows is illustrated in Fig. 27.

Two houses

Participants: 2 cats, 2 dolls, a dog. Stage decoration: Two houses with open windows, with porches facing each other. Between the houses free space (about 75-100 cm.). Near the houses are bushes, trees (made from cardboard, plywood, or branches). The windows are open. Nobody is seen.

PLAY AND ACTIVITY: SECOND AND THIRD YEARS   163

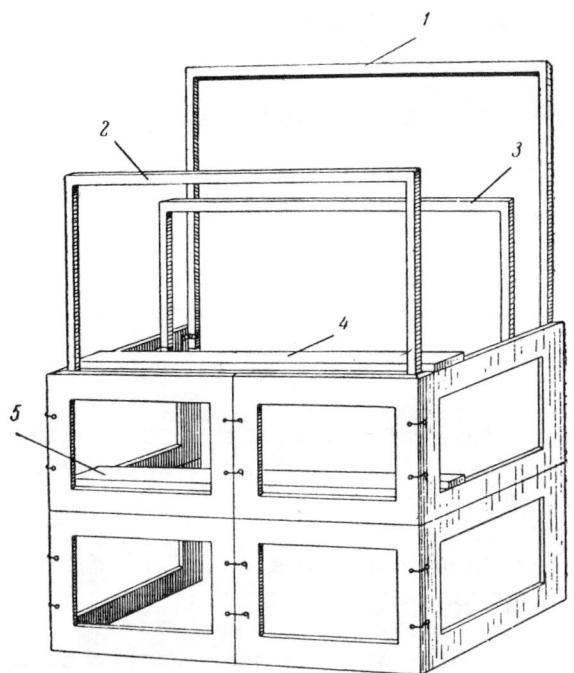

Fig. 27. A stage for puppet shows. 1-lath (rod) for the backdrop; 2-lath for the curtain; 3-lath for stage decorations; 4-shelf for stage; 5-shelf for props. (Constructed by M.I. Voskresenskoi)

The leader (*standing near the stage*): there are two houses. Who lives in them? Soon we shall know. We'll knock... Knock, knock, knock. Open!

A cat is seen in the window.

The leader: The cat looks out of the first window. Look at her. She is white and she wears a bow.

A cat looks out from the second window.

The leader (*in amazement*): Another cat looks out from the second window! Let's call the cats to go for a walk.

The cats come out of the houses through the porches.

The leader: What lovely cats, what meow! I'll stroke them.

The cats approach each other.

The leader: Children! Do you want to see how the cats are bouncing a ball (or a piece of paper)?

The children: Yes-yes...

The leader plays with the cats. Suddenly a dog appears on the stage, it barks and disappears. The cats run away.

The leader: Oh-oh-oh! The cats hid themselves, they can't be found!

The leader (*searching for the cats*): Let's knock again! Knock-knock. Open, answer our knock (twice).

Two dolls show themselves in turn.

The leader: Oh, who lives here - Marusia and Katia? Marusia and Katia! Come to us... Children invite Marusia and Katia!

The children: Come to us! Come to us!

The dolls (*from the window*): Well, alright, we'll come. Marusia, let's go, Katia, let's go.

The dolls (*coming out of the houses*): Hello, kids! Here we are. Kids, have you seen our kitties? Ks-ks-ks (*the cats appear*). Here are our cats! How nice, nice! We love them so much! (*They stroke the cats*). We have to feed the cats some milk. (*They give them a saucer with milk.*) Drink, drink! Now, we'll take the saucer away. (*They take it away.*)

The dolls go back into the house, the barking of a dog is heard, the cats run away.

The dolls: What a dog! He came again, and the kitties ran away, and hid themselves. Let's play ball. (*The children clap, and the dolls return with a ball*). Catch, Marusia! Catch, Katia! Again, again! (*about 10 times*) Enough! We have played enough, and now we'll put the ball back in place... We want to dance now. Clap your hands for us, kids.

The dolls dance, the children clap. The dolls bow; thank the children and give them a beautiful small package. They say: "Here you have a beautiful kerchief. Now you shall dance".

The children: Thank you, thank you.

The dolls: Good-bye, bye.

The children part from Marusia and Katia, and a children's dance begins with colored kerchiefs.

The whiskered and striped

The participants: A girl, a boy, a cat. Stage decoration: A bed on the right, and a table with dishes on the left. The bed is 25 cm. long, 10 cm. wide. The dishes, from which the girl feeds the cat, should be made of wood or of papier-maché. The adult who plays the girl should put the dishes on the table, and make the bed and put the kitten in it. The kitten should be very mobile, all the time playing and being naughty.

The leader (*comes out from behind the stage*).

Once upon a time there lived a little girl,
And what was she called?
Those who named her knew, but you don't know...
And she had... What did she have?
It is gray, whiskered, and striped.
What is it?

A cat appears on the stage. The leader stands up and strokes the cat. She continues stroking the cat's head between the ears until the children calm down, and stop talking about the cat. Then the kitten, surprising the adult, sniffs and walks away to the opposite side of the stage. Next a little girl appears. She holds a pillow, a sheet, and a blanket, and begins to make the bed.

    The girl: Here you have a feather-bed.
             On the feather-bed
             A clean sheet.
             Under your head,
             White pillows.

(*Comes near the kitten and puts it on the bed, with its face towards the children.*)

    A blanket on the feather-bed, covered with a kerchief.

    (*Covers the kitten with the blanket*)

    The leader: She puts the kitten to sleep, and goes to have dinner.

    The girl goes away. The kitten hides its head under the blanket and unobserved by the children turns around, so that its head is where its feet are supposed to be, with it's tail on the pillow. The girl comes in, and throws back the blanket.

    The girl: What is this?

On the pillow a tail,
On the feather-bed ears,
Who sleeps this way?

(*She shakes her head disapprovingly and puts the kitten back on the bed as before.*)

Under the bed – a feather-bed,
On the feather-bed – a sheet,
Under the head – pillows.
(*Walks away.*)

The kitten jumps up and begins to play with the blanket, throws it off the bed, and throws the pillow to the spectators, throws off the sheet, and crawls under the bed. Now only the end of its tail is seen.

The girl (*comes in*): What is this? (*Looks around, throws up her hands, and strokes her head.*)

Neither the feather bed, nor the sheets,
Nor can the pillows be seen.
And the whiskered one with the stripes
Has moved under the bed.

Who sleeps this way? What a dumb kitten! (*Pulls the kitten out from under the bed.*)

The leader: Our little girl begins to teach the kitten to speak.

The girl:(*Placing the cat in front of her*): Kitten, say: "Grandmother".

The kitten: Meow.

The girl: Say: "Horse".

The kitten: Meow.

The girl: Say: "Daddy".

The kitten: Meow.

The girl: What a dumb kitten!

The leader: Now she begins to feed the kitten.

The girl: Here, in this cup there is oatmeal.

(*Takes a cup from the table puts it in front of the little kitten. The kitten smells it and walks away.*)

  The girl: Well now he doesn't like it.
      Here in a saucer,
      You have onion and radishes.

(*Puts it in front of the kitten. The kitten comes near, sniffs and goes away.*)

  The girl: And still he doesn't like it,
      Here is a saucer full of milk.

(*Puts the saucer in front. The kitten moves slowly. The girl calls him: "ks-ks-ks". The kitten comes back and laps up the milk.*)

  The girl: Oh, what a dumb kitten! (*Caresses the cat, strokes its head. The kitten finishes drinking and washes its fur.*)

  The leader: The girl covers the kitten with a scarf and goes with the kitten.

The girl puts a scarf on the kitten and leaves. Everything is taken off the stage and a tree is put there. The girl comes in, holding the kitten in her arms like a small child. She sits down and sings a lullaby. From the left side a boy comes in and approaches the girl.

  The boy: Who is it? (*He tries to look under the scarf.*)

  The girl: This is my daughter.(*She swiftly turns away from the boy. The boy runs to the other side, and looks under the scarf.*)

  The boy: Why does your daughter have such a gray face?

  The girl (*Turns away from the boy*): Because she has not washed in a long time.

PLAY AND ACTIVITY: SECOND AND THIRD YEARS   169

The boy: Why does she have such fury paws and whiskers like a father?

The girl: She has not shaved for a long time.

The leader: And suddenly the kitten jumps and runs and all saw that it was a kitten.

The kitten jumps out from under the cover, the girl runs after him. The boy claps his hands. All of them go away.

The bear's den

The participants: A hare, a fox, a bear, a snow-maiden. Stage decoration: fir trees covered with snow, 3 shovels, a lantern a broom. The hare appears.

The leader: Children, look a hare came hopping in. What nice fur, how fluffy, and white like snow.

The hare (*bows, hops and sings*):

I am a little hare,
But what a brave one.
I am never cold in winter,
In my warm fur coat.

Dances and runs away. A fox and bear appear.

The leader: Now the fox and bear have come. Kids let's listen what they are talking about.

The fox (*shivers*): Hello clumsy bear. My paws are frozen!

The bear (*growls*): Hello, red-headed fox, the frost froze my ears and nose!

The fox: Let's go, bear, let's go to your den and warm up a little!

The bear: How can we find the house? It's dark all around.

The fox: Hare, hare, come here. Lighten the way for us!

The hare comes out with a lantern.

The hare: Here is a lighted lantern. Where is your home, bear?

The bear (*growls*): I lost the way in the snow. I cannot find my den!

The hare: Enough bear, don't growl. We'll go and search for your den.

The fox: Hare, go-go-go. Lighten the road for us.

They walk. First the hare, after him the fox, and hobbling at the end the bear. They go and sing.

> Winter, winter, cold, cold winter,
> Snow drifts high over everywhere,
> We cannot find our way,
> To the den of the big brown bear.

A snow-maiden appears.

The leader points out to the children what the snow-maiden is dressed in.

The snow-maiden: About what are you crying, animals? Your ears, your poor frozen ears.

The bear: Snow-maiden, please help me. Please find the way to my home.

The snow-maiden: Don't, don't growl, good bear. Let's clear the road.

The hare (*carrying shovels on its back*): Here are the shovels!

PLAY AND ACTIVITY: SECOND AND THIRD YEARS   171

  The fox: Here is a broom.

  The snow-maiden: Thank-you, red fox!

  The bear: Give me the broom. I'll clear the road.

  The fox: And I'll remove the snow with the shovel.

  The hare: I too will help!

They all clear the road and sing.

  We all clear the road,
  We clear the road.
  And proudly sing a song,
  We warmed up a bit.
  We can see the den.

  The bear: Snow-maiden, thanks, thanks for your help.

  The hare: You found the way to the house!

  The snow-maiden: Let's meet again all of us, let's meet on New-Years!

  The hare: I'll light the fir-tree. It will be joyous here!

Hangs the lantern on the tree. They all sing.

  We worked a bit,
  And found the den,
  What a lovely home,
  The bear has.

They dance and all the animals follow the bear into his den.

Our garden

    Participants: A watchman-grandfather, a hare.

    Stage decoration: Green leaves to represent a garden, a carrot.

    The watchman (*walks around the garden and stops*): What a green garden we have! Soon we'll have carrots! I'll watch the garden, so that nobody will steal the carrots. (*turns to the children*) Children, I'll rest on the grass for a while and if you see somebody coming, you'll call out to me: "Uncle Nicolai, get up". Well, what will you say?

    The watchman: That's good, kids (*makes another round and goes to sleep*).

    A hare appears, first in one place, then another, runs through the garden and begins to nibble a carrot.

    The children: Uncle Nicolai, get up!

    The watchman does not wake up for some time, then jumps up, and looks around. In the meantime the hare runs away.

    The watchman: Who came? Who is here? Nobody is here. Why did you wake me up, children? (*The watchman falls asleep again; the hare comes back. The children wake the watchman, he wakes up, sees the hare and calls out.*) Catch him! Catch him! Shut the gate! (*runs and catches the hare*) Well, well, I finally caught him. Now the hare will live with me. I'll build a cage for it. (*strokes the hare*) Here, I'll sing a song for you. (*sings a song*).

    Hare, dance,
    Gray one, dance!
    This way, that way dance,
    Dance, dance, dance!

The hare doesn't dance, only looks around.

PLAY AND ACTIVITY: SECOND AND THIRD YEARS

The watchman: Why don't you dance, hare? Perhaps you want some carrots?

The hare nods its head. The watchman brings a carrot, the hare grabs it with two paws, and begins to nibble. When he is done, it begins to dance while the watchman sings.

The watchman (*sings*):

Hare, hare clap your hands, gray one clap your hands. This way, this way clap your hands (*twice*). Hare, stamp your feet, gray one stamp your feet. This way, this way stamp your feet (*twice*). Hare, dance, my gray one dance. This way, this way dance (*twice*).

You danced well, hare. Now let's go. I'll show you your house. (*The watchman leaves with the hare, and returns without it.*) The children introduce themselves, the teacher dresses one of them like a hare and the child dances. Thus the dances are repeated a few times. Some children are chosen to be watchmen.

The watchman: Well, kids, fine fellows! Well, good-bye. I'll go home, and you have a fine time, and watch my garden! Leaves.

HOLIDAYS IN CHILDREN'S HOMES

Entertainment is part of the children's holiday celebrations. Holidays are celebrated 4 times a year: The Holiday of the Fir-tree, The Holiday of the 1st of May, The Summer Holiday, and the Holiday of the Great October Revolution.

The content of the holidays are related to the four seasons of the year. The events of general life are also reflected in the May Day and Revolution Day Celebrations.

During the holiday celebrations the children play games which they like best, sing songs and dance. The program is carefully prepared ahead of time.

Methods for the celebration of holidays are described in a book by T.S. Baladzan, "Holidays for children in children's centers and homes", M., 1957.

PLANNING OF PLAY AND ACTIVITIES

Plays and activities are planned a month in advance.

For one-year old children plays and activities are planned: 1) separately for each age group, taking into consideration their level of development; 2) individually, giving special care to children who are in need of it.

In a group of one-year old children there may be several regimes, and each age group will be engaged during different hours of the day (according to schedule) in addition to morning and evening periods. During waking time the teacher has to carry out activities with a subgroup. Individual activities are carried out mainly with regard to movement development. Demonstrations and musical activities are carried out in a subgroup of 3-4 children. Each activity is practiced for a few days until the desired results are achieved. For instance, "showing a doll", is practiced until the children turn their heads and follow a doll with their eyes when being asked "where is dollie?"

An approximate plan for play and activities for one-year olds

Natasha Ivanova 2 months	Teach to search for a rattle
Petia Petrov 3 months	Teach to follow movements of a red flag.
	Place on belly and hold in arms, to promote head control.

PLAY AND ACTIVITY: SECOND AND THIRD YEARS

Luisa Semenova 3 1/2 months	Teach to catch and hold a toy.
Lidia Kruglikova 3 1/2 months	Teach to turn from back to belly, encourage crawling.
Sasha Gubin 4 months	
Olia Stepanova 6 months	Teach to turn from belly to back.
Igor Titov 7 months	Teach to repeat syllables, demonstrating a doll, cat, dog, bear, "pat-a-cake", good-by, play hide and seek.
Sasha Gruzdev 8 months	
Lena Shorova 8 1/2 months	
Grisha Ilin 9 months	Teach to walk over barrier, to put spherical objects in a container.
Tamia Orlova 10 months	Play "who lives in the house?"
Goja Lukina 10 1/2 months	Hiding and finding toys.
Vera Drozdova 11 months	Teach to thread rings on a rod, closing and opening of nesting toys.
Oleg Muthin 12 months	First steps, collecting of scattered toys.

For two-year olds one has to enumerate the different activities during the (semester) and make bimonthly plans for children from the age of 1 year to 1 year and 6 months and from 1 year and 6 months to 2 years. The number of activities during a week are distributed as shown in Table 1.

In children's homes, where they spend 24 hours, the number of activities has to be increased by one in each division.

When planning activities with children older than a year and 6 months one has to consider that the children are outdoors every day. Therefore, in winter half of the activities take place in the yard, and during summer all the activities should take place outdoors in the fresh air.

The group of 2 year old children (the middle group) live with two regimes. Children up to 1 year

TABLE 1. An approximate plan of activities with children from 1 year up to 2 years of age

Name of the activities	Until 1 year and 6 months	Until 2 years
Development of speech and orientation to surroundings	4-5 activities	7-8 activities
Developing play with objects	3-4 activities	4 activities
Entertainment	2 activities	3 activities
Musical activities	2 activities	2 activities

and 6 months are activated twice: at 13 o'clock (after dinner) and at 14.30 (before putting them to sleep). Children from 1 year and 6 months are activated at 9 o'clock (after breakfast) and at 16.30 (after tea). The content of the first part of activities in both subgroups should be more complicated, and require more concentration, than will the second part. Besides these two activities, additional ones with the older group (from 1 year and 6 months) should be carried out which consists of motor games or organized observations.

Since two-year olds have still a low level of receptivity for special activities, the same games and activities have to be repeated 2-3 times a week.

Gymnastics are carried out every week with a third of the group, considering that each child should participate twice a week. Gymnastics is not put into the weekly description of the activities but is fixed in the planning of the day.

PLAY AND ACTIVITY: SECOND AND THIRD YEARS

AN APPROXIMATE ENUMERATION OF PLAY AND ACTIVITIES WITH TWO YEAR OLD CHILDREN

Development of speech and orientation in the environment

    Demonstration of objects with names: "wonderful bag" (using 3 objects until 1 year and 6 months and 4-5 objects after 1 year and 6 months).

    Topical demonstrations: up to 1 year and 6 months: "Who lives in the little house?", "fetching of dolls", "swimming ducks".

    From 1 year 6 months: "the hare and the carrot", "A bird sat at the window", "the girl and the hen".

Showing of live animals

    Oriented walks: until 1 year and 6 months in the playroom - learn to know with dishes, from 1 year and 6 months in the yard - learn to know about driving in cars.

    Activity with pictures: until 1 year and 6 months, naming pictures, from 1 year and 6 months telling stories from pictures.

    Activities for imitation: imitating the sounds of animals.

    Obeying orders: "give", "bring", "show".

    Story telling, conversation: stories about cats, or other topics chosen by the child-care worker.

    Development of movement: gymnastic exercises, motor games: up to 1 year and 6 months: rolling a ball to each other, "I'll catch-up, catch-up", hiding, from 1 year and 6 months: "Kids and a dog", let's play "hide and seek", thowing a ball into the basket.

    Developing actions with objects: play with blocks, nesting toys and with towers.

Entertainment: reflection of a sunbeam, toys with motors.

Tables 2 and 3 give an approximate monthly plan for children's activities.

TABLE 2. An approximate monthly plan for play and activities with children from 1 year to 1 year and 6 months.

Days of the week and dates of the month	Activity	
	1st	2nd
Monday: 6,13,20,27/1	Wonderful bag	Threading rings on a rod
Tuesday: 7,14,21,28/1	Wonderful bag	Threading rings on a rod
Wednesday: 8,15,22,29/1	Musical activity	Wonderful bag
Thursday: 2,9,16,23,30/1	Demonstration "Who lives in the house?"	Threading rings on a rod
Friday: 3,10,17,24,31/1	Same as above	Rolling a ball to each other
Saturday: 4,11,18,25/1	Musical activity	Game "I'll catch-up"

TABLE 3. An approximate monthly plan for play and activities with children from 1 year and 6 months to 2 years.

Days of the week dates of the months	First activity	Observation walks	Second activity
Monday: 6,13,20 27/1	Looking at pictures	Driving in a sled	Activity with nesting toys
Tuesday: 7,14, 21,28/1	Musical activity	Feeding birds	Throwing a ball into a basket
Wednesday: 8,15, 22,29/1	Demonstration: "The little girl and the hen"	Shoveling snow	Activity with nesting toys
Thursday: 2,9, 16, 23, 30/1	Looking at pictures	Driving in a sled	Activity with building material
Friday: 3,10,17, 24,31/1	Musical activity	Feeding birds	Throwing a ball into a basket
Saturday: 4,11, 18, 25/1	Demonstration: "The little girl and the hen"	Shoveling snow	Game, kid and the dog

For three-year olds the same as two-year olds, a quarterly plan is made. A calendar plan is made for each month. The number of activities with children for two-year olds for a week is organized in this way:

Name of activity	Number of activities within a week
Developing of speech and orientation within the environment	9-10
Motor games	2-3
Didactic games	3-4
Painting and modelling	2
Construction activity	1
Entertainment	1
Musical activity	2

Gymnastics take place in the same manner as with 2 year old children.

Accepting the fact that 3 year old children already acquire some personal experience and orientation within their environment has considerably widened activities once a week. Activities with new materials may be introduced for instance, working with clay for the first time or some didactic games. New activities should be performed in a subgroup of 10-12 children. The other activities may be executed in the third year with the whole group. The activities are carried out in the building from 9 o'clock and outdoors at 16.30. After these games the children play independently for some time.

AN APPROXIMATE PLAN FOR PLAY AND ACTIVITIES WITH 3 YEAR OLDS DURING THE SPRING (MARCH, APRIL, MAY)

Development of speech and orientation to the surroundings

Planned observations: The sun is shining, the snow is thawing, puddles are formed, the birds chirp in the spring; there are buds on the trees, the first flower and the appearance of grass.

Sightseeing walks and excursions: To see how the buildings are decorated for the 1st of May; see a shop window; see a kitchen. Play: "The bears' holiday"

PLAY AND ACTIVITY: SECOND AND THIRD YEARS

"A ladder" (E.Yu. Shabad), "Before going to sleep".

Activities with pictures: Looking at pictures, "Katia in the nursery" by L. Aleksandrovi and "Toys" by A. Barto; showing a film, showing slides, "The wolf and the seven goats", "The hares' house".

Conversation: Where did the children go on Thursday? About the children's many holidays.

Poems: "Sparrows", "Holiday".

Stories: "About a little girl", "Bird".

Didactic games: "What is missing?", "A lot - a little", "Say who is it?", "Guess", "What is ringing?"

Recognizing the toys by touch. Rolling of global objects. Matching pictures. Embroidery.

MOTOR DEVELOPMENT

Gym exercises. Motor games (The "Red-chicken", "Holding hand firmly", "Take care of the flag", "Sparrows", "With the bear in a pine forest").

PAINTING AND MODELING

Construction activity: Putting a little house together.

Entertainment: Films, dolls' theatre.

The monthly plan is described on page 171, Table 4.

TABLE 4. An approximate plan with children in the third year of life

Days of the week dates of the month	1st activity	1st observation and walk	2nd activity	2nd observation and walks
Monday: 4,11,18, 25/	What is missing?	Observing buds on branches	Modelling	Game: "Sparrows"
Tuesday: 5,12,19, 26/	Musical activity	Game: "Holding hands firmly"	Demonstration: "Teddy bear's holiday"	Observing the first flowers
Wednesday: 6,13, 20,27/	Story: "The bears' house"	Playing with sand	Painting	Game: "The red chicken"
Thursday: 7,14, 21,28/	Recognizing toys by touch	Observing birds	Projector story	Stepping over a board
Friday: 8,15,22, 29/	Musical activity	Playing on sand with sticks	Game: "What is the sound?"	Observing transportation
Saturday: 9,16, 23,30/V	Activity with pictures "Katia in the nursery"	Observing the unfolding of leaves	Putting houses together	Walking on a log

TABLE 1. Orientation index of speech development in children from 1 year to 3 years constructed by the Pediatric Department (by Docent N.M. Aksarina)

Understanding	Ability to imitate speech sounds	Vocabulary
Index of speech development of 1 year old children		
Understands the name of several objects and actions (by hearing the word without gestures) for instance; mama, aunty, meow, give, hand, dolly, take, sit, stand up, good-by, etc.	Easily imitates pronounced words which are familiar to him. One can arouse imitation to new basic sounds.	Pronounces a few words (within them 10 meaningful) that means, which designate some persons, objects, actions, for instance, bow-wow-dog, m-m-m-food, etc.
From 1 year to 1 year 6 months		
The vocabulary of meaningful words is increasing rapidly, that means, that contact is established between objects and their name. Child understands names of objects and actions, carries out simple verbal requests.	Easily imitates sounds, which are heard often. In his babbling he reflects the speech of an adult.	The vocabulary is about 30 words. Some words begin to have a general meaning, for instance, a dog means any dog (a white, black, a live or toy a big or small dog). There are many easily pronounced words (beep-beep, tu-tu, etc.)

TABLE 1. Orientation index of speech development in children from 1 year to 3 years constructed by the Pediatric Department (by Docent N.M. Aksarina) Continued.

Grammar	Use	Intonation	Articulation
Index of speech development of 1 year old children			
		Babbles emotionally expressively	In his babbling there a are many various sounds and their combinations
From 1 year to 1 year 6 months			
Speaks with separate words, which have the meaning of a sentence	Continues to babble, he uses basically words in moments when he's very interested, happy, surprised or during some other emotional experiences		

TABLE 1. Continued

Understanding	Ability to imitate speech sounds	Vocabulary
From 1 year 6 months to 1 year 10 months up to 2 years		
Understands the meaning of a whole sentence, describes happenings and events of his life. With a word one can change the child's condition and complicate his actions.	Easily repeats words pronounced by adults, words and simple sentences (understands them in a mechanical way).	The active vocabulary is rapidly increased and at the end of the second year a child uses around 300 words. The simplified words are exchanged for the real words.
From 2 years until 2 years and 6 months		
There is continuous development in the understanding of adult speech about his surroundings. One can speak with a child not only about events at the moment, but also about the past and future. But	Easily repeats whole sentences and short songs.	Properly incorporates unknown words and whole sentences into his vocabulary. Begins questioning: Where? Why? When?

TABLE 1. Continued

Grammar	Use	Intonation	Articulation

From 1 year 6 months to 1 year 10 months up to 2 years

| Begins to use sentences of 2-3 words and around 2 years, sentences of 4-5 words. Grammar changes appear in the words. | Speech begins to be a meaningful communication with an adult. A request, a wish, an impression is expressed by words. Speaks a lot during his play about his actions. | The speech is emotionally expressive. | |

From 2 years until 2 years and 6 months

| The sentences contain many words, complex sentences appear, although not always in correct grammatical form. | Speech is now not only a way of communicating with adults but also with other children. Speaks a lot about various occasions on his own initiative. | Great variety of emotions are reflected in speech. | |

TABLE 1. Continued

Understanding	Ability to imitate speech sounds	Vocabulary

From 2 years until 2 years and 6 months

to understand this kind of speech it is necessary that things which are said should have existed in the child's own personal experience.

From 2 years 6 months to 3 years

| Can understand the meaning of an adults' speech about events and occurences which he personally has not experienced. | Easily repeats songs and poems. | In his vocabulary he uses all particals of speech (besides the participle and the verbal adverbs). The vocabulary increases rapidly and at the end of the third year it reaches 1200-1500 words. |

TABLE 1. Continued

Grammar	Use	Intonation	Articulation

From 2 years 6 months to 3 years

Grammar	Use	Intonation	Articulation
Speaks with complex sentences, begins to use subordinate sentences (although grammatically the sentences are still built incorrectly).	Tells about things seen by him in a few short sentences. When questioned can tell the content of what was told him. Stories (through pictures and without pictures). Can understand the content of adult speech when spoken to directly.		Pronunciation mostly correct except r, l, and the hissing sounds.

TABLE 2. Indices of motor development in children aged 1 year up to 3 1/2 years

The child's age	Walking	Crawling	Throwing at a target
From 1 year and 1 month–1 year and 2 months	Walks without sitting; at the beginning 3–6 meters then 10 and more meters	a) Crawls on a step-ladder of 1 m height (the distance between the steps is about 10 cm) and comes down b) Climbs over a log on all fours	Throws a ball with two hands (diameter of 15–20 cm) while sitting
1 year and 3 months–1 year and 4 months	a) Walks alongside a 30 cm strip of carpeted floor then along a 25 cm wide board b) Steps over a stick lying on the floor	a) Climbs on a step-ladder of 1 m height, then comes down b) Climbs over a log	a) Throws a big ball 15–20 cm in diameter with both hands (from a sitting position) b) Throws a small ball (5–6 cm in diameter) with one hand from a standing position at a target 50 cm away
1 year 5 months–1 year 6 months	a) Walks up a sloping board (width 25 cm, length 1.5–2 m), which is raised 15–20 cm from the floor on one end, walks	Climbs a 1 m high step-ladder	Throws small balls with one hand into a horizontal target (a basket 60 cm in diameter), which is on the floor at a

TABLE 2. Continued

The age of a child	Walking	Crawling	Throwing at a target
	down to the floor b) Steps over a stick or a cord which is 5-10 cm raised from the floor		distance of 20-40 cm)
1 year 7 months– 2 years	a) Climbs over a sloping board (width 20-25 cm) and climbs down from the end of the board b) Climbs on an overturned box (width 50×50 cm, height 15 cm) and climbs down c) Steps over a board or cord which is raised 12-18 cm from the floor	Climbs a 1.5 m high step-ladder (the distance between the cross pieces is 15 cm) and goes down	Throws small balls with one hand into a wide horizontal target (diameter 60 cm) which is at chest level and at a distance of 50-75 cm
2 years 1 month– 2 years 6 months	a) Climbs up a sloping board (which is 20 cm wide and 1.5-2 m long) raised at	Climbs up a gymnastic ladder (height 1.5 m, distance between the cross	Throws small balls into a horizontal target (diameter 40 cm) which is at

TABLE 2. Continued

The age of a child	Walking	Crawling	Throwing at a target
	one end 25-30 cm from the floor, climbs down from the end of the board to the floor b) Climbs on a stool (40×40 cm high) 20 cm and climbs down c) Steps over a stick or a cord raised 20-25 cm from the floor d) Walks over a board 20 cm wide, which is horizontally raised 25-30 cm from the floor	pieces 15 cm) and comes down, step by step	chest level and at a distance of 80-100 cm
2 years 7 months– 3 years	a) Climbs up a sloping board (width 15 cm, length 2 m) raised at the end from the floor 30-35 cm	Climbs a 1.5 m high step-ladder and goes down	Throws small balls with one hand into a vertical target (diameter 50-60 cm) which is at a level of 80 cm, at a distance of 100-125 cm

TABLE 2. Continued

The age of a child	Walking	Crawling	Throwing at a target
	b) Climbs on a stool (40×40) and climbs down c) Walks over a board, which is horizontally raised 30-35 cm from the floor		
3 years 1 month- 3 years 6 months		Climbs a 2 m high gymnastic ladder and climbs down	Throws small balls with one hand into a vertical target (diameter 50 cm) distance 125-150 cm

*Pre-school education, edited by A.Ya. Goldfeld and Schelovonova, Medgiz, 1962 (pp. 240-242).

REFERENCES

AIZIKOVICH, R.S., Work on speech development with children ages 2-3 years, Kiev, 1961.

AKSARINA, N.M. and LADIGINA, N.F., Speech development of children in children's homes, *Pediatria*, 1954, 3.

ANUFRIEVA, A.I. and MITJUKOVA, O.M., Play and activity for youngsters, Gorkii, 1952.

BABADZHAN, T.S., Organized motor games for children at an early age, Moscow, 1950.

BABADZHAN, T.S., Holidays in day nurseries and children's homes, edited by Schelovanova, N.M. and Aksarina, N.M., Moscow, 1957. Early education of children in preschool institutions, *Methodological indexes*, Uchepedgiz, 1962. Early education of children in preschool institutions. Schelovanova, N.M. and Aksarina, N.M. (ed), Moscow, 1960.

CUBERT, K.D. and RISS, M.G., Gymnastics in early childhood, L., 1963. Games with rules in kindergartens. A collection of didactic and motor games. Program for education in kindergarten. Uchepedgiz, 1962.

KASATKIN, N.I., Essay of the development of the higher nervous activity in early childhood, Moscow, 1950.

KOLTZOVA, M.M., About the formation of the higher nervous activity in the child, Moscow, 1958.

KAVERINA, E.K., About the speech development in the first two years of life, Moscow, 1950.

LADYGINA, N.F., Methods of story telling through pictures with children from 1 year to 3 years, Moscow, 1961.

LEKHTMAN-ABRAMOVICH, R.Ya and FRADKINA, F.I., Stages of development in play and activity with objects in early childhood, Moscow, 1949.

MARKOVA, T.A. and PENEVSKAYA, L.A., Education of children in their third year of life, Uchepedgiz, 1962.

MINKEVICH, M.A., SERODICK, R.G. and UVEROVA, L.S., Physical exercises for children in early childhood, Moscow, 1958.

MITINA, A.D., About education in early childhood. The Saratov Book Publishing House, 1956.

PETROVA, V.A., Methods of activities of speech development in the second year of life, Moscow, 1962.

Programs of education in the kindergarten, Uchepedgiz, 1962.

A guide for preschool physicians in children centers and kindergartens. Goldfeld, A.Ya. and Schelovanova, N.M. (eds), Moscow, 1962.

ROSENGARD-PUPKO, G.L., Speech and the development of perception in early childhood, A.M.N., SSSR, Moscow, 1948.

SAPOTNITZKAYA, B.Ya., Carrying out organized activities with breast-fed children, Kiev, 1961.

The Nurse-educator in children's homes and the younger group in the children's homes and kindergartens, Kovrigina, M.D. (ed), Moscow, 1963.

SLAVINA, L.S., Some questions on the perceptiveness of speech by young children, *Preschool*, 1949, 12.

SOROKINA, A.I., Didactic games in the kindergarten, Uchepedgiz, 1955.

FEDIAJEVSKAYA, V.M., For the little ones with joy, Moscow, 1953.

FEDOSEEVA, T.N., Methodological guide for outdoor activities with children in their third year of life, L., 1961.

FONOREV, M.I., Physical education in early childhood, L., 1963.

FRADKINA, F.T., Stages of development in play and activities with objects in early childhood, Moscow, 1949.

EIGES, N.R., Organization of children's activities in the second year of life. In: *Questions About Child Education in Children's Homes and Centers*, Moscow, 1957.

EIGES, N.R., "Speech development in a child", *Medical Nurse*, 1958, 3.

METHODS OF KIBBUTZ COLLECTIVE EDUCATION DURING EARLY CHILDHOOD

Section Two: Early Child Care in The Israeli Kibbutz

METHODS OF KIBBUTZ COLLECTIVE EDUCATION

DURING EARLY CHILDHOOD

Translated from the Hebrew which was

assembled and written by

YONA BEN-YAAKOV, *Kibbutz Degania A*

CONTENTS

THE CHILDREN'S HOUSE IN EARLY CHILDHOOD 203

THE FIRST YEAR 204

    Work Regulations and Rights of the Mother in the Year of Birth 206

FROM TWO TO FOUR YEARS 212

    Organization of the Environment From Ages One to Four 217
    Toys to be Supplied to the Child at Different Stages 219
    The Daily Routine 222
    Educational Means – In Speech and In Action . 224
    Activity With Materials and the Manner of Their Presentation 230
    Training For Eating Habits 233
    Toilet Training 237
    The Story 241
    The Walk 243
    Holidays in the Children's House 244
    The Sabbath 245
    Birthdays 246
    Nightime in Collective Sleeping Arrangements . 248
    The Parents and the Children's House 254
    The Training of Educators 260

THE YARD 267

    Equipment and Installations 269
    Illustrations 277

THE CHILDREN'S HOUSE IN EARLY CHILDHOOD

There are three principles which shape the children's house:

a. A permanent physical surrounding.
b. A continuity of the work of the metapelet.*
c. A social unit of 4 to 5 children.

Permanent surroundings and continuity in the work of the metapelet provide a sound basis for the development of the young child's personality. Changes from house to house and from metapelet to metapelet during each age period and stage of development undermine the child's security and trust, distort the rhythm of his growth and cause disturbances, such as: fears, unquietness at night, regression from previous achievements, loss of appetite, etc.

Continuity of the metapelet for 3½-4 years contributes to the development of the relationship between her and the child, and to the child's security in her and in the surroundings in which he is growing up. The permanent metapelet observes, studies and becomes acquainted with the individuality of the child, his growth rate, his reactions, and his abilities, and in accordance with this knowledge she can pattern her reactions towards him and prevent complications in his further development. The presence of a consistent personality and a consistent educational approach and behavior help the child adjust to the surroundings and its demands, and thus prevent embarrassment and insecurity. One must also appreciate the contact which is formed between the permanent metapelet and the parents which allows for collaboration and mutual understanding in both thought and action regarding the child's education. This common understanding and sociable atmosphere contributes to the child's adaptation to reality.

---

*Metapelet is the Hebrew term for infant nurse and child-care worker.

The ability of the small child to live in a social group is limited and his adjustment to the group slow. His egocentric mentality doesn't allow him to be in constant contact with his peers. On the other hand, a degree of contact with a small group of peers is important for his general development. The urging of his needs is great and their immediate gratification gives him security, trust in his environment and emotional balance. The small child needs warmth and personal attention from the metapelet, and it is difficult for him to recognize the rights of the other children to receive the same attention. Therefore a small social unit is most appropriate for this young age.

The structure of the comprehensive children's house must meet the needs of both the infant and the toddler. The children live in two separate units until the age of 2½–3 years. At that time one should aim at obtaining cooperation of the children in each unit in activities such as: play in the yard, Sabbath and holiday parties, common walks with two metaplot*, physical care, eating, washing, etc. After 3–3½ years of age one can let the children of both units be together in activities such as walks and storytelling, but eating and physical care should continue to be carried out in the separate units.

THE FIRST YEAR

The mother: The relationship between the mother and the infant during his first year of life provides the basis for his security, his emotional stability and the formation of his personality. The children's house with its arrangements and customs and the interpersonal relationships between the metapelet and the parents (especially the mother) help cultivate that primary relationship. In order to strengthen this tie one should encourage extended breast feeding and feeding by the mother till the late months of weaning. It

---

*Metaplot = plural of metapelet.

is important to secure the individual mother's intimacy with her infant by the use of a screen, a separate room, or scattered nursing hours. The hour given to the mother permits her to leisurly feed and play with the infant. The mother feeds, bathes and diapers her infant and puts him to bed. We encourage the mother's feeding the child in the morning and the evening until that time when the children begin to eat together - by the age of one. Another area of contact between the mother and the infant is bathing. The mother should be allowed to bathe her infant until he is six months old.

Bathing is done before meals, and the mother can arrange the bath time according to her convenience. But she should avoid anything which would upset the schedule of the children's house or disturb the children. After six months the mother may continue to bathe the child if she wishes, but then she must do it on her own time. When weaning starts, the mother feeds the child, and she is free to visit the children's house at any time she wishes. She has the right to participate in all visits by the doctor and to express her wishes. The children's house must create a pleasant and free atmosphere, encourage the mother to visit, and include her in all that goes on with and around her child.

WORK REGULATIONS AND RIGHTS OF THE MOTHER IN THE YEAR OF BIRTH

1. A chavera* who has had a normal pregnancy should work a regular work day until the end of the eighth month of pregnancy. In the ninth month she should work only 6 hours daily.

2. The chavera should integrate rest periods into her work day, according to the specific hygienic and climatic conditions.

3. Following delivery the chavera is free of all work for a period of six weeks.

4. She shall then work a four hour day, until the child is 6 months old.

5. As the number of feedings which are given over to the metapelet increase, the mother's work day should be increased - until she works for seven hours when the child is nine months old. After the ninth month, she should return to a full work day. During the period the child is 9-14 months she should continue to give the morning and evening feedings on her own time and should she thus be late to work, her occupation with the child should be taken into account.

6. The mother has the right to her full yearly vacation, just like any other chaver.

7. In the child's first year, she should spend her vacation within the kibbutz.

---

*Hebrew term for comrade; i.e. a member of the kibbutz. Chaver (masculine) Chavera (feminine) Chaverim (plural).

8. A non-breast feeding mother has the same rights as a nursing mother.

9. The mother of twins shall receive two months vacation and her work day should be one hour less than that of other mothers.

10. A nursing mother who is working a short day should attempt to arrange her work hours according to the kibbutz work schedule - either in the morning or the afternoon.

11. A mother should not be given evening or night work shifts and during the first six months of the child's life she should be freed of all special duties or work mobilizations.

The provision of justified and recognized opportunities for the encouragement of the relationship between the mother and her infant constitutes the basis for the development of security and trust in the infant and provides for the personal needs of the mother.

The child: The nucleus of the human's ability to adapt is created during the first year of life. Adaptation is the mutual fitting together of the organism and the environment. Already in the first year, the infant is required to adapt to the non-human environment - to food, to temperature, etc. - and to a routine of life. This age is characterized by the infant's complete dependence upon the adult. On the other hand, the urgency of his needs and the difficulty of his adaptation require consideration and adaptation on the part of the adult world. The feeling of security in the providing and caring environment creates his emotional stability, strengthens his personality and encourages his healthy development.

During the first 6-8 weeks the feedings are determined according to the individual infant's ability to adapt. One should not attempt to keep a rigid schedule. After this period one should aim at establishing a regular schedule – every 3-4 hours, with a longer break at night. In special cases one should be flexible and continue with short breaks.

Infants who wake at night should be given fluids (tea or milk) by the night watch, but with the agreement of the mother. Should the infant fail to stop crying, the mother should be woken and she should then feed the baby. The night feeding should be stopped in accordance with the infant's need for longer periods of sleep. At approximately 3-4 months of age the infant will sleep for 7-8 hours at night and will eat four times during the day – every four hours. When he becomes 9-10 months old, one should try to change to three basic meals, with a light supplement (fruit juice) in the afternoon.

Weaning: Weaning is a double process.– from the mother's breast to solid food, and from the mother's overall care to that of the metapelet. In each of these areas we must act with care and gradualness. Beginning in the first two months we should give the child small quantities of juice from a spoon or a soft plastic cup, so as to let the child become used to different forms of feeding. All supplementary food should be given from a spoon or a cup. When feeding from a bottle, one must be careful to keep the nipple hole of proper size (according to the consistency of the food) so as to assure the infant satisfactory sucking. When the child is 6-7 months old (period of teething – individual variations taken into account) and his gums are sensitive, one should give him bread crusts or cookies. Chewing these may provide the infant with pleasure and satisfaction. An infant who has not suckled from his mother's breast will be weaned from the bottle in the same manner as a breast fed baby. One should aim at completing weaning by the age of one year. If the child has difficulty, one should not worry and should delay the completion of weaning until the child is ready for it.

Thumb Sucking: Thumb sucking is a source of satisfaction and enjoyment. Most children suck their thumbs and one should not view this with concern and should not wage a war against it. When the child's activities and interests become wider and he begins to gain satisfaction from them, he will give up his thumb sucking. One should see to it that the infant gets sufficient satisfaction which suckling at his mother's breast or sucking from a bottle. One should not use a pacifier as a standard procedure, but only in special instances. It's constant use may distract us from discovering the the real cause of the crying and discomfort. The child can become dependent on the pacifier - and also develop increased dependence on the adult (who then must always return the pacifier when it falls out of the baby's mouth - especially at night). In addition the dependence on the pacifier limits the child's activity and restricts his awareness and interest in the surroundings.

The process of transition from mother to metapelet: The metapelet plays an important role in the process of the child's adaptation to life patterns and adult behaviors. The pattern of interrelationships which is knitted between the mother and the metapelet during the child's first months of life when the mother plays the major role in caretaking, forms the psychological background for the transfer of caretaking functions - especially feeding - to the metapelet. As the child grows and his needs become wider, the sphere of contact with the metapelet as a providing object increases, and with this so the emotional relationship between them. This will then provide the basis for the metapelet becoming an educator and will make it easier for the child to adjust to the demands of reality.

Beginning at 6 months, the metapelet begins to feed the baby one meal a day. After a month she adds an additional meal. By 12-14 months she feeds him all his meals. From 9-10 months one should go over to regular food with much variety; vegetables, cereals, meat balls, noodles, etc. The local pediatrician is responsible for the nutritional program. New foods should be introduced gradually, carefully and consistently. If the child refuses, one should not force him. Feeding should be carried out in a calm atmosphere, when the child is clean and dry. When he is capable of sitting steadily, he should be seated in an arm chair. Until then he should be fed while being held by the mother or the metapelet. When the children reach greater independence and are less dependent on the metapelet, they are seated together for the meal. One should start with two children, and gradually add the others. The eating arrangements (means of serving and supervision) should be made in accordance with the needs of the young child: use large bowls, a medium-sized spoon, a soft pleasant napkin which covers the whole chest. The food should be ready on the table, so that the metapelet need not leave the table during the meal. Her presence, quietness and willingness to help will encourage the child and add to his quiet and security. If the educational method and the environment are positive and age-appropriate, the children will achieve enough independence in eating by the age of 1½-2 years to allow them to sit together in a group.

The physical surroundings: A positive, quiet and balanced physical environment provides the child with stimuli which are appropriate to his stages of development and this is an important precondition for his healthy growth. Restful colors on the walls, pictures, flowers and pleasant curtains contribute to an aesthetic and pleasant home. When the child and his mother return from the maternity hospital, they should find a nice placard with greetings from the children's house to the parents, a cake baked for the occasion, etc. From the age of two weeks (weather permitting) the infant should be placed in a playpen in the fresh air. At the age of 1½-2 months a colorful toy should be hung over the crib. Other toys are given to the infant according to the development of his senses and his motor abilities. From six months he needs to be in movement, and a small playpen is not large enough for this. Thus he should be provided with a wide

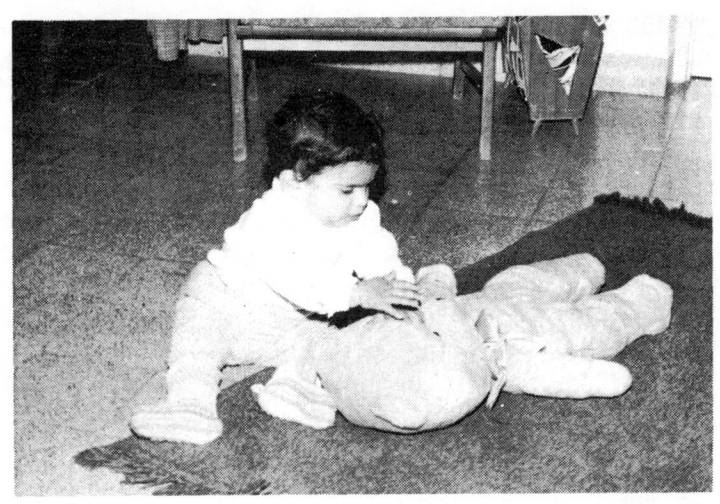

fenced-in area, a small paved yard which is fenced in and covered with soft linoleum or other plastic material which is also simple to keep clean. Inside this "yard" one should provide various toys which help develop his senses and his muscles. Once he takes his first steps, he should be allowed unrestricted movement. He will train his muscles by walking, and should find support in the infant's house and in the

yard, such as: a small dividing wall 60 cm high made of wooden slats, a buggy with a handle at the same height as the child, etc. In order to develop the full sense of family one should allow the brothers and sisters to visit and play with the infant. But these visits should not disturb the routines of the infant's house or the rest of the other infants. The contact and cooperation of the father in caring for the child during this early period completes the network of family relationships for the child, and supports the mother in her maternal feelings.

FROM TWO TO FOUR YEARS

At the turn of the second year the child achieves increasing control of his muscles and a growing ability to willingly direct his movements and obtain things in his surroundings. He can walk, even run and climb, but without specific goals. He shows the wish to be independent though his ability is limited, his balance precarious and his dependence on the adult still strong.

His activity and play has a clearly motor quality. He pushes, pulls, drags from place to place, palpitates, tears, throws, picks up and throws again. His ability to express his needs in words is very limited. His vocabulary is small, and is assisted by movements, hints and various vocalizations. One needs intuition and patience in order to understand and fulfill his needs. Yet he understands what is said to him. From the social point of view, his relations to others are determined by the wish to satisfy his own needs. He does not recognize the rights of others, and acts towards his peers as towards non-human objects. He takes and doesn't know how to give. The taking is not always useful - he may take something and immediately throw it away. His instinctual drives are strong and it is often difficult for him to defer their immediate satisfaction. The presence of the metapelet and her willingness to help the child in every instance prevents tension, anger and various collisions and in large part assures quiet in the house and relaxation for the children. His needs for movement and activity will be satisfied if he is permitted to move about in all parts of the children's house. The doors should be open and not form a barrier as he moves around in the whole area available to him - in the playroom, bedroom, shower room, porch and yard. The surroundings should be made interesting with varying toys. Everywhere he comes he should find something to take, to hold, to roll, to exercise his muscles. He will exercise and enjoy himself. At this age one should guide the child gradually, carefully and slowly towards good eating habits, cleanliness and a daily schedule which is appropriate to his needs.

When the child becomes two or two and a half his security in his own abilities increases, he becomes motorically stable and no longer requires constant adult supervision. Vocabulary increases substantially and he can now express his wishes. His ability to wait becomes greater and if necessary he can get over slight disappointments. His social aims change. Occasionally he will forego the right to play with a

certain toy or will make some other concession. He appears more relaxed and comfortable and more capable of accepting demands which are consistent with the level of his abilities. At this age one must still guide his upbringing carefully and slowly.

From two and a half to three years he goes up to a higher level of development and reveals a very strong need for independence and expression of his own power and skill. He refuses help, saying "me, me" or "myself". He persistently demands his own way, resists changes in his schedule and likes to keep to a routine. His emotional drives are strong, complex and conflicting. He has difficulty in making choices and gets caught between conflicting wishes - "do want, don't want, won't do..." He is full of contradictions, stubborn and conservative. Every new thing in food and clothes arouses his resistance and causes conflict. He is active, persistent, controlling, and knows how to utilize things and situations. With all of that, he is highly dependent on the adult's attitude towards him and will be willing to perform as requested if this assures him of the adult's friendliness and appreciation. Patience, understanding, friendliness, warmth and sincerity and educational creativity in the behavior of the adults will help him master this difficult period in his development.

At three, three and a half and four years he will be more balanced and less suspicious of change. His growing maturity gives him still further security in his own abilities in the environment and in his relations to others. He shows outstanding development in speech control. Speech can be used to influence, and entertain him, and to move him to carry out social tasks. His ability to perceive and understand things widens and enrichens his concepts, and he then translates this into activities and varied games. His verbal ability and his wider vision help him in social relationships. He will be ready to relate to one or two other children and will be ready to share and to give. He will attain much in his adjustment to reality and in learning habits and accepted rules of behavior. And yet he still gets caught in conflicts and disappointments due to his overestimation of his own abilities. These disappointments often upset his

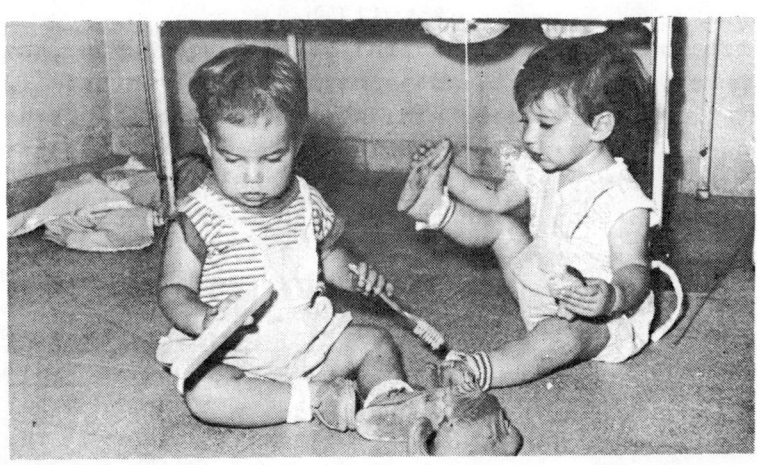

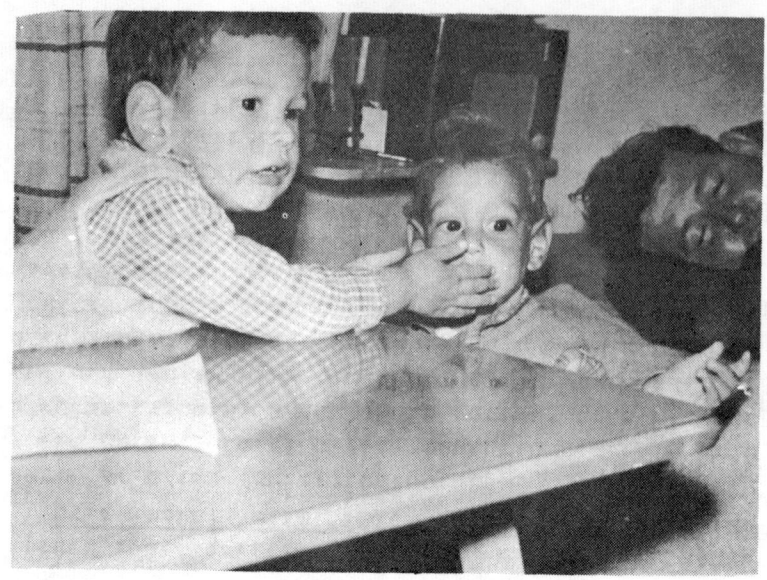

feelings of self security and belief in his acceptance by others. Seeing this behavior as part of normal development will help us gain the patience and understanding which the child so badly needs from us.

We have tried to describe in general terms the behavior of the child in his stages of development up to the age of four. This will help us also understand the personality of the child. One shouldn't view every stage as something clearly defined. The manner in which each child goes from stage to stage is something individual and is dependent in large part on the environment.

One of the goals of the educator is to understand and appraise the child's personality. This helps us know how to adapt our own behavior and reactions so as to provide an environment which is optimal for the child's development.

EARLY CHILDHOOD EDUCATION IN THE KIBBUTZ

ORGANIZATION OF THE ENVIRONMENT FROM AGES ONE TO FOUR

The inner arrangement of the children's house is determined according to the child's needs during the different stages of development. Our first concern is for the child's freedom of movement and constant activity. Everywhere he turns, he should find something to involve him in quiet and enjoyable activity.

His ability to engage in shared activity is limited. Thus one must spread out many corners for play in all parts of the house so as to minimize conflict and to permit the child freedom in his play.

To encourage independence, the child should be allowed to take toys by himself. The toys should be arranged in such a way that the children can reach them and use them without the help of an adult. The child will use them as he wishes, and move them from place to place. But we should see to it that at the end of activities (at mealtimes, before going to bed or going outside for a trip) we will return the toys to their places. In this way the child will learn about order. One should immediately remove and repair any broken toy.

A good way to increase stimulation is to change the image of the toys by painting them, exchanging toys, adding accessories - such as a new bell, reins, or propeller, etc. A toy is an instrument of play which enriches the child's activity and acts as an important means for his general development - both emotional and physical. He learns the characteristics of the materials from which the toys are made, develops his senses and learns to use the material according to his changing needs.

Also, one should be sure that materials are available which are appropriate for the child's age. There is special importance for sublimative materials, such as clay, glue, sand and water.

Age 1-2

The character of the child's play is principally motoric at this age. He will move things, push, pull, put inside and take out, throw and lift. At this stage one should not have complicated play corners with many elements, and one should take care of the order and make sure that every toy has its permanent place.

Age 2-4

During this period the child develops new skills, his world of concepts becomes wider and his curiosity increases. He observes and gains impressions from what is going on around him, imitates what he sees and thus learns thru play the meaning and manner of execution of these new activities. As we provide the child

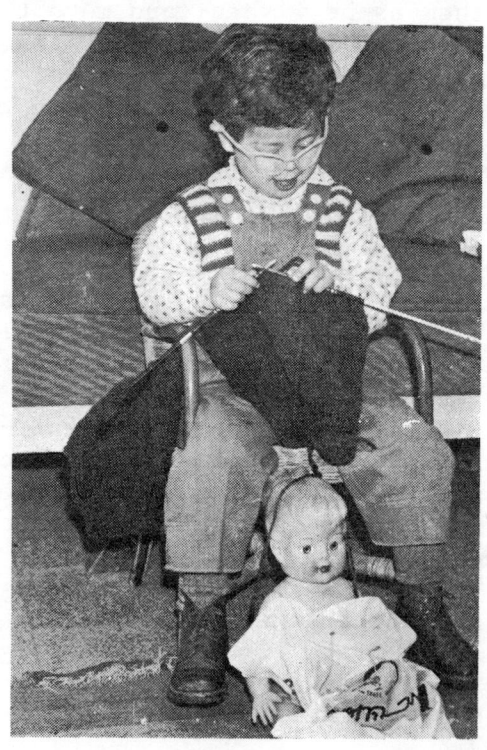

with plentiful and varied possibilities for activity we will help him learn the ways of life, widen his concepts and develop his ability to think and make conclusions.

Fears, disappointments and insecurity which bother him occassionally, find their expression in the play language of the child. Play helps the child "repair" the disappointing reality and turn it into a satisfying fantasy. He then becomes the sole ruler in his fantasy world.

The play corners should be increased gradually, and their content widened according to the changing needs of the child. We should try to make full use of all the available space and fill it with rich content full of variety.

Following is a list of play material for each age.

TOYS TO BE SUPPLIED TO THE CHILD AT DIFFERENT STAGES

Room toys

1. *First year*

Clanging toys, with or without a handle.
Plastic or rubber rings.
Rubber dolls and toy figures.
Small, soft plastic blocks.
Small balls of varying materials and colors.
Small carts which are easy to push (when crawling).
Beads.
Carriages with high handles (to use when child begins to walk).
Small boxes.
Smooth, colorful pieces of cloth (end of first year).
Boxes of all kinds and sizes, with or without steering wheels.

2. *Second year*

One should gradually add:

Various vehicles inside the house.
A steering wheel for every child.
Various dolls from cloth, soft and hard plastic.
Small table and chairs for the children to sit – as the beginning of a doll corner.
Sofa for the dolls (and also the children).
Large, soft animals.
Various towers.
Wooden cubes of varying sizes and colors.
A large pleasant box with old equipment familiar to the children – such as old farm tools, etc.
Picture books.
Balls of various sizes in a pleasant box or basket.
Large, colorful wall board.
Blackboards and chalk.
Materials: colorful cloth, paper for painting, magazines, etc.

Toys under the care of the metapelet: table games such as: 2-3 piece jig-saw puzzles, form boards, picture books, paints, clay, glue, colored chalk.

3. *Third year*

Gradually add:

Bedding for the sofa (dolls corner).
Small closet with drawers.
Clothes for dolls.
Clothes hangers.
Small kitchen utensils.
Doll's carriage.

For the building block corner:

Wooden blocks for toddlers (set of 25).
Small ladder, wooden planks, etc.

For the costume corner:

Plentiful and varied clothes, and hangers for clothes.

For the book corner:

Special shelf for books for free use.
Small pillows on which to sit in corner.
Building blocks made of soft plastic.
Large Beads.
Simple percussion instruments - from nature as well as manufactured.

Toys under care of the metapelet: table games, such as Lotto (matching colors, animals, etc.), jig-saw puzzles (5-6 pieces), color domino, hammering boards, crayons, clay, plastiline, glue.

4. *Fourth year*

Add:

To dolls' corner - mirror, dressing stand, various dolls, small closet with first-aid materials (small dropper, plastic bottles, rubber nipples, etc.) dolls' clothes.

For the costume corner: symbols for playing roles of men and women, such as: soldier's hat, head kerchiefs, aprons, etc. There are never too many clothes. Keep them clean and orderly.

For the building block corner:
Various accessories such as bells, propellor, etc.

More books.
Jig-saw puzzles (5-6 pieces).

All the toys are freely available to the children except for special books, finger paints and glue.

Toys for the yard

In addition to the various pieces of equipment (see paragraph on yard equipment) one should add: vehicles of all sorts and sizes in which to ride, wheelbarrows, tricycles, carts, etc.

For sandbox

Tools such as: shovels, funnels, buckets, boxes, molds and old kitchen utensils. At the end of the third year one should add small, but real tools: shovels, rakes, picks (not sharp), wheels, etc. These should be kept in a permanent place and gathered together at the end of activity in the yard. One should also have boxes of various sizes and from various materials: wooden and cardboard boxes which are used to pack vegetables, large tin boxes etc. These are valuable toys for children.

THE DAILY ROUTINE

We should try to create a homely, free, relaxed and pleasant atmosphere in the children's house. A flexible daily routine will make it much easier for the metapelet to fulfill her educational function to supply the individual needs of each child and will avoid tensions, clashes and anger.

The creation of foci of work such as the bathing of children at certain hours, feeding at the same hour (when they are still small) carrying out of housework etc. lead to tension, impatience, nervousness and anger, cloud the atmosphere and affect the mood and behavior of the children are resting. One should not leave the children alone in the house. This will allow the metapelet to forstall conflicts before they blossom out, supply the children's needs the moment they express them, and thus prevent difficulties in the child's security. Such tasks as going to the laundry, bringing food, etc. should be organized ahead of time. Minor treatments (such as first aid for skin lacerations etc.) should be carried out in the children's house by the metapelet or the nurse, and visits by the pediatrician should be made in the children's house. It is not good to drag young children to the clinic, except when the child is in need of treatment which can't be done in the children's house. Also such things as haircuts, clothes fittings etc. should all be done at home.

Rest hours and activities should be organized according to the physical development of the child. Children from 18-22 months should be permitted a short rest during the morning (8:30-9 a.m.). This is especially important during the summer. During the summer, walks should be taken during the early morning hours and in the winter later on in the morning. There is no need to take walks every day; 2-3 times a week is sufficient. The metapelet should spend time with the children in the yard, and may clean and arrange the yard at this time. The purpose of walks is to vary the impressions of the child and to widen his world and give him pleasant experiences. One should take care not to tire the children with excessively long walks, and the metapelet should not try to carry out other tasks during her walks.

One should not try to establish "periods of concentration" with groups of children until the age of 2½-3 years. Individual play will allow the child to concentrate his interest on areas which are appropriate for him and to his personal liking. The metapelet should take out materials such as clay, dough, chalk, table games etc. and make them available to the children in addition to toys which are scattered about the various corners of the children's house. Care for continuous activity of the children will forestall frustrations, aggression, crying and anger and will bring about a proper educational environment which permits of continuous, well-grounded educational activity. In the summer, bathing during the morning hours may be refreshing and relaxing. In the winter, one should bathe the children after lunch. Visits of parents should be organized and scattered during the morning hours. This also helps assure a continuity of activity in the children's house. The metapelet arrives in the children's house before the children awake in the morning and she should bring the food for breakfast with her. She dresses the children as they awake. In order to prevent tension, she may give children up to 1½ years something to drink when they wake up. At this age, the children still do not sit all together at meals. It is possible to arrange to have all the children eat breakfast together only towards the end of the second year. No matter what the age, one should never feed children when they are wet or still in their pajamas. Already from the early hours of the morning the children should be given proper activities and should be free to move about in the house and the yard. Meals should be given at rational intervals and in accordance with hygienic needs. One should not push them together into too short a span of time. The permanent metapelet should give full information about the individual children to the helper who wakes the children in the morning and should instruct her in all the routines regarding dressing, giving children something to play with, keeping other children quiet until all have woken up, etc. Following the afternoon nap one should dress the children in their evening clothes, but protect them from dirtying themselves by dressing each with an apron. They may then play in the house or on the shaded porch, as they wish. Supper should not be given before 4.00 p.m. in the winter, and 4.30-5.00 p.m. in the summer. All the children's houses and all the parents should arrive at an agreement as to the hour when the children go to their parent's rooms. In those kibbutzim where supper is given later, it should be given by the permanent metapelet or her assistant at 7.00 p.m. One should not arrange a rotation of parents to give supper to the group.

EDUCATIONAL MEANS - IN SPEECH AND IN ACTION

The manner in which we approach a child and the words we use have special meaning for him. One must take into consideration the mentality of the young child.

A *positive approach* arouses less resistance to

the demands of the educators. This is a more constructive manner than restricting or interfering in the child's activity. By stressing a positive suggestion we lower the child's attention to his negative activity and we refrain from stressing its importance. We are "helping" him and not stopping or interfering with him and at the same time we are also providing him with a healthy model to copy when he himself wishes to approach his peers. One should remove from usage negative approaches and speech. All guidance and every suggestion should be stated in a positive manner. For example: "Throw the ball over the fence" instead of "don't break the window!" Or, "eat the meat" instead of "don't play with your food."

When, how and under which circumstances one makes a demand from the child is often more important than the content of the demand itself. One fails in one's demand if the timing is wrong (when the metapelet has just been changed, when the child has just been moved to a new house, when the child is sick, while the parents have gone away for a trip, etc.) When a child fills a demand of an adult before he is developmentally ready for it, he loses the enjoyment of mastery and develops resistence. However he also loses a chance for enjoyment thru mastery if demands are made too late.

Children like to solve problems themselves and not be dependent on adults. In other words, one should just give the child a chance to try to solve problems by himself, serve himself, get things for himself, do things by himself - and not solve everything for him. Give the child a minimum of help so that he will have maximal opportunity for self growth. In other words, explain to him what to do - don't do it for him. Of course this does not mean we should withhold help if he really needs it. If a child says "help me" when he is capable of doing something by himself, he may be testing the adults relationship and willingness to help. One should not say: "You can do it yourself". We will give him greater security if we help him freely and conscientiously. Also, when a child asks for help we should listen and reply to him. That will make him less anxious and fearful of his own inability and his dependence on us. This doesn't interfere with our efforts to refrain from giving unnecessary help and to give him opportunity to act by himself. But excessive support, especially when it is not requested puts the child under the adult's protectorate, leaves him dependent and weakens his personality.

The use of many words and several demands at a single time: The reason for failures by parents and metaplot is often the use of too many words and the making of several demands together, when a single demand would be sufficient. Children develop defenses against too many words. It is better to use several means of request rather than to use words alone.

The voice is an educational tool. The speech which makes the strongest impression on a child is that which is simple, clear and quiet. Children get angry when they are yelled at. A good rule is to never yell or call to a child from a distance. It is better to come close. Our words will be accepted if they are said quietly and face to face. Speech transmits feelings just as thoughts do. Children are sensitive to the quality and to the strength of one's voice. They sense unfriendliness or fear in an angry tone - irrespective of the content of the words. Here the educator gives an example of himself - just as in other areas. Children will yell if their educator yells.

Guidance of behavior succeeds when it is consistent and congruent with the interests and motivations of the child. We can succeed in changing behavior of a child if we try to bring to his attention an activity which is of value or interest to him, or will provide him with a solution to a problem. It is important to be acquainted with each child, and to guide him in accordance with his own particular interests and motivations. The suggestions will differ for each child and his own special needs.

One should use words and tone which will help the child feel secure. The words we use and the way we use them are most important. One should not use words which will cause the child to feel fear, guilt or shame. These feelings do not change a child's behavior, but they may cause damage and create greater problems for the child. Good behavior is not the result of fear and guilt. Such improvement is only superficial, and will be accompanied by submerged resistence, anger, and feelings of hate and vengence.

For example: "You are a bad boy", "nasty", "dirty" won't change the child's condition. One should stop all use of the words, the tones and the gestures which cause children to feel fear, guilt or shame.

Helping a child at the proper moment means supporting him before he looses balance, finding a compromise before two children begin to fight over something, or suggesting a new activity before children show weariness from the present activity. An alert and intuitive metapelet can create conditions that will prevent fights and other negative occurances among the children.

One can make suggestions more emphatic by stressing them thru one's own actions. A verbal suggestion may not suffice in itself, even if it is made in a positive way. For instance: "Go inside as it is time for dinner". Sometimes it is necessary to add: "I will help you put your building blocks back in place". A positive suggestion accompanied by actual help, and made at the proper moment, will help make an effect on the child.

One should give a child a choice only when it is clear that the situation permits a choice. As the child grows and develops, the possibilities for choice increase. The ability to make a decision is a sign of maturity. There are decisions which the young child is still unable to make, due to his limited ability and experience. Thus we must be careful not to suggest that he make a choice when we ourselves are not sure we are willing to leave the decision to him. Example: "Do you want to go to sleep"? He will answer: "No".

Yet we expected and wanted his agreement. Instead of asking a question, we should have said: "Now it is time to go to sleep"! One should be careful about the tendency to ask questions, except when the question is truely in place and appropriate to the situation. One shouldn't ask the child when to go to sleep, to eat or to wash. The child can not be free to change the schedule of the children's house or to ruin property, etc. On the other hand, there should be freedom for the child to decide where and with what to play.

To control children's behavior: When there is a need to restrict behavior, one should explain, define clearly and consistently, and to stand upon one's demands. There are several things which cannot be done. The important thing is to be sure that the restriction is really necessary and to define it with complete clarity. The child will feel greater security if the adult is responsible for him and his actions. He will be freer in his activities when he knows there is an adult who will stop him before he will do things that afterwards may cause sorrow or pain.

One should avoid comparisons and the creation of competition between children. They will damage the child's self-esteem and his social relationships. It is important that the child not overestimate either failure or success. He should feel that he is loved and accepted whether he succeeds or fails, that our relationship with him is not dependent upon success or failure or upon his being "the first" or "the best".

Example: "Who will finish eating first"? Such a question will cause a slow or motorically less developed child to be tense, insecure in his own abilities, disappointed in himself, and consequently inactive, apathetic, etc. Competition leads to arguments between children and spoils the atmosphere.

Example: "I finished first"! "I arrived first"! etc. Such feelings prevent the children from having quiet play and pleasant recreation, and encourage aggression and unfriendly relationships.

The metapelet must always be aware of the overall situation. It is important to develop the ability and the talent to observe what is going on between the children, so that there will be ample opportunities to help the children.

Equal attitudes to children. A negative attitude of a metapelet towards a certain child may promote negative attitudes in the other children towards this child and spoil the mutual relationships in the children's house.

Participation in the child's world

Participation in the child's world brings the child closer and supports him. His world is full of experiences and fantasies which are far removed from the world of the adult. The child cannot reach our world and we must go into his. Relationships of parents and educators with the children are largely determined by the amount of communality which exists between these two worlds.

Do not sneer at the failures, weaknesses and fears of the child. He enjoys when you laugh with him, but not when you laugh at him. He views this as ridicule and becomes angry and bitter.

Private property and hoarding. The small child is egocentric, and he is unable to give in to others or recognize their rights. We must overlook these expressions of ownership and permit the child to become attached to a toy, or play with all the blocks or dolls and we should find a way to compensate the other children.

Every type of punishment or threat of punishment is inexcusable. The young child does not yet possess the capability of logic and he doesn't relate his actions with our reactions. Punishment merely arouses anger, hatred, and aggression and does not help change the condition of the small child. It may only cause him feelings of isolation within an unfriendly environment and he may look for compensation in autoerotic activity which will inhibit his growth and development.

The children's health is very important. Unhygienic arrangements which lead to frequent sickness may create an unsatisfactory educational situation and interfere with the child's general development. The metapelet should be aware of changes in the weather and make proper changes in clothing, time of bathing, etc. She should remove all objects which might cause damage or wounds. She must be constantly aware of dangers.

On the other hand, she shouldn't show excessive wariness or fear. Let's remember that the child counts on her, and revelation of weakness on her part will weaken his security and personality.

ACTIVITY WITH MATERIALS AND THE MANNER OF THEIR PRESENTATION

Activity with various materials permits the child to use and develop his muscles and to learn about the materials and their characteristics. Through touching and using materials, he obtains positive sublimating instinctual satisfactions. The child doesn't set out goals for himself when he plays with materials. He has no plan before his eyes. He simply enjoys the activity, the use of his muscles and his control over the material. As he develops, the child goes from instinct satisfying activity to creative activity. One should stress especially play with water and wet sand - materials with which nature has plentifully provided us - and let us not take them away from our children. These materials should be available every day of the year. In the winter one may use a high sand box or a sand table on the porch. From the age of 1½-2 years we can give the child finger paints and dough. We can make variety by adding food coloring to the materials.

Clay: We should put clay on a table covered with tin or oilcloth. For the ages 1½-2 years, we should use large hunks. The children will knead it with their fingers, will pound on it and take out aggression, will roll and cut it and make various forms. From such experience they will learn about the clay.

Paint: We should try to arrange things so that the child can have free and unhampered activity. Sufficient space for each child will prevent frictions. The child should paint while standing and should not have to worry about dirtying his clothes (each child should be given an apron with sleeves). In the summer he should work when naked from the waist up. We should give him the paint on a large piece of paper or cardboard. At his age one should provide only a few basic colors which the child can mix with his fingers, hands, fists, forearms or elbows. We shouldn't bother him, guide him or restrict him.

Dough: This should be prepared so that it won't stick to the child's hands and it can be colored with food coloring. It is best prepared with a large amount of salt.

White chalk: The child can draw on a blackboard or on the floor. He should be taught not to draw on the walls. The child should have free access to chalk at all times.

From 2 1/2-3 years, after the child has attained complete mastery of these materials, we may permit him free, independent access to the materials.

Paint: We should provide it in large, convenient bowls into which the child can put his fingers or hands and which the child may choose and use as he wishes. We should add additional colors which will interest and encourage him, as well as give him pleasure.

Clay: One may add toothpicks, buttons, beads etc. These the child will stick into the clay, will experiment with and will learn from experience.

Glue: One may now add work with glue, such as gluing scraps of cloth and colored paper, etc.

Plastaline: This can also be used, but not instead of clay.

Crayons: Crayons should be freely available. Use large pieces of paper, which should be in plentiful supply on a special shelf or folder.

Age 3-4 years: At this age all the materials should be freely available to the children. One may add wide brushes. In addition to tables, one should also provide easels with a place to keep the paints. One can also add soft colored pencils. The proper paper is plain, 8½ × 11 inches.

At this age children like to keep their creations, and we should provide them with a way of doing this. Our relationship to the child's work should be a positive, supportive one and we shouldn't interfere or ask the "meaning" of his "creations".

Our presence during the work period encourages and supports the child. We should be willing to help him when he requests. The sincere interest of the surroundings brings security to the child and arouses creative forces.

TRAINING FOR EATING HABITS

The relationship of the child to food is not dependent solely on his appetite, hunger or nutritional needs, but also acts as a source of pleasure and satisfaction. Thus one should take care of the child's positive relationship to food.

The infant's adjustment is slow and is connected with his emotional and motoric development. Our aim is to provide him with socially acceptable eating habits. But in teaching proper eating habits, we must be cognizant of the individual rate of development of each child. Correct eating habits during the nursing and weaning periods underlie the child's relation to food and to habits which he will have to learn in the future. Beginning in the second year of life, all the feedings are turned over to the metapelet and consistency in her educational approach will provide a good chance for success in training. Quiet and peacefulness in the children's house during meal times help provide the proper educational atmosphere. The metapelet must have a practical approach to feeding and be free from emotional responses regarding food and from any sort of forcing. A child who cannot yet sit up comfortably should be fed while being held on the metapelet's lap.

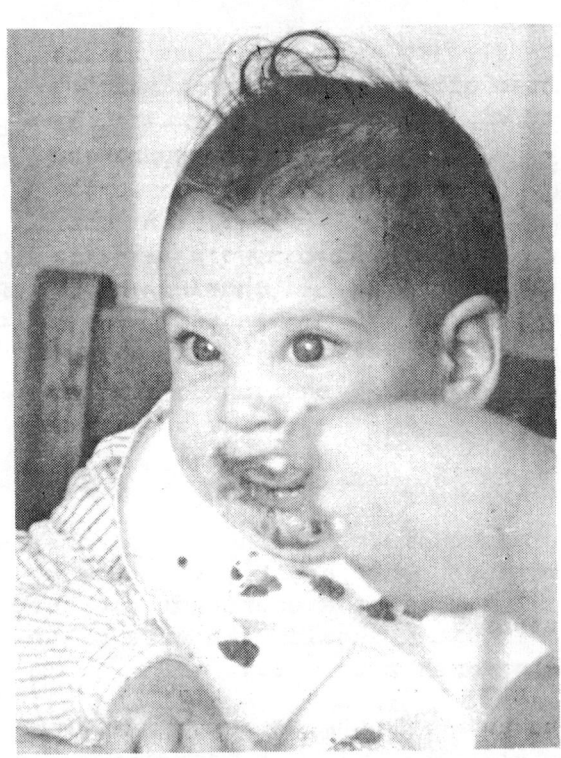

The transition from eating alone to eating in groups should be gradual: start with two children and gradually add until the whole group is eating together. After the children have all achieved preliminary eating habits (under proper conditions and with a permanent metapelet) they will be able to sit together orderly and eat together at the age of 1½-2 years. One should closely watch that there is a quiet atmosphere during meals and that the table and dishes are aesthetic. Eating utensils should be adapted to the child's ability to use them: a deep dish, a medium sized spoon and chair and table of proper height. The amount of food put on the plate should be in accordance with the child's appetite and like or dislike of the particular food. It is better to give an additional portion, if the child wishes, rather than have him leave food on the plate. Food should be prepared according to the child's taste, and the metapelet should be in contact with the cook regarding this. The child should be given each course separately, so that he can taste each food and become accustomed to it. A mixture of different foods increases the amount, dulls the child's sense of taste and leads to repulsion at the unaesthetic manner in which the food is served. One should not have too many different foods in a single meal. We must also take into consideration the special tastes of children from different backgrounds with different culinary customs. From an early age one should already get the children used to a varied diet. New foods should be introduced gradually and in small quantities. The child will taste them and will slowly become accustomed to their taste, smell and form. The child shouldn't be overburdened by the introduction of too many new foods at once. The metapelet should organize the mealtimes in such a way that she won't have to run around and so that she can sit quietly with the children at the table. She will thus prevent tension - both in herself and in the children. The tray and all the eating utensils should be close to the table, possibly on a small table set there for this purpose. The process of developing cultured eating habits is a slow one: In the beginning the child will eat with his hands

and will smear the food on the table and on himself. As he becomes more independent his motor abilities will develop, he will be able to control his movements and develop proper and pleasant eating habits. In the initial stages of group eating one should not burden those children who still have difficulty in sitting for prolonged periods. In order to prevent tension, one can offer the child some solid food, such as: bread and butter, a meatball, etc. and he may also eat this while walking around. When the child has reached a stage of motor maturity which allows him to control his motoric impulses, he should eat his whole meal while sitting at the table. He shouldn't be forced to wait at the table until all his "chaverim"* are finished, but one should aim at having all the children start their meal together. One shouldn't scold a child who is late. Also, food should not be used as a means of punishment, such as: leaving food from one meal to another, withholding favorite dishes, removing the child from the tables, etc. One shouldn't pressure the slow child, nor encourage competition. Always consider the individual rate of development of each

---

*The Hebrew term for comrade or friend. All members of the collective are termed "chaverim".

child. After 2½ years, one sets the table and puts the food in pleasant serving dishes. (Never set the kitchen pots on the table.) The metapelet then hands out portions according to the children's wishes. From the age of three, the child should be permitted to take his own food, and we should only watch that he eats in an aesthetic manner. We should provide him with a fork and spoon and thus educate him to eat in a pleasant and orderly manner. Beginning at the age of two, the metapelet should eat two meals a day with the children, acting as a model from which they may learn the proper eating habits. Her presence and active participation also adds to the pleasant, sociable atmosphere. One shouldn't prevent quiet conversations during the meal. The children should also have free access to food - such as bread and fruit - between meals, and they should be encouraged to serve themselves. It is worthwhile having the children take part in the preparation of certain foods, such as making salads, buttering bread, etc. and in the setting of the table and the cleaning up after the meal.

Proper conditions and organization and a positive and supportive educational approach help the child adjust to proper eating habits.

TOILET TRAINING

A child's adjustment to his surroundings is dependent on the control of his instinctual drives and the relinquishment of pleasure. Acceptance of demands for cleanliness is indeed a difficult relinquishment. The child's approach towards his excrements is simple and natural. He has none of the disgust or nausea which exists in adults. He regards them as part of his body and attaches to them great importance. The negative feelings are acquired, they are the fruit of an educational process related to the relationship of the metapelet and the mother, and to the methods used during toilet training. The child won't be willing to relinquish his excrements unless he receives a compensation for his "giving" - some expression of a warm,

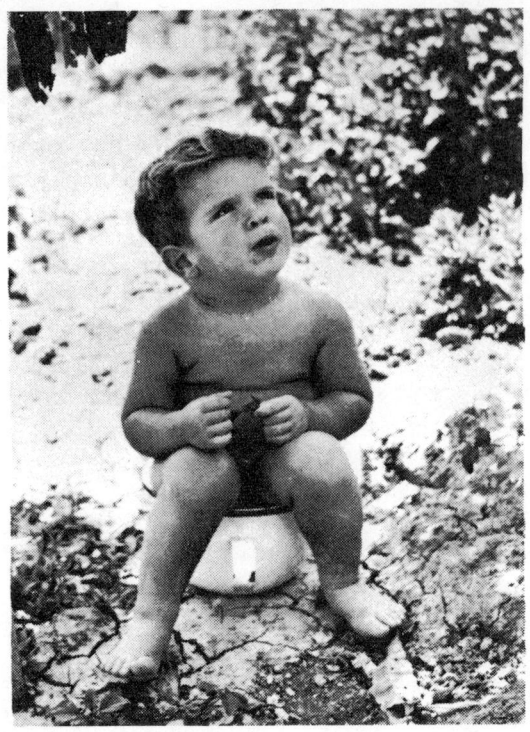

supportive relationship on the part of a closed, loved person.

One should not begin making demands on the child during a period of stress - such as following the birth of a sibling, during a trip of the parents, during or following a sickness, during a family crisis, etc. Everything which causes a shock in the child's life causes a regression in his accomplishments. Scaring, threatening and punishing cause damage and effect the healthy development of the personality. There is a definite connection between toilet training and character development, both in positive and negative ways. Toilet training should be done with patience, courtesy and consistency, and in a quiet, practical manner. During the initial stages the metapelet should be the only person who makes demands on the child. Once some

headway has been made, the parents should be included and a common educational approach achieved.

When should toilet training be started?

From the earliest age, keeping the infant clean is a primary and basic stage in toilet training. One should try to see that the infant enjoys being dry. One should never feed an infant while he has a soiled diaper. Demands for toilet training are dependent on the child's general development: muscle control (walking, sitting and rising) and sphincter control, mental development which allows him to understand the demands made upon him, and willingness to cooperate with adults who are close to him. The proper age is about 1½-2 years, depending on the individual development of each child. One should neither start too early nor too late. The first association towards the potty should be a pleasant one, so we will take care about all the technical details: the potty should be comfortable. The potty should be on the floor and not on some high spot, so that the child will feel secure. It should be placed outside of the eating area so that the child will have the proper associations regarding eating and elimination. One shouldn't try to intice the child to sit on the potty by giving him games, toys, food or other activities. On the other hand, one should not take away a toy which he might be holding. Sitting on the potty need not be done at specially organized times (before or after meals, etc.). One should instead arrange it according to the individual needs of each child. This will prevent collective potty sitting. One need not be strict about the child's activities with the pot (sliding it on floor, exchanging pots, etc.) as the child merely enjoys his motoric abilities, and this stage will pass with time. The initial training should be aimed at control of bowel movements. Introduce the pot gradually and consistently – beginning once a day and going up to 3-4 times a day. In cases of obstinate refusal, stop and wait for 3-4 weeks, without even mentioning the pot. Then start again slowly. Make sure that the child becomes independent in caring for himself by providing him with proper clothes (pants without suspenders, etc.), by keeping the pots in a convenient spot, by having a convenient place to wash hands, etc. When the child achieves full independence and no longer needs our help, we can suggest that he use a regular toilet. If a child happens to soil himself, we should change his clothes without making any negative remarks. Don't show any affective reaction to his achievements or his failures. The metapelet's reactions should only be practical and to the point. During this period make plentiful use of sublimative play; sand, water, clay, glue, dough, and paint – and divert the child's instincts and pleasures into creative activity. During the period of toilet training pay attention to bodily cleanliness, and the washing of hands and face. Encourage the child's pleasure in "being clean" instead of pleasure in playing in dirt.

Incorrect methods and excessive demands may cause fears and constipation. There are fears which are related to childhood fantasies – fear of the toilet and of the flushing water, fear of falling into the toilet

or loosing part of his body in the toilet, etc. The
child cannot overcome these fears by himself, and usually cannot even express them. Thus we must follow him
in different ways, understand the reasons for his fears
and try to help him overcome them. Strictness and re-
strictions are not limited to the child's relationship
to toilet habits, but spread into other areas of the
personality as well and determine his general development.

THE STORY

Stories are a source of pleasant and entertaining
emotional experiences for the small child, and teach
him to express his feelings and knowledge in words.
The story concretizes in words the child's experiences
and his knowledge about his surroundings.

The small child from 2-2½ years likes to see himself or people close to him as the center of each
"tale". A story accompanied with gestures, sound and
rythm, and told in correct and simple language, speaks
to the heart of the child. He is willing to listen to

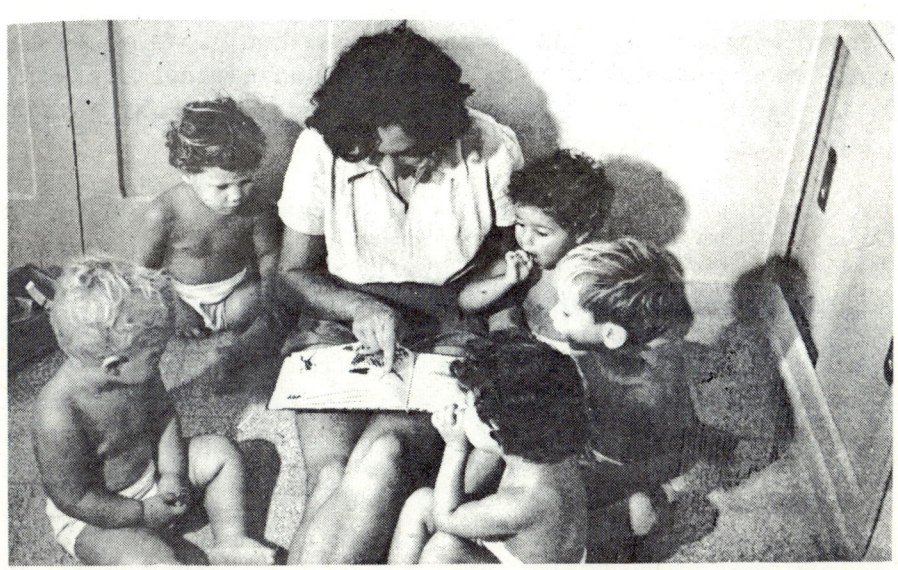

it endlessly. And takes part in it, watching carefully each detail of the form and content. Repetition concretizes the "tale", and brings the child closer to it.

At the age of three the child's world widens, his intellectual comprehension develops, and his interests grow beyond the limits of his own daily activities. Animals, people, and various vehicles (especially those related to people who are close to the child) comprise the contents of stories for this age. Fantasy stories that are entertaining and not fearful, are pleasant to the child and good for him. The story is an experience for the child, and should be told in a pleasant, comfortable and free atmosphere. One shouldn't create a rigid "story-telling hour" that is constant and at the same time for all children. Tell stories at various appropriate opportunities to one or several children, as they wish. Tell the story by heart, while looking at the children, and not in the book. In this way we take an active part in the child's reactions and liven his experiences. One may make use of pictures and animal dolls during the stories, but this should not interfere with the direct contact between the metapelet and the child while she is telling the story.

Each metapelet should choose and work out for herself a modest number of stories which are appropriate for the children in her care. At early ages the picture book may be made out of various materials, such as plywood, plastic, or cardboard.

At three years one can introduce appropriate picture books (with a number of objects) of such a size that the child can handle the book by himself without damaging it. Caring for the book, keeping it clean and whole, and handling it correctly teaches the child the special attitude and attention which this cultural property deserves.

THE WALK

As with any activity with young children, walks should essentially be a pleasant experience.

A walk widens and enrichens the child's environment, acquaints him with new objects, persons and phenomena. It deepens his observations and searching and enrichens his world.

A well equipped yard may also serve as an additional source of such enrichment.

Up to the age of two years it is enough to walk around the yard, a lawn near the children's house or some other nearby, shaded spot. The children enjoy the freedom to move about and the play with the metapelet (with a ball, a wheel, etc.). Walks with small children in a carriage, the child being restricted in movement do not fulfill the needs of the child and should be avoided.

At the age of 2½ years we can take the children for walks to more distant places, such as the cowsheds, the chicken runs, the school yard or a nearby woods. There is no need to plan ahead, and the children will find things of interest on the way and linger where they wish, observing and investigating. Don't bother them or drag them away, and don't tire them. The metapelet should remember that her participation in the child's experiences and in the childhood world gives the child more security and encourages him in his investigation and activity. Thus the walks should be devoted strictly to the children and their needs, and not be used by the metapelet as an opportunity to carry out errands or duties of her own.

HOLIDAYS IN THE CHILDREN'S HOUSE

The general holiday atmosphere in the kibbutz blends in with the atmosphere of the holiday in the children's house and gives the child a feeling of belonging and of closeness with his parents, the kibbutz members and the place itself. The small child absorbs impressions of the holiday atmosphere which is expressed in the cleaning up of the house, the special dress (his own, and that of the metapelet and his parents) and the special signs of the holiday: decorations, food and song. The holiday becomes a deep experience to the child which effects his tender soul and leaves imprints for the rest of his life. From the first year of life he will be impressed by and absorb signs, symbols and decorations. An excess of symbols are a burden, however, and may confuse his impressions.

The tradition of each holiday, with its symbols and customs, which repeat themselves each year crystallize in the child's mind the special image of each holiday. Verbal explanations are in place only from the age of 5-6 years. From the age of 2½ the children will participate in the preparations for the holiday. The formal decorations should be prepared by the metapelet herself and the child should be left to be spontaneous in his creations. One shouldn't give him "suggestions" or "plans" for decorations and symbols. On the other hand the children should help to clean the children's house, get the table and prepare the typical holiday food. The appearance of the young child in plays or pagents is a burden to him and is damaging. Remember that we are supposed to give the child a pleasant experience, not he give us.

The parents should be part of the holiday making in the children's house. They should be invited to take part in the preparations for each holiday. Their participation tightens their relationship with the children's house. The mutual feeling of belonging gives the child security and strengthens his personality.

THE SABBATH

We will pay special attention to the Sabbath. A continuity of repetitive weekly experiences makes a deep impression on the young child and leaves a definate emotional imprint. Therefore we should give the Sabbath a particularly festive color. On Friday one should feel the preparation for the coming Sabbath: the child should be present during preparations and should participate in them as much as possible. The children's house should be thoroughly cleaned. The toys should be cleaned, and the doll's clothes washed and ironed, and the dolls dressed in holiday clothes. Flowers should be put on the table. And the children should be dressed in clothes which differ from their daily ones.

The metapelet should also wear festive clothes. The tables should be covered with white (not plastic) tablecloths, and colorful flowers which the children like should be put on the table. Sabbath candles should be lit while all the children are sitting around the table, and Sabbath songs will add to the pleasant atmosphere. This ceremony should not exceed 5-7 minutes. For children from 3-4 years one can play Sabbath songs on a recorder, or on the phonograph.

The day's schedule on the Sabbath should not differ from that on weekdays, except that the children will be with their parents during the morning hours. After this playtime with the parents, the children should return to the children's house at an appointed hour. The metapelet should greet each child and help the parents separate from him. Then she should see that the child gets back into the routine of the children's house.

Housework should be kept at a minimum on the Sabbath, and one should not try to use the Sabbath to carry out special cleaning or other arrangements which would spoil the relaxed atmosphere of the day of rest - the Sabbath.

BIRTHDAYS

Birthday parties have special meaning to the young child. The concept of an additional year being added to his life is incomprehensible but the feeling "I'm already big" which accompanies the birthday is clearly absorbed in his young soul, and this encourages him and adds to his feeling of security. On this special day he is not merely one of the group, but the only one upon whom is focused the attention of the metapelet, the parents, the siblings and all other members of the family. We should put stress on this particular day by making the birthday party on the exact date and by not combining several birthdays into one party and by

not trying to combine the birthday party with a celebration of the Sabbath or some other holiday. The content and character of this modest family celebration should be different and special. The birthday of each child is a day of joy and celebration for everyone in the children's house, the workers, all the children and all their parents.

The first birthday should be celebrated by everyone sitting together in the children's house over coffee and cake. The "child of the day" should be dressed in holiday clothes, his bed decorated, and a large sign hung on the wall greeting all the parents. It is a good custom to photograph the child before his birthday and to present the picture to his parents during the party, on this day of their happiness. A copy should also be kept for the children's house. The second birthday should be celebrated in such a way that all the children take an active part. They are impressed by the pleasant atmosphere of the family "togetherness". The "host's" chair should be decorated with flowers and greenery. Songs and games, and common dancing with the children and the parents will add to the joy and satisfaction of the occasion. Each child should be given a small present wrapped in colorful paper (a doll, a toy, car etc.). The toys need not be the same, and the metapelet should choose toys which she feels are particularly appropriate for each individual child. The special present for the child whose birthday is being celebrated is the traditional photograph. At the 3rd and 4th birthdays we can elaborate on the content of the party by adding a puppet show, or a movie about a story which is familiar to the children. A good custom is to have the parents of the child tell a humorous story to all the children and one should instruct the parents and prepare them for this.

Special importance should be given to presents from the parents to the children's house. Thus from a tender age the child can absorb the joy of giving. This experience will help him as time goes on to respect others and to develop good social behavior.

NIGHTIME IN COLLECTIVE SLEEPING ARRANGEMENTS

Customs of putting to bed, sleeping and night-watch

The child's relaxed state directly effects his willingness to go to sleep and his ability to sleep well. Conditions which contribute to such a state are as follows: The evening hours should be devoted to quiet play with the family. The family room should be prepared during this period so as to be compatable to the needs of the child for free movement and play, with a minimum of prohibitions and restricting or critical comments. The parents should devote this time to the child only and not occupy themselves with other things.

In each children's group the parents and metapelet must arrive at a common agreement the time of going to bed (in accordance with medical-educational regulations). There should be regulations and customs which assure a quiet and relaxed transition for activities of the day to rest of the night, such as:

a) Preparations for going to bed should be carried out in all parts of children's house, and not just in the bedrooms.

b) The parents should put their children to bed in a relaxed, pleasant, short and "down-to-business" manner, but without being rigid.

c) Only modest use should be made of bedtime stories and songs, and one shouldn't become involved in other distracting activities.

In order to help the parents separate from their children, the metapelet should come into the room and say good-night to the children.

This method should start from the age of 1½-2 years. At younger ages the metapelet stays with the children until they are all asleep. With older children, the metapelet should come back to check on the children after she has finished her supper, and the children should know of this arrangement. After the metapelet leaves for the evening, one parent (by rotation) should stay in the children's house until the night watch comes on, so that there should be constant watch over the children. This assures a feeling of security to the children and the parents. From the age of 2½-3 it is worthwhile to arrange to have a parent or other kibbutz member in the children's house, especially in border settlements and during times of war tension, etc. Their bed should be comfortable; and should be in the playroom and not in the children's bedroom. The adult should come to the children's house no later than 10.30 in the evening. The children should know ahead of time which adult will be sleeping in, and should be acquainted with him.

Miscellaneous comments

The children's house should be well lit while the children are being put to bed, and afterwards a small light should be left on in the bedrooms and the bedroom doors should be left open. One shouldn't prohibit the children from talking quietly before falling asleep, yet one shouldn't encourage dragging this out too long.

Night-watch in children's house

One member of the kibbutz's education committee should be in charge of arranging adequate supervision of the children's houses at night. She should carefully inform each watch-woman of the permanent regulations as well as the specific and changing orders; according to the situation. Every watch-woman should be well known to the children and one shouldn't use temporary visitors or new members in the kibbutz who are not completely familiar with the routines of the children's house. In border settlements the night-watch should also be coordinated with the kibbutz security committee. The supervision at night should be continuous. It should start not later than 8.30-9.00 p.m. and end at 6.00-6.30 a.m. when the metapelet comes to work. It is important that the children know ahead of time whose turn it is to be nightwatch and this woman should visit all the children and all the children's houses before she starts her tour of duty.

She should also be given full information about each child by the metapelet, especially when special problems exist. The watchwoman should inform the metapelet about any technical problems which disturb the children at night (such as squeaky doors or dripping faucets) so that the metapelet can have them repaired. The nightwatch's base should be the infant's house, or some place very central to all the children's houses. She should visit each house once an hour, and should immediately attend to any child who calls her through the "electronic baby-sitter".* One should see that the children's houses remain quiet during the night, and one shouldn't suddenly turn on lights when the children

are sleeping. A flashlight and a pencil should be kept in a permanent place in each children's house, so that the nightwatch can leave a note regarding any special events which occurred during the night. The nightwatch should not be given any additional tasks. She should eat her night meal in the children's house or some appointed central place. There should be a small electric lamp in each children's house for the

---

*See page 252.

use of the nightwatch, as well as a kerosene lamp in case of an electricity failure.

Getting the children up in the morning

We should be concerned with seeing that the child has a gradual transition from night to day, and not confront him with drastic changes which will spoil his mood upon rising in the morning. Thus we should see that: the metapelet is in the children's house by the time the first child wakes up, so that when he opens his eyes in the morning he sees the familiar and loved adult by his side. If he knows ahead of time that he can expect this, then he will be able to sleep quietly. The presence of the adult is doubly important during the period of toilet training, and the importance of this should not be underestimated.

Finally we should add that the condition of the child during the day affects his sleep at night. The relationship between himself and his surroundings, the degree of satisfaction from motor activity and play, and the general atmosphere in the children's house, all contribute to the emotional balance of the child, to his ability to adjust to social demands, to his willingness to go to sleep and the possibility of achieving rest and relaxation during sleep.

"Electronic baby-sitter"

An "electronic baby-sitter" should be used to make the nightwatch more efficient. The base of this intercom system should be in the infant's house. Some central place near the infant's house. It should be located in such a way that it will not disturb the infants and should have connections to all the children's houses, including those of the school age children.

Between each round which the nightwatch makes among the children's houses, she can keep track of exactly what is going on in all the children's houses by listening to this intercom, and can thus go and help wherever she is needed. At the early ages, one only uses the intercom to hear what is happening in the infants' house. As the children grow older they can be taught how the intercom works and the nightwatch can then converse with them through the intercom.

Regulations

1. There should be one person on watch for every 50-60 children. If there are more children, then there must be an additional person working on the nightwatch.

2. Additional help is also necessary in such situations as: stormy nights, states of emergency, or during periods when many children are sick.

3. Special watch in cases of night crying should be approved by the education committee.

Family sleeping arrangements

In those kibbutzim that are undergoing a transition to family sleeping arrangements, these should start from infancy and gradually include older age groups. The children's houses are exactly the same as when they are used for collective sleeping. The children's house is a general framework for all the child's activities. The metapelet remains responsible for the emotional and physical care, just as before, and all the physical care of the child is done in the children's house. All meals should be had in the children's house. The children's clothes are kept in the children's house and are cared for by the metapelet. The metapelet also continues to look after all the health needs of the child, and keeps in contact with the nurse and the doctor when he is sick. The children's house remains a positive educational factor which encourages the child's general development, in which a full life experience is to be had, both on weekdays, and on the Sabbath and holidays.

The parents

Family sleeping arrangements put additional educational responsibility on the parents, and give added importance to the relationship and collaboration between family home and the children's home. Communication of various kinds, exchange of information and personal contact between the family and the metapelet are necessary for the education and adjustment of the child. The family apartment must consist of two rooms with separate entrances and with sanitary facilities. One should never permit any child, no matter what his age, to sleep in the same room as his parents. Do not permit both collective and family sleeping arrangements in the same kibbutz. There should be a common, agreed hour of going to bed for each age, in order that all the children get enough sleep and arrive at the children's house on time in the morning. Children should not be left alone in the evenings without someone watching them. In all instances, a sick child should be kept in the children's house.

THE PARENTS AND THE CHILDREN'S HOUSE

Parents are the central emotional factor in the formation of the child's personality. Their influence on the child's education and adjustment can be crucial. On the other hand, the child spends most of his day in the children's house. The congruence or incongruence between these two centers of the child's life may be fateful for the child's future. The parent's participation and integration within the child's life are fundamental bases of education in general, and collective education in particular. The demands and reactions of the family and the children's house should be coordinated. The parents can be brought close to the children's house in the following ways: Discussions between the metapelet and the parents, familiarize the parents with the child's problems and help in finding solutions to them. These discussions should be held after working hours, and should be arranged ahead of time with the parents. Visits of the parents to the

children's house - either at the initiative of the metapelet or themselves - are important. But the parents should avoid interfering with or commenting about the work of the metapelet. Participation of parents widens, and adds variety, to the child's environment and gives a feeling of togetherness, cooperation and mutual responsibility in the children's house, which then becomes "the house of all of us". One should encourage all sorts of common activities in the children's house, such as "Children's Day", common preparation for holidays, etc.

Saying good-morning

During the first year of life the needed contact between mother and child is satisfied by constant meetings - in feeding, bathing, etc. After the period when all the care goes over to the metapelet, one must encourage additional daily contact between the mother and the child over and above that which occurs in the evening hours. A consistent, routine visit accompanied by gratifying and pleasant behavior, which does not take the child out of his other routines, is a proper framework of common enjoyment and helps the child separate from his mother with a feeling of satisfaction and emotional balance. Visits of all the parents at an identical time is an unsatisfactory arrangement, as it causes difficulties in their places of work, interferes with the intimacy of the mutual recreation of the child and his parent, interrupts the routine of the children's house and causes noise and pandemonium. Taking the child out of the house for a walk or for other reasons - takes him out of his routine and makes it more difficult for him to reintegrate into the children's activity. It is best to visit in the children's house, to take part in the child's play and to be busy with him. Then the separation will be easier and the transition simpler.

Generally this morning visit is during work hours and therefore it must be short - 10-15 minutes. Its purpose is the attainment of emotional satisfaction, and thus its character is more important than its length. The educational value of the visit is its ability to impress on the child that mother is working - something which can't be changed. This helps the child adjust to reality. The metapelet should always be by the mother's side in order to lighten the task of separating and should help the mother where this is necessary.

The child's corner in the parent's room

The child should have a special corner for his toys in the parent's room - a corner all of his own. There should not be too many toys but the corner should be attractive to the child. The child should keep order in his corner and become attached to his toys and enjoy his ownership of them. It is best to have toys which have been made by members of the family together with the child. One should also help the child develop a need to give (to give presents to friends, neighbors and the children's house) but the parents should not interfere with or "guide" the child's acts in this area.

Parent's travel

It is not advisable for both parents to travel out of the kibbutz for extended periods of time during the child's first years of life. Their absence causes tension and disappointment in the child and undermines his confidence in their love for him.

Children's travel

It is not advisable for small children to travel outside the kibbutz and this is definitely not to be done during the first year of life. During the second year, it is advisable to limit such travel to the minimum. This should be only on special occasions and with the approval of the education committee.

The metapelet and her role

The child spends most of the day in the children's house and his needs are cared for by the metapelet. His relationship to her and the basis for his social adjustment are built upon her patient approach, her understanding and her warmth towards him. She should also keep her eyes open for opportunities to provide him with physical stimuli that will encourage his activity and his curiosity and will widen his world.

A a warm and quiet atmosphere encourages the child and gives the child a feeling of security and trust.

In her relationship to the parents, the metapelet should show understanding and a willingness to include them in the educational efforts and in the concern with the child's health.

The metapelet should have frequent talks with young mothers, in particular. She should inform the young mother of each change in the child or in his routines, and explain all new signs of the child's development. She should also try to avoid making decisions and changes without consulting with the mother.

Mothers who come to the kibbutz from the city have certain difficulties in adjusting to collective education. The metapelet should understand these difficulties, have patience and permit the mother express her feelings freely. Intimate discussions, explanations and a willingness to listen all help the mother adjust to and accept the ways of life of our society.

Common meetings of the parents and metapelet which are organized by the metapelet and the early childhood supervisor are important and should be held at least once every two months. They should be used to discuss such topics as:

    a. Report on the children.
    b. Description of their games and behavior.
    c. Explanation of methods of toilet training (at the appropriate time).
    d. Feeding habits.
    e. Daily schedule.
    f. Problems of sleep, naps, and nightwatch.
    g. Questions of hygiene and health.

      h. Recreation of children and parents.
      i. Explanations of changes in schedules, particular behaviors, etc.
      k. Discussion about appropriate stories and distribution of story material to parents.

Festive meetings with the parents may be encouraged on such occasions as a birthday in one of the families, the return of someone from the hospital etc. The development of relations among themselves and with the children of their friends helps develop a warm family-like atmosphere in the children's house and in an indirect way effects the relationships among the children themselves.

One of the central tasks of the metapelet is to be vigilant in developing the atmosphere in the children's house and in mobilizing the participation of parents in educational work.

Work of a metapelet who is also a mother

The metapelet should try to avoid any actions which will disturb the normal progress of the children's lives. During her pregnancy she should work as long as possible (until the middle of the ninth month) and should receive whatever help she needs. When she is out of work, she should continue her contact with the children to as great a degree as possible.

Upon completing her vacation, she should return to work with the children and concentrate her work in direct care of the children - in feeding, bathing and putting them to bed.

It is definately inadvisable to have a metapelet, work with a group which includes her own child. This can be damaging both to her own and to the other children.

Transition to kindergarten

Children are transferred from the children's house to the kindergarten at the age of 3½-4. In order to avoid crises and emotional shocks, this transfer should be made gradually. The metapelet should continue working with the children in the kindergarten until she feels that they have adjusted to their new environment. Before the children are transferred to the kindergarten, the metapelet will hold discussions with the kindergarten teachers and the education committee regarding the problems involved in preparing the children for the transfer and in helping them adjust and fit into the kindergarten children's group.

Before transferring the children one must check: 1. the proportion of boys and girls and 2. the placing of children in the bedrooms, following consultation with the parents.

THE TRAINING OF EDUCATORS

The permanent metapelet

1. A chavera who begins to work with a group of young children must undergo several months of practical training under the supervision of an experienced metapelet with *educational knowledge*.

2. Following this she must take a one-week's basic course and thereafter continue to take part in monthly study groups.

3. After she has worked for 1½-2 years and has demonstrated her talent and her special emotional attachment to young children, she should be permitted to take a basic theoretical course for three months at the Kibbutz Teacher's Seminary. This training widens and gives a stronger base to her knowledge about the development, needs and personality of the infant and young child up to the age of 4. Even more basic one-year courses are available at the eminary.

4. Medical training for 2 months in one of the hospitals completes the circle of the basic training of every metapelet.

5. A metapelet who has completed the foregoing stages of training and who continues to work with young children, should take part in the monthly study groups at the kibbutz Teacher's Seminary.

6. Each metapelet has the right, every second year, to take part in short refresher courses (5-6 days) which are given at the Seminary.

7. Each metapelet should be given 2-3 days every year to make observations in other kibbutz children's homes. If a metapelet has been unable, for family reasons, to leave the kibbutz to take part in courses, she should be given additional days for such observations.

8. Each metapelet who has worked for three years has the right to receive a special budget for professional literature.

9. Local self-education should be promoted through the establishment of education discussion groups and an educational library in each kibbutz.

10. *The substitute metapelet*: Every substitute metapelet should study the problems of the child and should learn to relate to them. Then she should be given some training.

In each children's group there must be a single, steady substitute metapelet. She should be part of the education team, should take part in all group discussions and parent's meetings. After she has completed a short training, she must continue to take part in the regional study groups.

After a period of successful work as a substitute metapelet, she may become a candidate to be a regular metapelet.

The substitute metapelet during hours when the metapelet is not working:

Even this substitute must be a constant person and she should take part in all the activities - just like other substitute metaplot.

The early childhood supervisor

1. Each kibbutz must have a supervisor for early childhood.

2. Her selection depends upon her social status in the kibbutz and her level of training. She does not necessarily have to work directly with young children but she must be completely familiar with the problems of early childhood (by having worked previously or having fulfilled functions related to this age).

3. Each chavera who is chosen as a supervisor must complete a course for supervisors given by the kibbutz movement. These courses are held for two days each month and last for 2½ years.

4. These courses include the following subjects: psychology, education, life activities in the children's house (singing, play, painting, etc.) problems of organization, problems of supervision, etc. The total number of hours in each course is 354.

5. Each kibbutz must give the supervisor time to carry out her job, according to the range of her responsibilities and the size and number of the children's groups.

The responsibilities of the supervisor

1. Her principle responsibilities are daily, practical guidance to the metaplot, induction of new metaplot into their jobs, clarification of problems arising in wake of work or in the interactions between metapelet-parents-children, etc.

2. She should visit the children's groups as needed, and discuss problems which she observes with each metapelet.

3. She must organize and participate in periodical meetings of the parents and metaplot of each children's group.

4. She should arrange regular supervisory meetings with each metapelet, which should be used to discuss problems arising in her work.

5. Additional functions: she is responsible for the organization and equipping of the educational establishment.

6. She is responsible for balancing the budget of each children's house.

7. She is responsible for the continuous work of the early childhood education committee.

Work hours of the supervisor

    3 hours/week for three groups of toddlers

    8 hours/week for three to six groups of toddlers

    12-16 hours/week for 6-12 groups of toddlers

Each kibbutz should prepare 2-3 supervisors and should allow them to obtain the proper training.

The absorption of young children into the kibbutz

When we talk about the absorption of young children into the kibbutz, we mean their absorption together, the absorption of their parents. Proper absorption of the family will ease the absorption of the children. The family should be brought close to the kibbutz and a specific liason person should be appointed to help the new family. Understanding for and acceptance of the special needs of new person will provide him with a feeling of trust and will strengthen his security, (which is inevitably disturbed when one comes to a new and strange environment).

A positive and accepting attitude of the metapelet towards the parents and the children is of particular importance. A warm manner of listening to their requests and of helping them will be more effective than simple verbal explanations such as "that is the way we do things here".

It is also important to understand the attitudes of the parents of the other children in the group and to encourage and stimulate the relationship between themselves and the new family.

In addition, before a new child is accepted one should:

1. Obtain health records of all members of the family.

2. Send any child over 3 years of age to the kibbutz Child Guidance Clinic for psychological testing.

The results of the psychological tests will be received by a qualified member of the Education Department of the kibbutz movement.

One should differentiate between the methods of absorbing infants under 6 months of age and those children who are older. There is also a difference between absorbing a family that comes from another kibbutz and one which comes from the city or from another country.

a) An infant who comes from another kibbutz will be put into the infants' home and his mother will care for him according to the accepted regulations for the first year of life.

b) An infant or toddler who comes from the city or from another country should sleep with his parents for the first ten days, but should eat, play and bathe in the children's house. As he gradually adjusts to the new environment, his mother should begin to leave him for short periods. Her absence should be gradually increased, until the child is left in the children's house for his afternoon nap. He should begin to sleep at night in the children's house only after he has become accustomed to and feels relaxed in his bed there.

This final stage will be determined mutually by the parents, the absorption committee and the education committee. If the particular group does not have an adult sleeping in at night, this should be arranged during the period in which the new child is becoming adjusted.

The work of the mother: During the initial period following the arrival of a new family in the kibbutz, the mother should be freed of all work and her subsequent availability for work will be dependent upon the degree of her child's adjustment to life in the children's house and his ability to be without her. At the beginning, it is wise to have her work somewhere nearby the children's house, so that she can visit her child according to his needs.

The education committee is responsible for all the arrangements necessary for the absorption of the new family:

1. Appointment of a liason person to the family;
2. Making sure there is a permanent metapelet;
3. Making the initial arrangement of the child's play corner in the family's room.

During the period that a new child is being absorbed the metapelet should not be burdened with any additional tasks outside the children's house (such as kitchen duty, guard duty, etc.). She should also delay any vacation or trip until the child's absorption is complete.

The janitor of the children's houses

The work of the janitor or yardkeeper of the children's houses is of highest priority among the trades, and must include within it many different skills. The janitor is "an artist for everything", "a jack of all trades", the man whose "hands are in everything": carpentry, metalwork, painting, gardening, driving, etc.

Broken toys and run-down installations should be repaired and painted with bright colors, so that they seem new, different and attractive to the children and stimulate the children's play and activity.

The talented and blessed hand of the janitor fixes, paints and rejuvenates a broken screen, a smashed window, a lonely hole in the wall which reminds us of the picture which hung there before the nail fell out, a door hanging crooked on a single hinge, a chair with a broken leg - all those little things which irritate everyone and spoil the aesthetic effect of the house. If he needs the help of more expert tradesmen, we will arrange this for him. Each house should have regular repair days, say once every two weeks.

But the janitor does not only repair. He should transport food from the central kitchen, take the children's clothes to the central laundry, and so on.

In the winter he should store away equipment which must be kept inside and bring fuel to heat the children's house.

The janitor should plan the landscaping of the children's house together with kibbutz gardener and landscaper and when doing so should take the needs of the children (for play and living space on lawns, etc.) into consideration.

In one short sentence, we can say that the janitor is the good "man of the house" who takes care that his home is well kept and pleasant.

THE YARD

A richly equipped yard with a wide variety of playthings encourages the child's emotional and physical development. It invites him to take part in many activities which fulfill and sublimate his drives. The child will find such a yard to be full of content and interest, will become attached to it and will not wander away.

The yard is an extension of the children's house - an integral part of it. Their physical connection allows the child free and independent access to the yard and leaves the metapelet free of worry, as well as saving her time. The yard is designed with the comprehensive children's house in which two children's groups live from birth to kindergarten age. The area of the yard should be about 2 acres and it should surround the children's house. It is divided into two equal sections, with a gate between them. This allows the yard to be used as one or two units, according to the needs. Each unit consists of a separate yard with its own entrance and sidewalk to the door of the children's house. The yard should be surrounded by a wire fence with a concrete base or a fence of colorfully painted ironwork. A fence of shrubs is not appropriate. When building the yard, both evergreen and deciduous trees should be planted. The equipment and character of the yard should be adapted to each age group.

The western or northern section of the yard is the shaded and cooler part, and is used particularly in the summer and during the morning and mid-day. Most of the equipment and play corners should be covered with sand.

The eastern or southern section of the yard should also be equipped but with equipped, but with equipment which is adjusted and changed according to the time of day and the season. In the summer the children will play there only during the shaded afternoon hours. As the children are dressed up following their afternoon nap (in preparation for their visit to the family room) there should be available playthings which will not cause the children to get dirty. In the winter, the children will play in this section of the yard for some hours in the morning - when the sun is warm - and it should be properly equipped for this. The yard should have a network of concrete sidewalks which the children will use for driving or pulling their vehicles (tricycles, carts, toys on wheels, etc.). The rest of the yard should be covered by a lawn, except for a 3 meter wide concrete playfloor adjacent to the eastern porch. This is used for individual and group playpens, and it should be covered (this can be an awning).

EARLY CHILDHOOD EDUCATION IN THE KIBBUTZ 269

Equipment and installations (see following pages for illustrations)

1. SWINGING

   a. *Wooden swing.* Height 30-40 cm above ground.

   b. *Regular swing.* Medium height. Children like to be swung by adults. This is for that purpose.

2. BALANCING

   a. *Steps-slide.* A construction which has wide steps on one side and on the other side a slide and a ladder.

   b. *A board* for balancing, 40 cm wide, 30 cm above ground.

   c. *Movable low ladder.*

3. CLIMBING

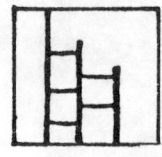

Climbing equipment.

4. DOLL HOUSE

a. *Doll house.* In order to save place, this can be put in the corner of the yard. It can be covered with colored fiberglass and the door can be draped with a pleasant curtain. The floor should be covered with a straw mat. Furniture includes a table, a sofa, a cupboard for play kitchen utensils, etc.

b. *A hiding corner.* A small tent or a large box with a curtain covering the entrance.

5. CRAWLING

A tunnel of barrels or of large asbestos pipes stimulates the young child to crawl.

6. SITTING

Table and benches - 1.20 m long, 80 cm wide, covered with stainless steel. A table can be built around the central tree in the yard. It is used for play with clay, paints, etc.

7. ROCKING

Rocking - various types of rocking toys.

EARLY CHILDHOOD EDUCATION IN THE KIBBUTZ 271

8. SHADE

A sunshade - used as an additional corner for play and activity, or as a spot to store carts and other vehicles at the end of the day. Several benches may be kept in this corner.

9. WATER

Wading pool and shower in which the children can play during the hot hours in the summer. The pool should be emptied in the afternoon. It should be 1.40 m square and 50 cm deep. The sides must be smooth and it can be lined with white or blue cement.

10. WATER-PLAY

Water-play equipment.

11. SAND

a. *Sandbox with water faucet*. Contact and play with water and sand helps the child lower his emotional tension and sublimate his drives. The sandbox should be next to the wall of the house. This allows for more hours of shade during the day. It should be 1½ × 2 m wide and 50 cm deep. A 40 cm wide concrete frame surrounds it, and is used as a bench by the children. A faucet above the sandbox is essential.

b. *Sandtable* - Even during the winter the child needs activity with damp sand but it is advisable that this is done while standing up. This is also worthwhile for playing with sand in the afternoon when he is dressed in clean clothes.

EARLY CHILDHOOD EDUCATION IN THE KIBBUTZ

12. MUD

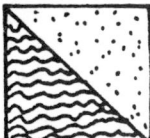

Water and mud corner. This should be made with a cement floor. The corner should contain: a half-barrel or water container on legs, the height of the child, two small metal holders for water basins, a clothes line for hanging wet doll's clothes, a soap dish and a box with old kitchen utensils such as pitchers, a strainer, etc.

13. ANIMALS

Pigeon nest – A nest gives a rural atmosphere to the yard and adds variety to the landscape. It should be painted in fresh, pleasant colors. Height = 2m.

14. FURNITURE (see furniture plans)

The furniture and its measurements, are adapted to the needs and comforts of the children, according to their age.

a. *The dining table* – Next to the regular dining table there should be an accessory table of the same length and height but not so wide. The two tables are used for feeding the children, as well as for work and table games. One can also use tables in the form of a trapezoid.

b. *The chair* – During the first stage of sitting, the child should be given a chair with removable protective shields on the sides. These can be removed when the child achieves more stable sitting and walking.

c. *Open cupboard* – This should be made to fit under the window in the dining room, so as to save space in the room. The cupboard is used for toys, which are changed according to the age of the children. Table games are kept locked in the closed section of the cupboard until the children are old enough to open the cupboard by themselves and use the games without damaging them.

    d. *Cupboard with drawers* - This is in the bedroom. Each cupboard is divided in two, and is used up till the age of 2½-3 years for clothing. After that age, the cupboard is used according to the personal wishes of the children, half of the drawer being used for clothes and half for personal belongings.

    e. *Infant dressing table.*

    f. *Table-bench in shower room* - This is used for dressing the children after the shower.

    g. *Crawling playpen* - For use in the yard, can be taken apart and moved. Once the infant reaches the age of 6-7 months he should be provided with safe and ample space to crawl. The floor should be covered with linoleum or other plastic material, so that it is easily cleaned.

    h. *Individual playpen* - These are put on the concrete floor or the southern porch. When the children outgrow them, they should be stored away. Never leave unnecessary furniture in the house or yard.

15. MISCELLANEOUS

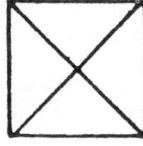

    a. *Tool shed* - This is for storage of the metapelet's tools - hoe, rake, broom, hammer and nails, paints, toys for repair, etc. The tool shed should be locked.

    b. *Hanger* for various tools used in sand play.

    c. *Colored tool box* - for additional tools.

    d. *Scrap corner* - This corner is for all sorts of scrap which can be found around the kibbutz, such as old tires and wheels, boxes, old plumbing or electric

EARLY CHILDHOOD EDUCATION IN THE KIBBUTZ

fixtures, ropes, etc. The corner is surrounded by shrubs and acts as another corner to hide in.

e. *Small garden* - This is used to permit 3-4 year olds to observe growing plants and to enjoy their fruits. The children's participation in the gardening is only token - such as occasionally watering the plants or picking the fruit.

f. *An old tractor* - or other vehicle.

g. *Faucet and basin for the metapelet* - This is for the convenience of the metapelet who sometimes needs to wash a child who has excessively dirtied himself during play.

h. *Old painted automobile*

i. *Bench for parents* - For the use of parents when they come to visit or pick up their children and who wish to sit and watch the children play.

j. *Shed for 6-8 baby carriages* - There should be baby carriages in the children's house to be used to take babies for rides in the evenings, or other times when the parents need them.

None of these installations should be higher than 60-70 cm. On should add logs, tires, steering wheels, boards and all sorts of boxes. There should be faucets in every corner and rubber hoses available in the yard.

Care for the cleanliness and improvement of the yard is one of the important responsibilities of metapelet. She should give this sufficient time.

SOURCES

E. Buxbaum - Your Child Makes Sense
A. Wolf - Parents Manual
K.H. Read - The Nursery School

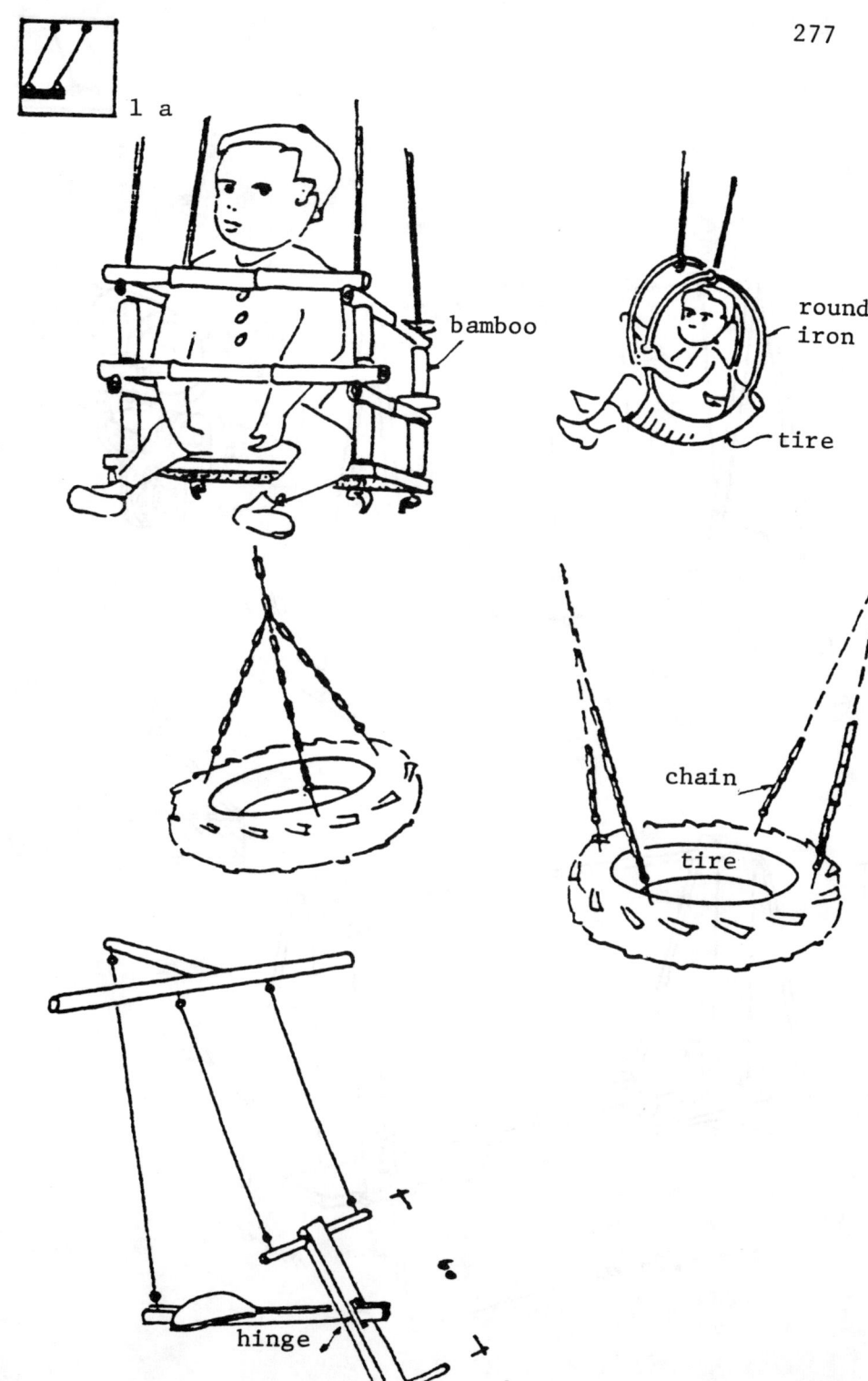

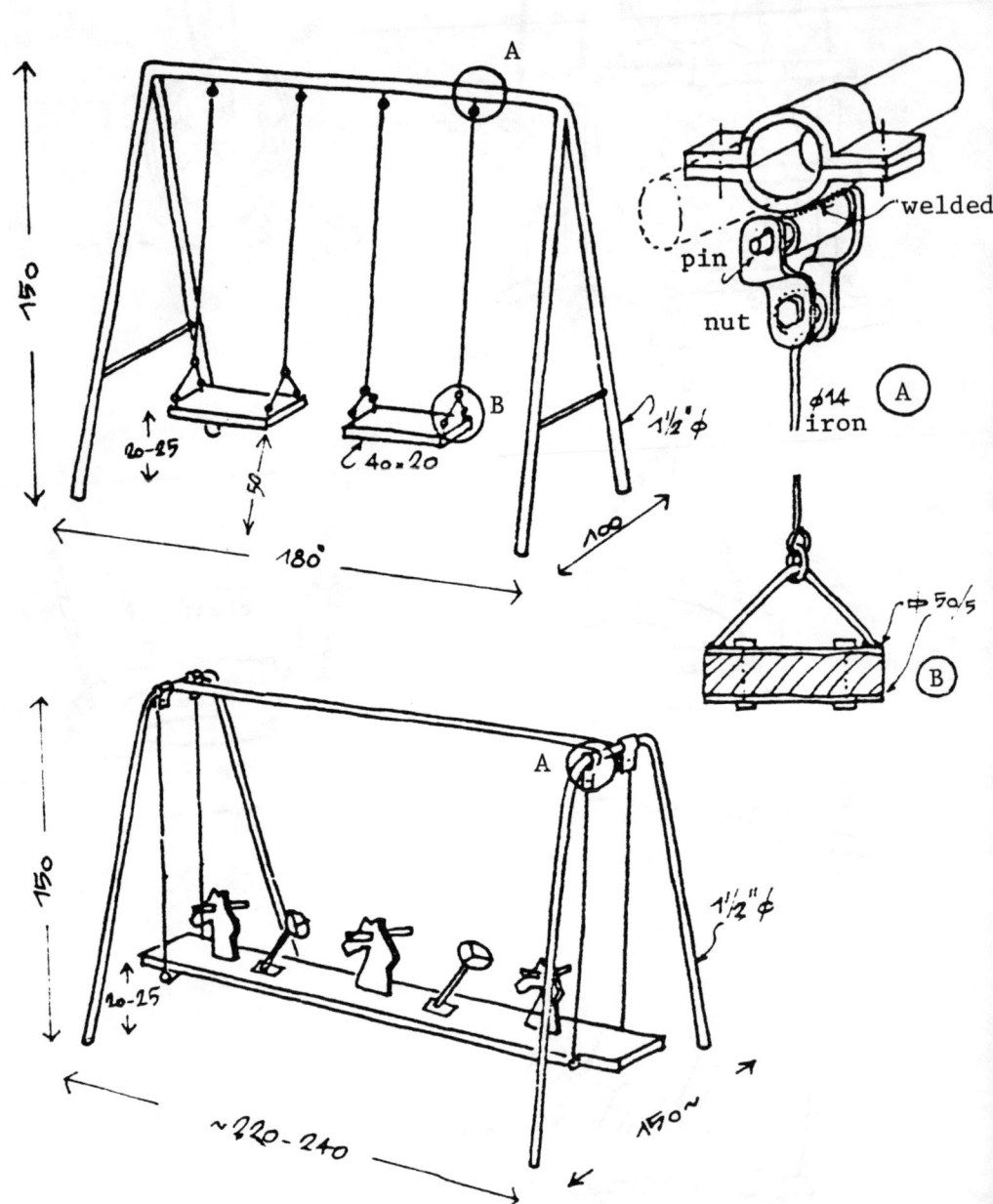

2 a

ladder
slide
tin, 5mm.
ϕ 1"
60
60
40
12

smooth 1' plank
ladder
2x3/3
3/4"ϕ

60
60
60-100

smooth 15/2" wood

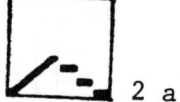

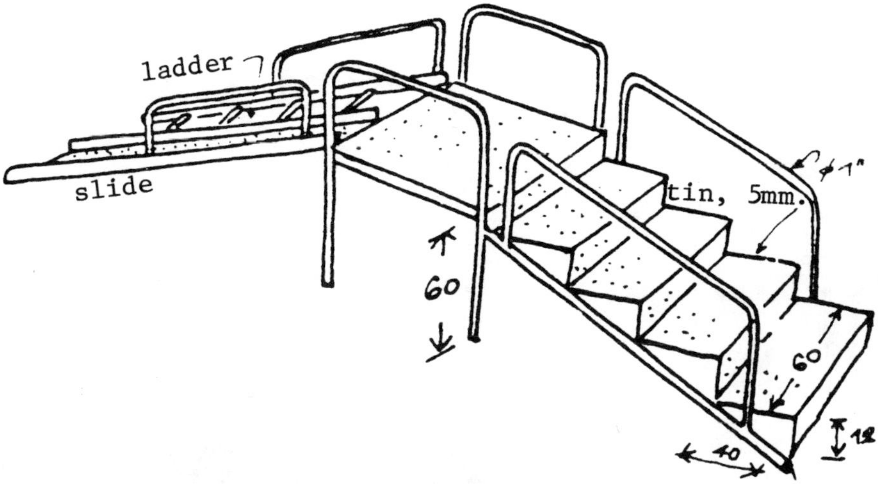

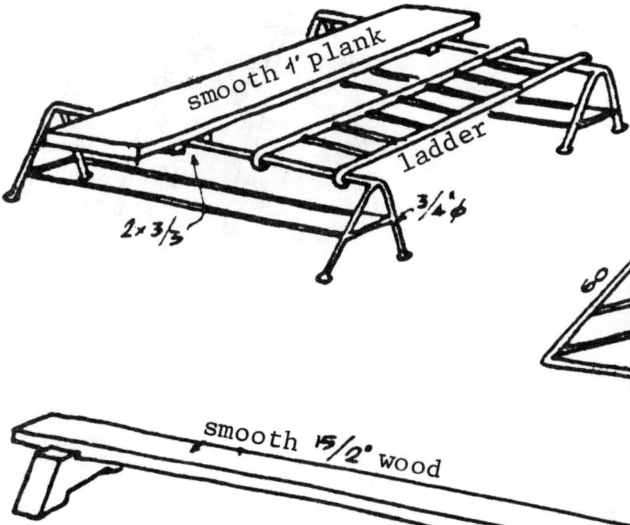

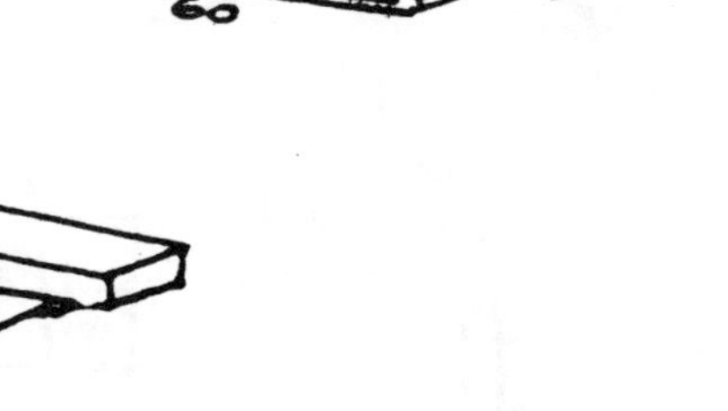

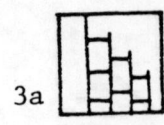

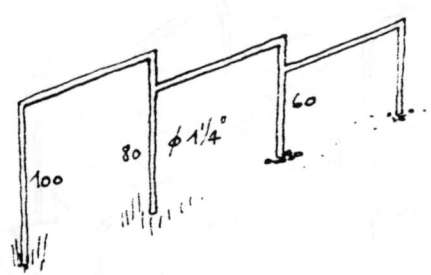

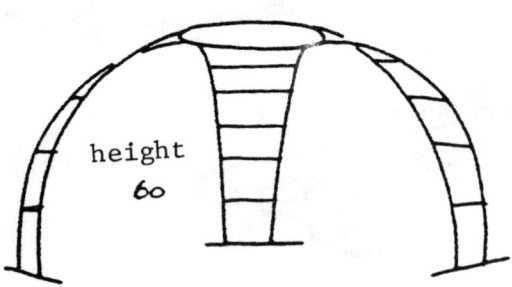

 4a

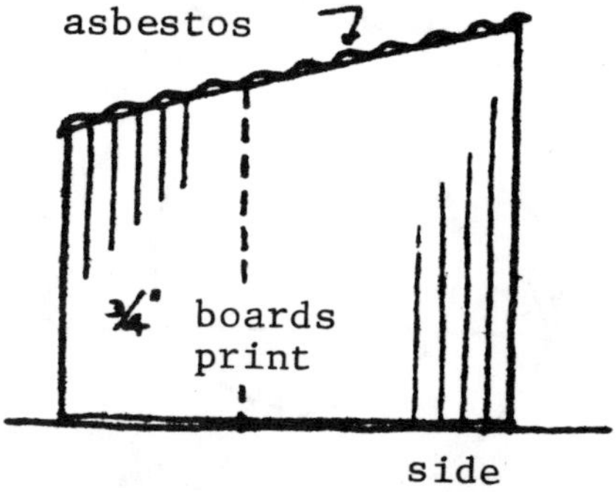

side — door — 50, 60, 15, 3, 3

asbestos
¾" boards
print
side

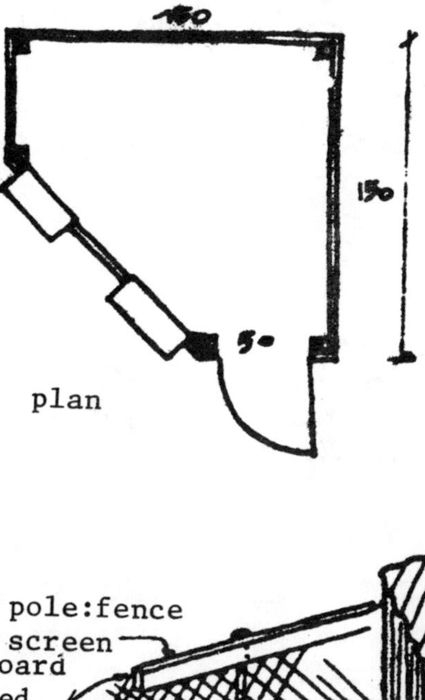

plan — 150, 150, 50

in the corner
of the yard

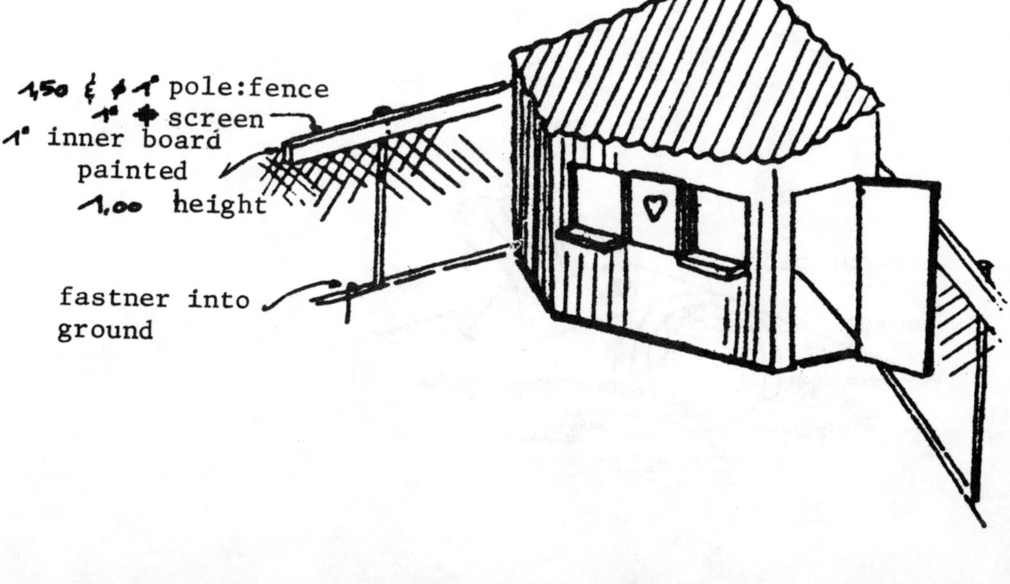

1,50 & ∅ 1" pole:fence
1" ∅ screen
1" inner board
  painted
1,00 height

fastner into
ground

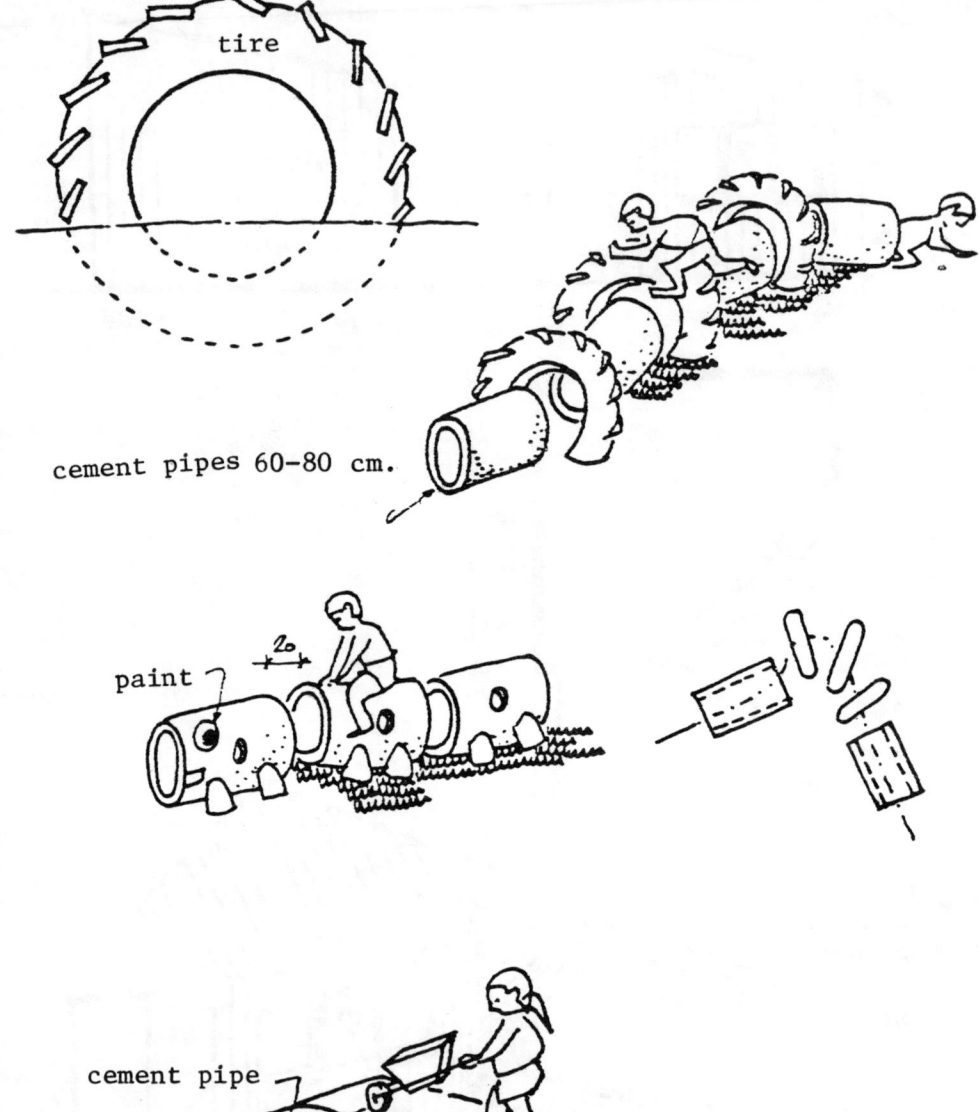

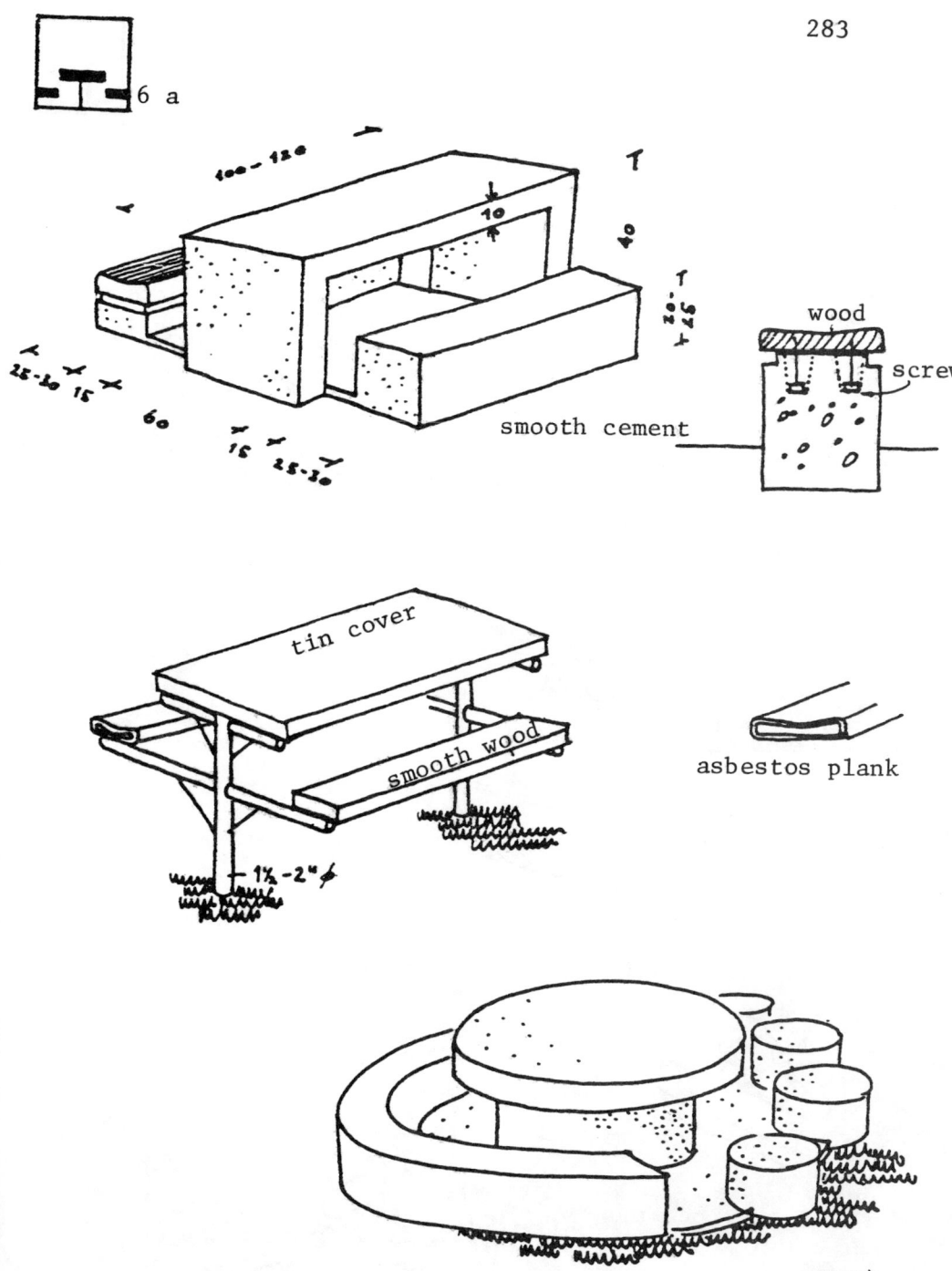

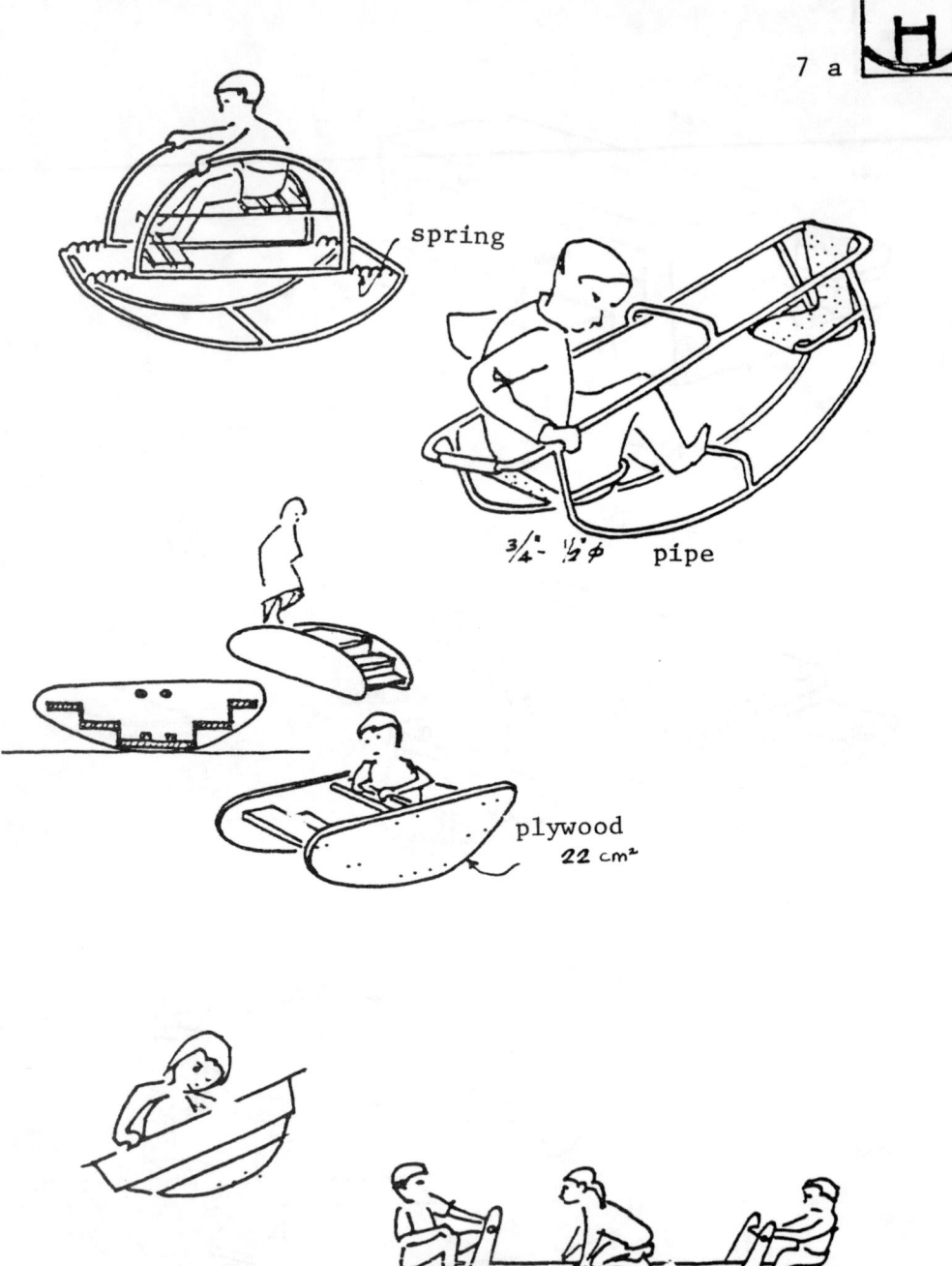

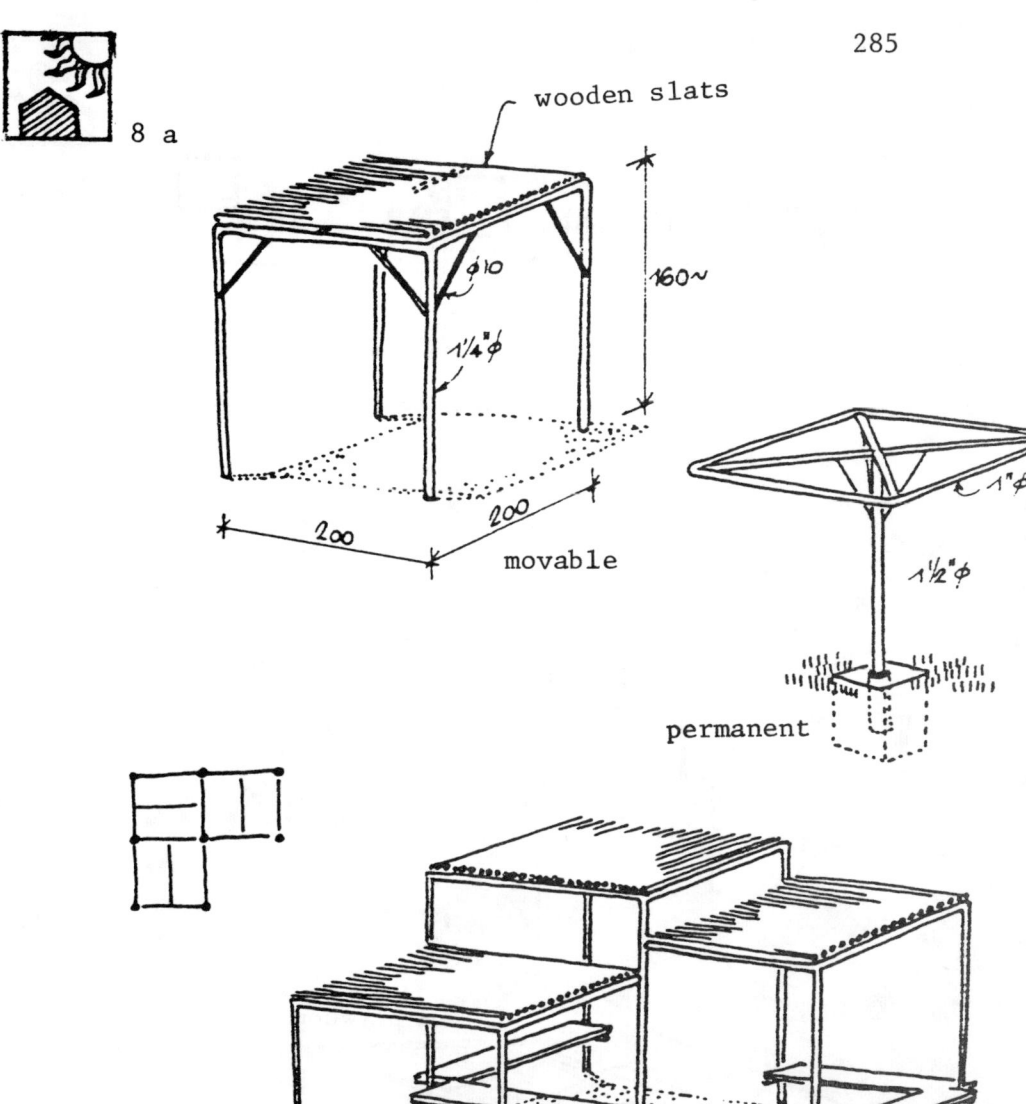

286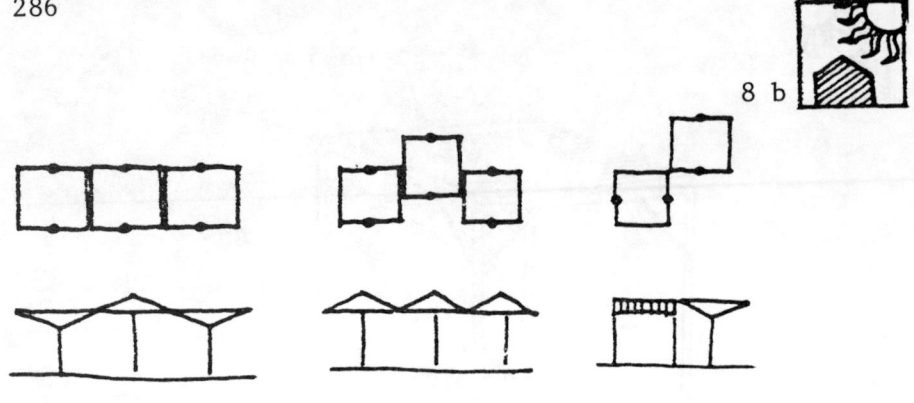

20 slats
20 plywood
100

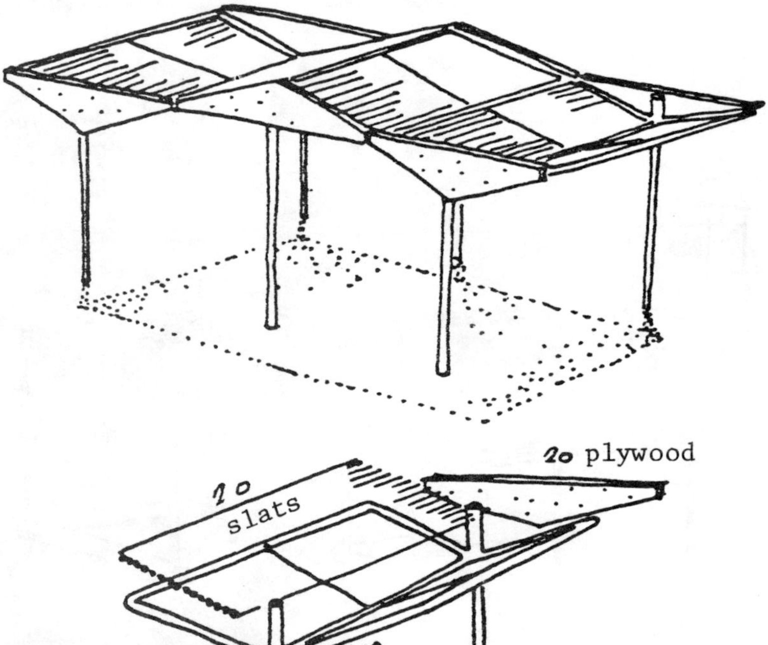

9 a

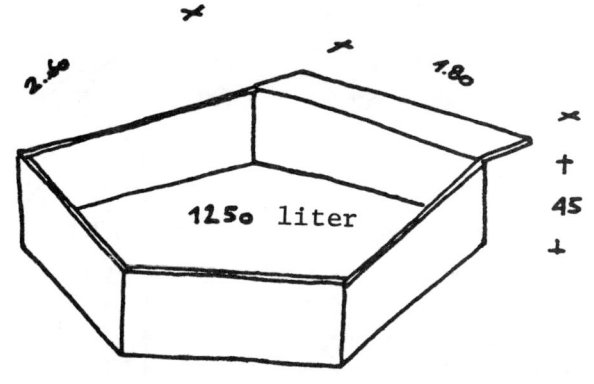

2.40   1.80
1250 liter
45

water pool

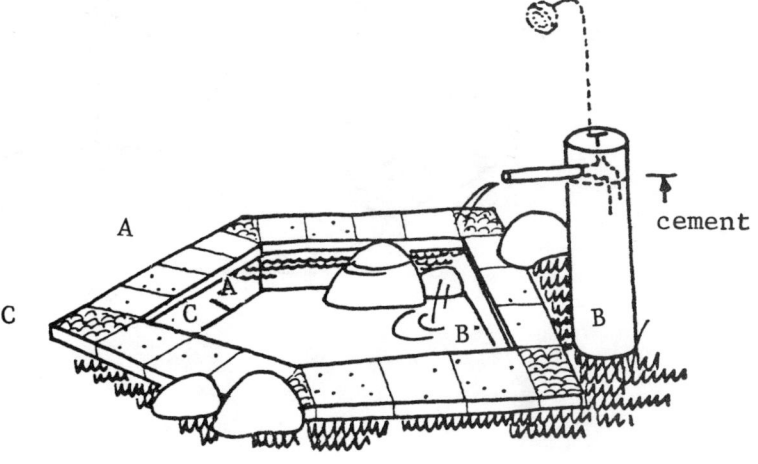

cement

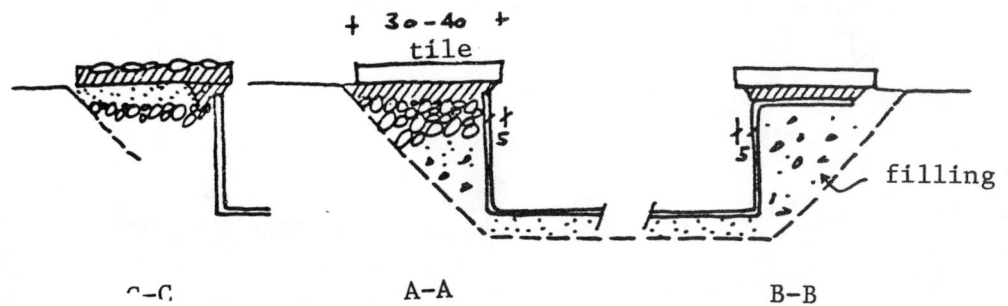

30-40
tile
filling

C-C   A-A   B-B

10 a

water play

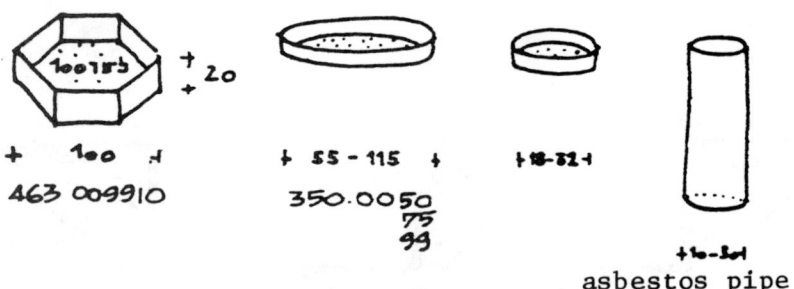

asbestos pipe

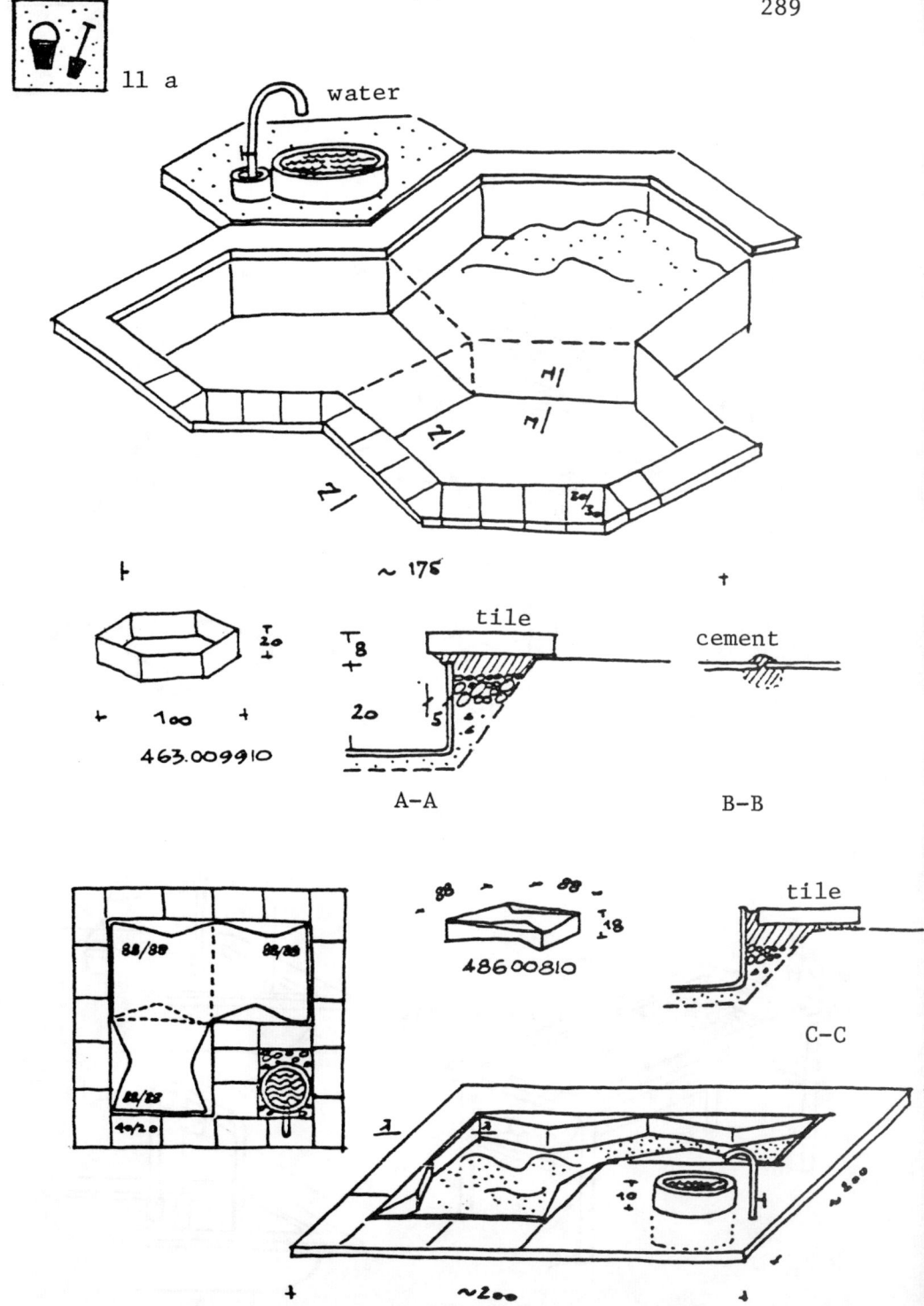

12 a

a wall for sticking mud
filled cement pipe
wooden frame
half barrel
cement floor
canals in floor

tin cover
wooden frame

lever or pulley

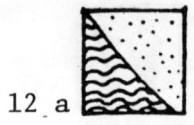

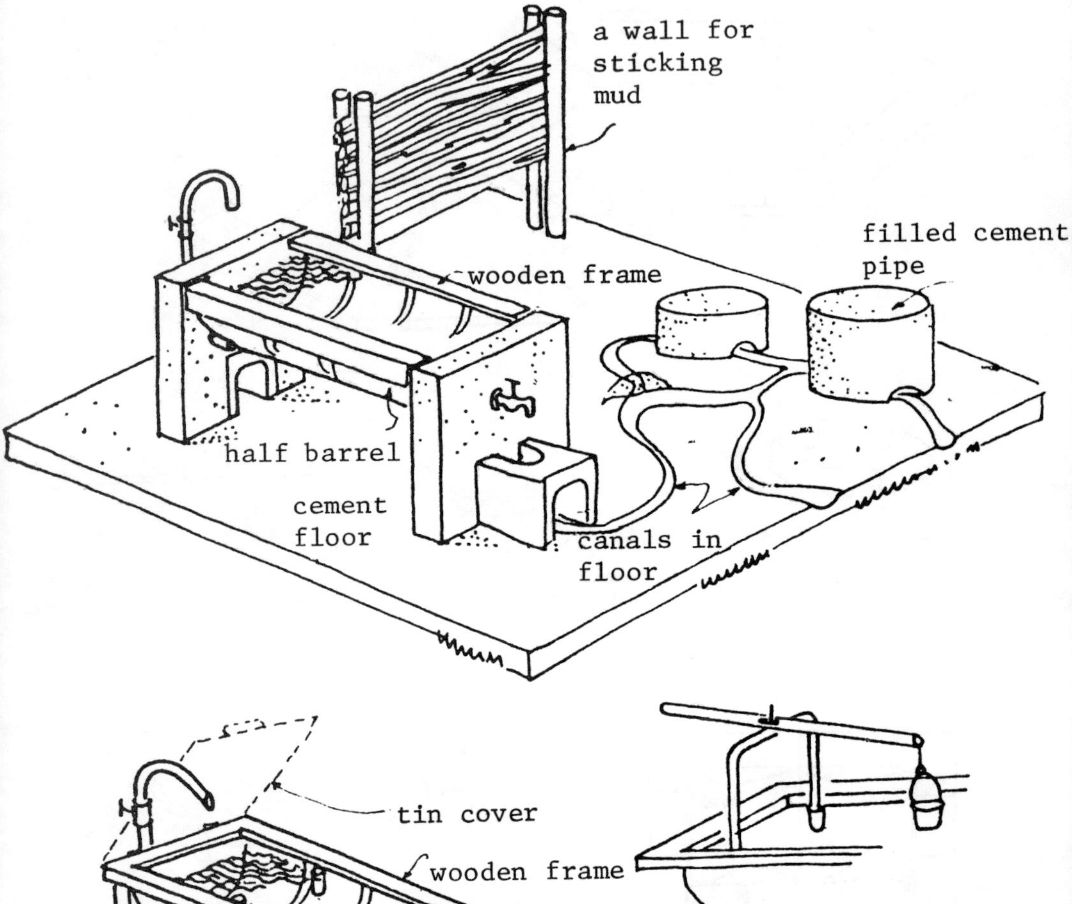

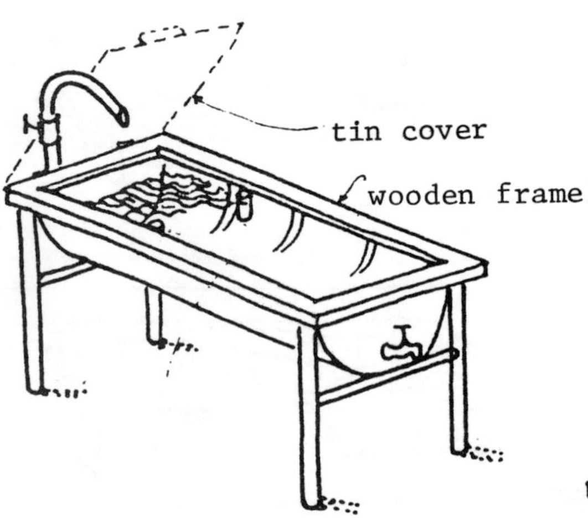

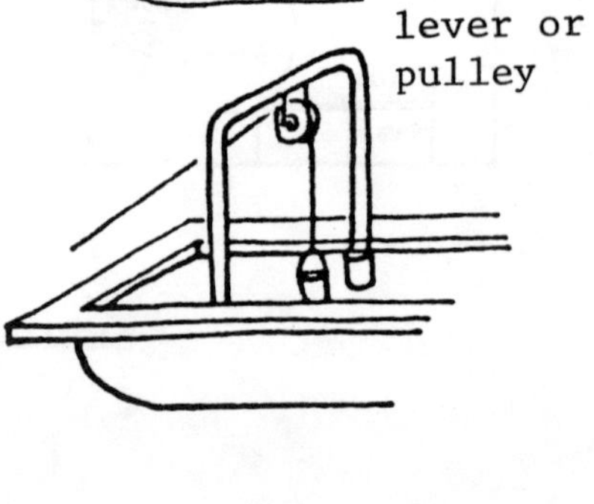

 13 a

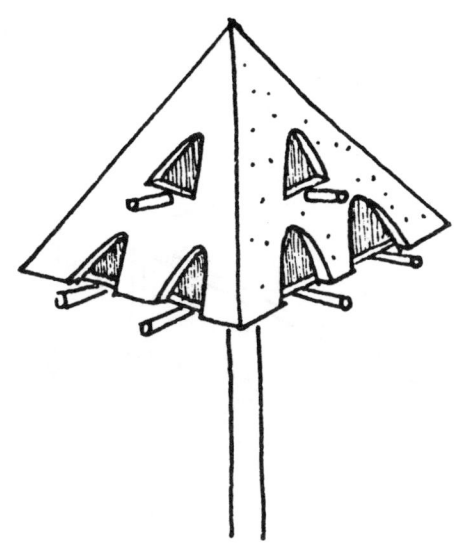

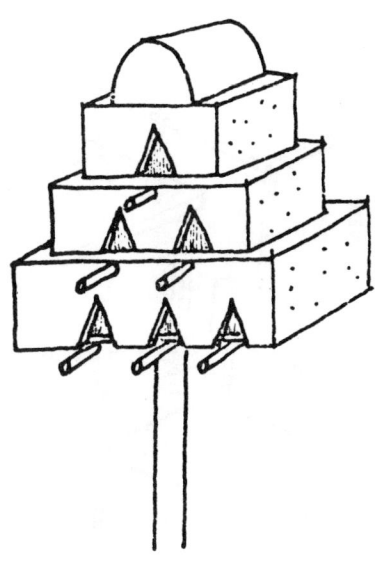

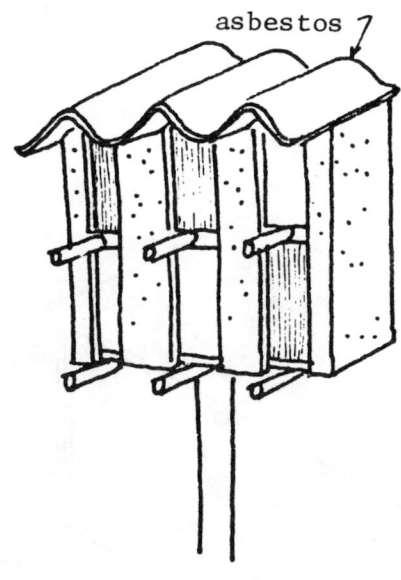
asbestos

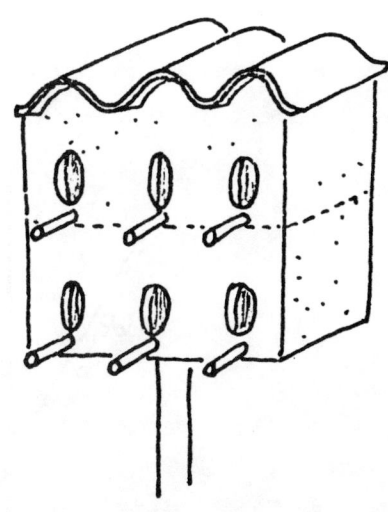

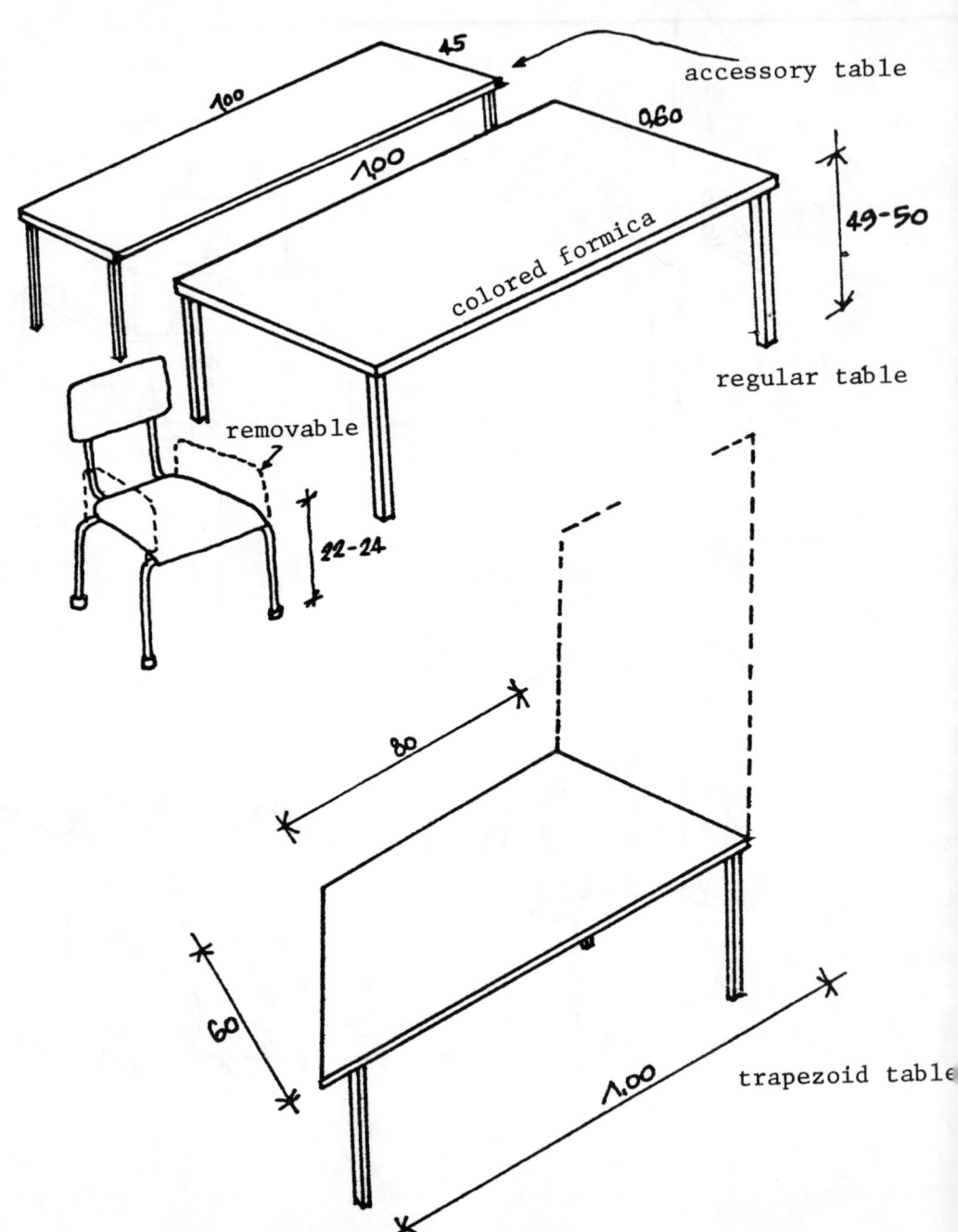

14 b

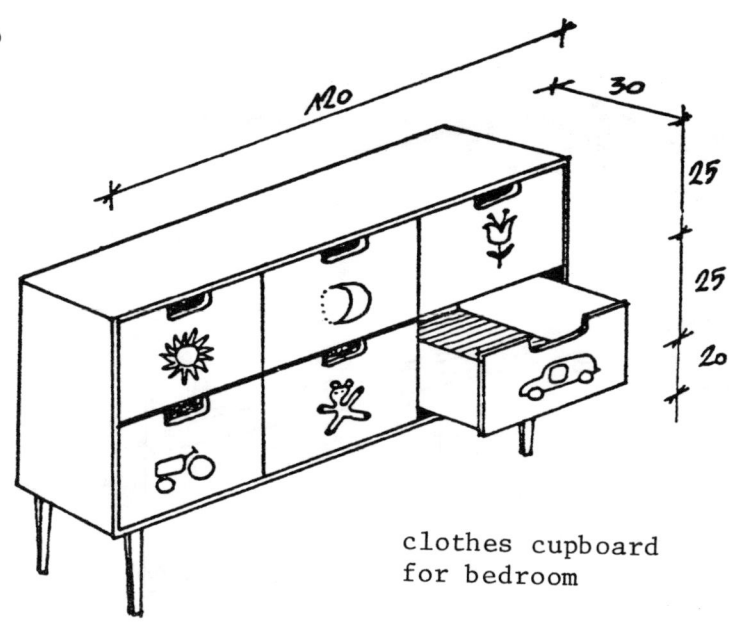

clothes cupboard for bedroom

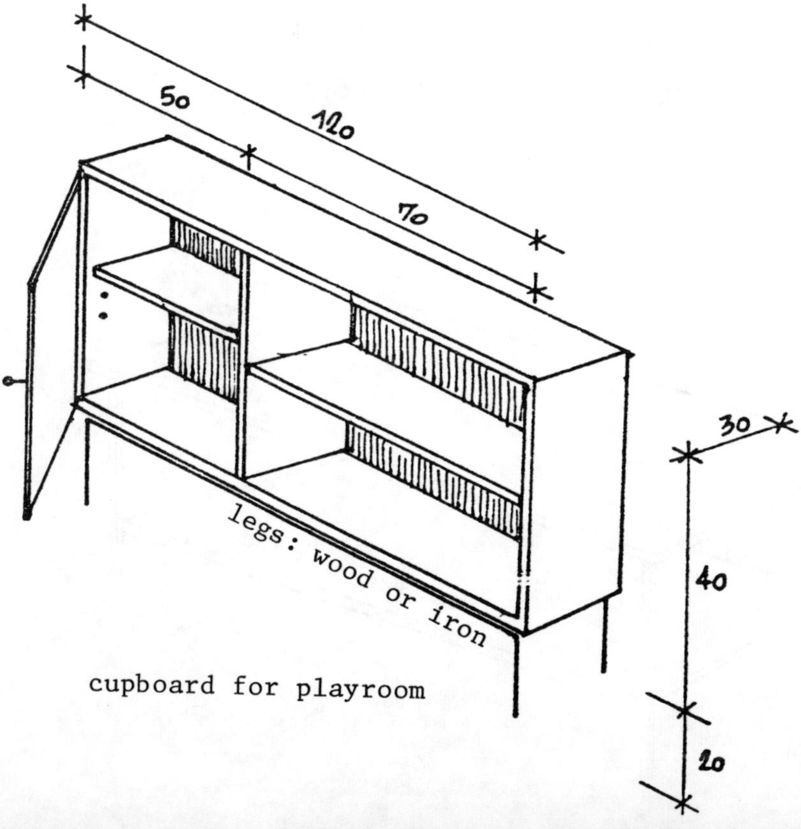

cupboard for playroom

legs: wood or iron

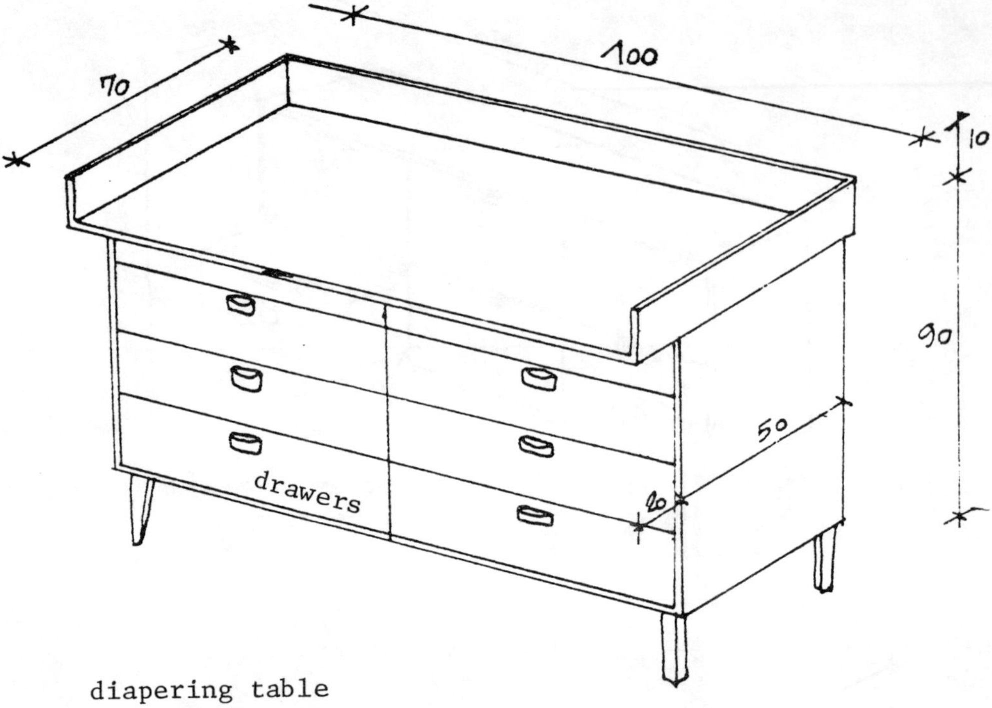

14 c

diapering table

drawers for diapers – divided in middle

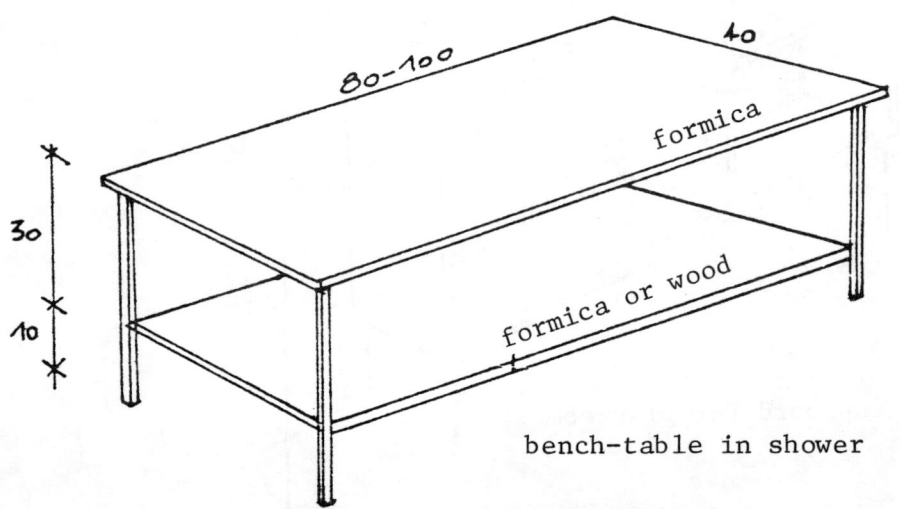

bench-table in shower

14 d

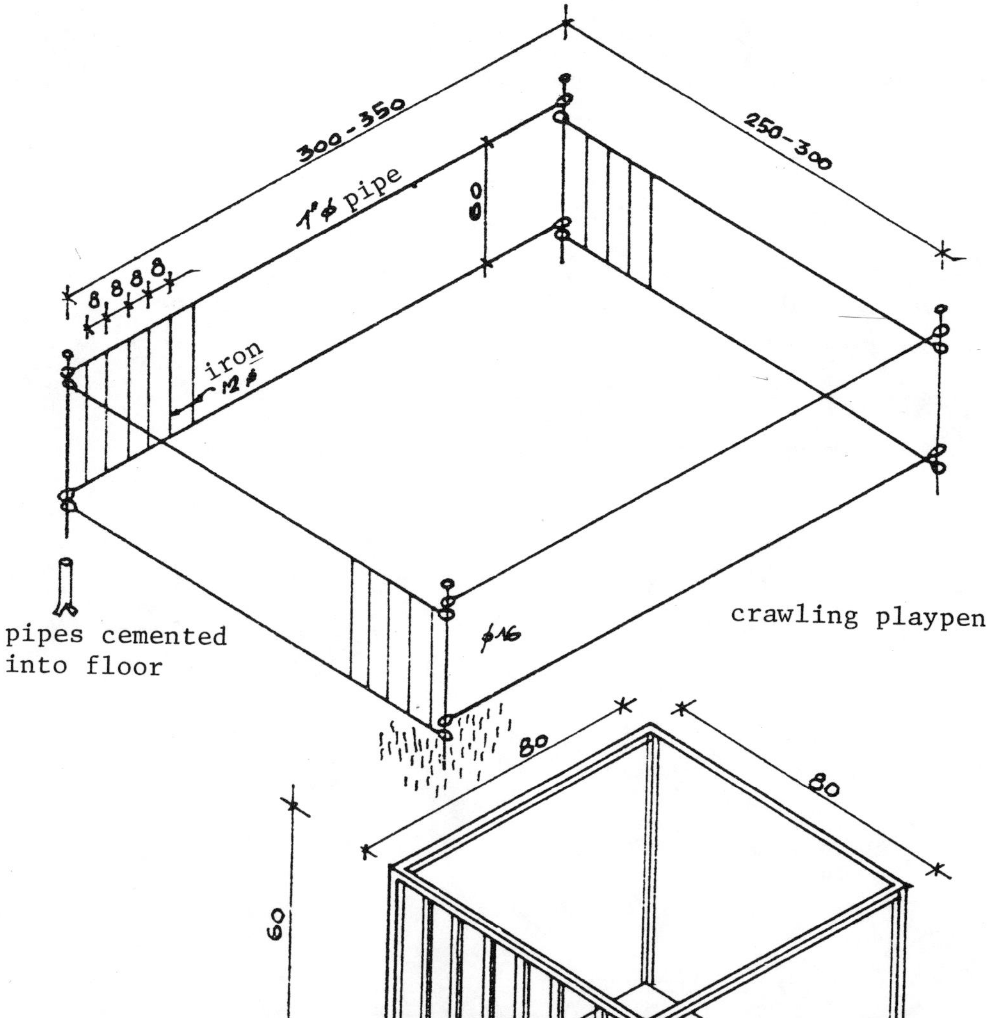

300-350
1"Ø pipe
250-300
80
8,8,8,8
iron 12 Ø
Ø 16
80

pipes cemented into floor

crawling playpen

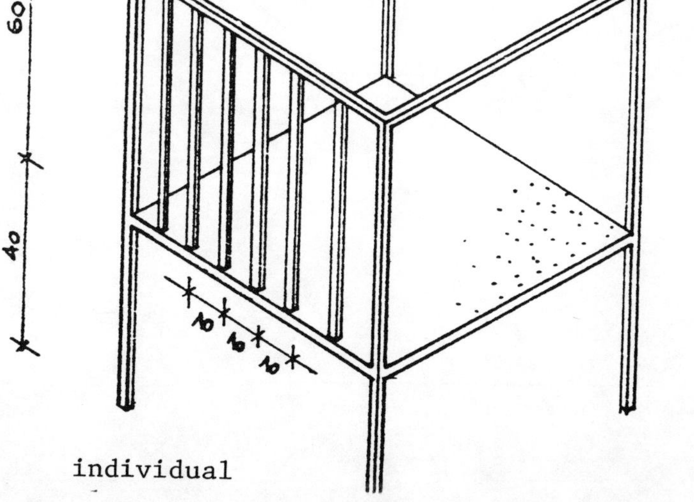

80
80
60
40
10, 10, 10

individual